928
B59

W9-ADR-621

Title Withdrawn

MAR - - 1996

BLACK AMERICAN WOMEN POETS AND DRAMATISTS

GRACE DIXON LIBRARY
18400 JOY ROAD
DETROIT, MI 48228

Writers of English: Lives and Works

BLACK AMERICAN WOMEN POETS AND DRAMATISTS

Edited and with an Introduction by

Harold Bloom

CHELSEA HOUSE PUBLISHERS
New York   Philadelphia

Jacket illustration: Horace Pippin, *Domino Players* (1943) (courtesy of The Phillips Collection, Washington, D.C.).

CHELSEA HOUSE PUBLISHERS

Editorial Director Richard Rennert
Executive Managing Editor Karyn Gullen Browne
Copy Chief Robin James
Picture Editor Adrian G. Allen
Creative Director Robert Mitchell
Art Director Joan Ferrigno
Production Manager Sallye Scott

Writers of English: Lives and Works

Senior Editor S. T. Joshi
Series Design Rae Grant

Staff for BLACK AMERICAN WOMEN POETS AND DRAMATISTS

Assistant Editor Mary Sisson
Editorial Assistant Scott Briggs
Picture Researcher Ellen Dudley

© 1996 by Chelsea House Publishers, a division of Main Line Book Co.

Introduction © 1995 by Harold Bloom

All rights reserved. No part of this publication may be reproduced or transmitted in any form or by any means without the written permission of the publisher.

Printed and bound in the United States of America.

First Printing

1 3 5 7 9 8 6 4 2

Library of Congress Cataloging-in-Publication Data

Black American women poets and dramatists / edited and with an introduction by Harold Bloom.
    p. cm.—(Writers of English)
    Includes bibliographical references (p.).
    ISBN 0-7910-2209-9.—ISBN 0-7910-2234-X (pbk.)
    1. American literature—Afro-American authors—History and criticism. 2. American literature—Afro-American authors—Bio-bibliography. 3. American literature—Women authors—History and criticism. 4. American literature—Women authors—Bio-bibliography. 5. Women and literature—United States. 6. Afro-American women in literature. 7. Afro-Americans in literature. I. Bloom, Harold. II. Series.
PS153.N5B547 1994
830.9'9287—dc20
                          94-4337
                          CIP

Contents

EDISON BRANCH LIBRARY
18400 JOY ROAD
DETROIT, MI 48228

◈ User's Guide

THIS VOLUME PROVIDES biographical, critical, and bibliographical information on the seventeen most significant black American women poets and dramatists. Each chapter consists of three parts: a biography of the author; a selection of brief critical extracts about the author; and a bibliography of the author's published books.

The biography supplies a detailed outline of the important events in the author's life, including his or her major writings. The critical extracts are taken from a wide array of books and periodicals, from the author's lifetime to the present, and range in content from biographical to critical to historical. The extracts are arranged in chronological order by date of writing or publication, and a full bibliographical citation is provided at the end of each extract. Editorial additions or deletions are indicated within carets.

The author bibliographies list every separate publication—including books, pamphlets, broadsides, collaborations, and works edited or translated by the author—for works published in the author's lifetime; selected important posthumous publications are also listed. Titles are those of the first edition; variant titles are supplied within carets. In selected instances dates of revised editions are given where these are significant. Pseudonymous works are listed but not the pseudonyms under which these works were published. Periodicals edited by the author are listed only when the author has written most or all of the contents. Titles enclosed in square brackets are of doubtful authenticity. All works by the author, whether in English or in other languages, have been listed; English translations of foreign-language works are not listed unless the author has done the translation.

The Life of the Author
Harold Bloom

NIETZSCHE, WITH EXULTANT ANGUISH, famously proclaimed that God was dead. Whatever the consequences of this for the ethical life, its ultimate literary effect certainly would have surprised the author Nietzsche. His French disciples, Foucault most prominent among them, developed the Nietzschean proclamation into the dogma that all authors, God included, were dead. The death of the author, which is no more than a Parisian trope, another metaphor for fashion's setting of skirt-lengths, is now accepted as literal truth by most of our current apostles of what should be called French Nietzsche, to distinguish it from the merely original Nietzsche. We also have French Freud or Lacan, which has little to do with the actual thought of Sigmund Freud, and even French Joyce, which interprets *Finnegans Wake* as the major work of Jacques Derrida. But all this is as nothing compared to the final triumph of the doctrine of the death of the author: French Shakespeare. That delicious absurdity is given us by the New Historicism, which blends Foucault and California fruit juice to give us the Word that Renaissance "social energies," and not William Shakespeare, composed *Hamlet* and *King Lear*. It seems a proper moment to murmur "enough" and to return to a study of the life of the author.

Sometimes it troubles me that there are so few masterpieces in the vast ocean of literary biography that stretches between James Boswell's great *Life* of Dr. Samuel Johnson and the late Richard Ellmann's wonderful *Oscar Wilde*. Literary biography is a crucial genre, and clearly a difficult one in which to excel. The actual nature of the lives of the poets seems to have little effect upon the quality of their biographies. Everything happened to Lord Byron and nothing at all to Wallace Stevens, and yet their biographers seem equally daunted by them. But even inadequate biographies of strong writers, or of weak ones, are of immense use. I have never read a literary biography from which I have not profited, a statement I cannot make about any other genre whatsoever. And when it comes to figures who are central to us—Dante, Shakespeare, Cervantes, Montaigne, Goethe, Whitman, Tolstoi, Freud, Joyce, Kafka among them—we reach out eagerly for every scrap that the biographers have gleaned. Concerning Dante and Shakespeare we know much too little, yet when we come to Goethe and Freud, where we seem to know more than everything, we still want to know more. The death of the author, despite our current resentniks, clearly was only a momentary fad. Something vital in every authentic lover of literature responds to Emerson's battle-cry sentence: "There is no history, only biography." Beyond that there is a deeper truth, difficult to come at and requiring a lifetime to understand, which is that there is no literature, only autobiography, however mediated, however veiled, however transformed. The events of Shakespeare's life included the composition of *Hamlet,* and that act of writing was itself a crucial act of living, though we do not yet know altogether how to read so doubled an act. When an author takes up a more overtly autobiographical stance, as so many do in their youth, again we still do not know precisely how to accommodate the vexed relation between life and work. T. S. Eliot, meditating upon James Joyce, made a classic statement as to such accommodation:

> We want to know who are the originals of his characters, and what were
> the origins of his episodes, so that we may unravel the web of memory
> and invention and discover how far and in what ways the crude material
> has been transformed.

When a writer is not even covertly autobiographical, the web of memory and invention is still there, but so subtly woven that we may never unravel it. And yet we want deeply never to stop trying, and not merely because we are curious, but because each of us is caught in her own network of memory and invention. We do not always recall our inventions, and long before we age we cease to be certain of the extent to which we have invented our memories. Perhaps one motive for reading is our need to unravel our own webs. If our masters could make, from their lives, what we read, then we can be moved by them to ask: What have we made or lived in relation to what we have read? The answers may be sad, or confused, but the question is likely, implicitly, to go on being asked as long as we read. In Freudian terms, we are asking: What is it that we have repressed? What have we forgotten, unconsciously but purposively: What is it that we flee? Art, literature necessarily included, is regression in the service of the ego, according to a famous Freudian formula. I doubt the Freudian wisdom here, but indubitably it is profoundly suggestive. When we read, something in us keeps asking the equivalent of the Freudian questions: From what or whom is the author in flight, and to what earlier stages in her life is she returning, and why?

Reading, whether as an art or a pastime, has been damaged by the visual media, television in particular, and might be in some danger of extinction in the age of the computer, except that the psychic need for it continues to endure, presumably because it alone can assuage a central loneliness in elitist society. Despite all sophisticated or resentful denials, the reading of imaginative literature remains a quest to overcome the isolation of the individual consciousness. We can read for information, or entertainment, or for love of the language, but in the end we seek, in the author, the person whom we have not found, whether in ourselves or in others. In that quest, there always are elements at once aggressive and defensive, so that reading, even in childhood, is rarely free of hidden anxieties. And yet it remains one of the few activities not contaminated by an entropy of spirit. We read in hope, because we lack companionship, and the author can become the object of the most idealistic elements in our search for the wit and inventiveness we so desperately require. We read biography, not as a supplement to reading the author, but as a second, fresh attempt to understand what always seems to evade us in the work, our drive towards a kind of identity with the author.

This will-to-identity, though recently much deprecated, is a prime basis for the experience of sublimity in reading. *Hamlet* retains its unique position in the Western canon not because most readers and playgoers identify themselves with the prince, who clearly is beyond them, but rather because they find themselves again in the power of the language that represents him with such immediacy and force. Yet we know that neither language nor social energy created Hamlet. Our curiosity about Shakespeare is endless, and never will be appeased. That curiosity itself is a value, and cannot be separated from the value of *Hamlet* the tragedy, or Hamlet the literary character. It provokes us that Shakespeare the man seems so unknowable, at once everyone and no one as Borges shrewdly observes. Critics keep telling us otherwise, yet something valid in us keeps believing that we would know Hamlet better if Shakespeare's life were as fully known as the lives of Goethe and Freud, Byron and Oscar Wilde, or best of all, Dr. Samuel Johnson. Shakespeare never will have his Boswell, and Dante never will have his Richard Ellmann. How much one would give for a detailed and candid *Life of Dante* by Petrarch, or an outspoken memoir of Shakespeare by Ben Jonson! Or, in the age just past, how superb would be rival studies of one another by Hemingway and Scott Fitzgerald! But the list is endless: think of *Oscar Wilde* by Lord Alfred Douglas, or a joint biography of Shelley by Mary Godwin, Emilia Viviani, and Jane Williams. More than our insatiable desire for scandal would be satisfied. The literary rivals and the lovers of the great writers possessed perspectives we will never enjoy, and without those perspectives we dwell in some poverty in regard to the writers with whom we ourselves never can be done.

There is a sense in which imaginative literature *is* perspectivism, so that the reader is likely to be overwhelmed by the work's difficulty unless its multiple perspectives are mastered. Literary biography matters most because it is a storehouse of perspectives, frequently far surpassing any that are grasped by the particular biographer. There are relations between authors' lives and their works of kinds we have yet to discover, because our analytical instruments are not yet advanced enough to perform the necessary labor. Perhaps a novel, poem, or play is not so much a regression in the service of the ego, as it is an amalgam of *all* the Freudian mechanisms of defense, all working together for the apotheosis of the ego. Freud valued art highly, but thought that the aesthetic enterprise was no rival for psychoanalysis, unlike religion and philosophy. Clearly Freud was mistaken; his own anxieties about his indebtedness to Shakespeare helped produce the weirdness of his joining in the lunacy that argued for the Earl of Oxford as the author of Shakespeare's plays. It was Shakespeare, and not "the poets," who was there before Freud arrived at his depth psychology, and it is Shakespeare who is there still, well out ahead of psychoanalysis. We see what Freud would not see, that psychoanalysis is Shakespeare prosified and systematized. Freud is part of literature, not of "science," and the biography of Freud has the same relations to psychoanalysis as the biography of Shakespeare has to *Hamlet* and *King Lear,* if only we knew more of the life of Shakespeare.

Western literature, particularly since Shakespeare, is marked by the representation of internalized change in its characters. A literature of the ever-growing inner self is in itself a large form of biography, even though this is the biography of imaginary beings, from Hamlet to the sometimes nameless protagonists of Kafka and Beckett. Skeptics might want to argue that all literary biography concerns imaginary beings, since authors make themselves up, and every biographer gives us a creation curiously different from the same author as seen by the writer of a rival *Life*. Boswell's Johnson is not quite anyone else's Johnson, though it is now very difficult for us to disentangle the great Doctor from his gifted Scottish friend and follower. The life of the author is not merely a metaphor or a fiction, as is "the Death of the Author," but it always does contain metaphorical or fictive elements. Those elements are a part of the value of literary biography, but not the largest or the crucial part, which is the separation of the mask from the man or woman who hid behind it. James Joyce and Samuel Beckett, master and sometime disciple, were both of them enigmatic personalities, and their biographers have not, as yet, fully expounded the mystery of these contrasting natures. Beckett seems very nearly to have been a secular saint: personally disinterested, heroic in the French Resistance, as humane a person ever to have composed major fictions and dramas. Joyce, self-obsessed even as Beckett was preternaturally selfless, was the Milton of the twentieth century. Beckett was perhaps the least egoistic post-Joycean, post-Proustian, post-Kafkan of writers. Does that illuminate the problematical nature of his work, or does it simply constitute another problem? Whatever the cause, the question matters. The only death of the author that is other than literal, and that matters, is the fate only of weak writers. The strong, who become canonical, never die, which is what the canon truly is about. To be read forever is the Life of the Author.

▨ Introduction

IN OUR CONTEMPORARY AMERICA many of us are mad on angels; it is something of a growth industry. Tony Kushner's *Angels in America,* possibly our best drama since the death of Tennessee Williams, is the major aesthetic consequence, so far, of a national mania. Very close in eminence are the visions of Thylias Moss, a remarkable poet by any standards. She concludes her poem, "Fisher Street," with a phantasmagoria of laundry taking the place of angels:

> Songs rise in vapor, white and bleached
> Like all that laundry struggling on the line
> like all of us
> to be free.
> I don't expect to see
>
> any other angels.

I don't often get the sense that Moss poetically needs much "struggling on the line . . . to be free" of influences, since she is so much an original. Her wit and metric alike have some relation to Elizabeth Bishop's, but she swerves from Bishop because in some inalienable sense Moss remains a religious poet, though with a differencé, as at the close of "Birmingham Brown's Turn," one of her irrealistic triumphs:

> Going there, we notice how Jesus
> can become Confucius without a hitch
> and can keep his parables if he wishes.
> We all keep salvation.

In another strong poem, "A Form of Deicide," Moss observes that "Between Elvis, God, and Santa Claus, some people / get everything they need." She rather clearly does not, if only because her God is "a shadowy ever-descending brother," as he is described in "The Warmth of Hot Chocolate," an immortal wound of a prose-poem. My particular favorite, for now, is the marvelous "Doubts During Catastrophe," where Ezekiel's vision of the valley of bones is amplified, with an exuberance all Moss's own:

Being in God's hand doesn't mean being in a full house. It means mother Hubbard being a grave robber cloaking herself in hood and cape dark as her act. This is what one does when one has dogs to beware of: Dig up the prize begonias, a femur, fibula, a tibia, phalanges. She didn't even love these bones when they walked the earth in her man.

As the Millennium approaches, I take comfort in the wisdom of this superb, younger poet: "Being in God's hand doesn't mean being in a full house."

—H. B.

Maya Angelou
b. 1928

MAYA ANGELOU was born Marguerite Johnson in St. Louis, Missouri, on April 4, 1928. Her life has been both remarkably varied and occasionally grim (she was raped at the age of eight by her mother's boyfriend), and she has won greater critical acclaim for her several autobiographical volumes than for her poetry and drama. She attended public schools in Arkansas and California, studied music privately, and studied dance with Martha Graham. In 1954–55 she was a member of the cast of *Porgy and Bess,* which went on a twenty-two-nation world tour sponsored by the U.S. Department of State. Some of her songs were recorded on the album *Miss Calypso* (1957). Later she acted in several off-Broadway plays, including one, the musical *Cabaret for Freedom* (1960), that she wrote with Godfrey Cambridge.

In addition to these artistic pursuits, Angelou held a variety of odd jobs in her late teens and early twenties, including streetcar conductor, Creole cook, nightclub waitress, prostitute, and madam. She has been married twice: first, around 1950, to a white man, Tosh Angelos (whose surname she adapted when she became a dancer), and then, from 1973 to 1981, to Paul Du Feu. She bore a son, Guy, at the age of sixteen.

When she was thirty Angelou moved to Brooklyn. There she met John Oliver Killens, James Baldwin, and other writers who encouraged her to write. While practicing her craft, however, she became involved in the civil rights movement. She met Martin Luther King, Jr., was appointed the northern coordinator of the Southern Christian Leadership Conference, and organized demonstrations at the United Nations. She fell in love with the South African freedom fighter Vusumzi Make, and they left for Egypt, where in 1961–62 Angelou worked as associate editor of the *Arab Observer,* an English-language newspaper in Cairo. She broke up with Make when he criticized her independence and lack of subservience to him.

In 1963 Angelou went to Ghana to be assistant administrator of the School of Music and Drama at the University of Ghana's Institute of African Studies. In the three years she was there she acted in several additional plays, served as feature editor of the *African Review*, and was a contributor to the Ghanaian Broadcasting Corporation. Returning to the United States, she was a lecturer at the University of California at Los Angeles and has subsequently been a visiting professor or writer in residence at several other universities.

Angelou's first published book was *I Know Why the Caged Bird Sings* (1969), an autobiography of the first sixteen years of her life; a tremendous critical and popular success, it was nominated for a National Book Award and was later adapted for television. Two more autobiographical volumes appeared in the 1970s, *Gather Together in My Name* (1974) and *Singin' and Swingin' and Gettin' Merry Like Christmas* (1976), along with three volumes of poetry: *Just Give Me a Cool Drink of Water 'Fore I Diiie* (1971), *Oh Pray My Wings Are Gonna Fit Me Well* (1975), and *And Still I Rise* (1978). She wrote several more dramas, including the unpublished *And Still I Rise!*, a medley of black poetry and music that was successfully staged in 1976; two screenplays (directing one of them and writing the musical scores for both); and several television plays, including a series of ten one-hour programs entitled *Blacks, Blues, Black*. She also continued to pursue her acting career and was nominated for a Tony Award in 1973 for her Broadway debut, *Look Away*. She was appointed a member of the American Revolution Bicentennial Council by President Gerald R. Ford in 1975.

In the last fifteen years Angelou has solidified her reputation with two more autobiographies, *The Heart of a Woman* (1981) and *All God's Children Need Traveling Shoes* (1986), along with two more volumes of poetry, *Shaker, Why Don't You Sing?* (1983) and *I Shall Not Be Moved* (1990). The peak of her fame was perhaps achieved when in 1993 she composed a poem, "On the Pulse of Morning," for the inauguration of President Bill Clinton. Angelou's latest prose work, *Wouldn't Take Nothing for My Journey Now*, a collection of essays and sketches, also appeared that year and, like most of its predecessors, was a best-seller.

Maya Angelou, who has received honorary degrees from Smith College, Mills College, and Lawrence University, currently resides in Sonoma, California.

❀ *Critical Extracts*

CHAD WALSH   Maya Angelou has had a versatile career—at various times an actor in *Porgy and Bess*, dance teacher in Rome and Tel Aviv, northern coordinator for the Southern Christian Leadership Conference— and at all times, a poet whose work is a moving blend of lyricism and harsh social observation.

Just Give Me a Cool Drink of Water 'Fore I Diiie is divided into two parts. The first is the more personal and tender, such as "To a Man"—

> My name is
> Black Golden Amber
> Changing.
> Warm mouths of Brandy Fine
> Cautious sunlight on patterned rug
> Coughing laughter, rocked on a whorl of French tobacco

Many of these poems have been set to music. The second part, "Just Before the World Ends," has more bite—the anguished and often sardonic expression of a black in a white-dominated world. "Riot: 60's" presents an angle of vision not shared by most suburbanites:

> Lightning: a hundred Watts
> Detroit, Newark and New York
> Screeching nerves, exploding minds
> lives tied to
> a policeman's whistle
> a welfare worker's doorbell
> finger.

Chad Walsh, "A Fact about Recent Poetry: Women First," *Washington Post Book World*, 9 April 1972, p. 12

UNSIGNED   The 36 poems in this book ⟨*Oh Pray My Wings Are Gonna Fit Me Well*⟩ are grouped, arbitrarily it seems, into five parts, the first four of which contain pieces that are all surface. The themes, chiefly lost or wronged love or frustrated desire, and their treatments are akin to country-western music. It is in the treatment that the superficiality is most obvious: motives not explored, little depth or interpretation of feelings, no sense of time or change, no allusion or any rich ambiguity, little melody.

Some are merely cute. Most could be as effectively stated in declarative sentences. A few poems capture some sense of loneliness, but without conveying any insight or universal values. The twelve poems in part five are generally better, containing some developed images, a degree of music, while also finding deeper meanings in man's actions or inactions.

> Unsigned, "Notes on Current Books," *Virginia Quarterly Review* 52, No. 3 (Summer 1976): 82

SANDRA M. GILBERT   I can't help feeling that Maya Angelou's career has suffered from the interest her publishers have in mythologizing her. *Oh Pray My Wings Are Gonna Fit Me Well* is such a painfully untalented collection of poems that I can't think of any reason, other than the Maya Myth, for it to be in print: it's impossible, indeed, to separate the book's flap copy, with its glossy celebration of "Maya Angelou . . . one of the world's most exciting women . . . Maya, the eternal female" from the book itself. All this is especially depressing because Angelou, "eternal female" or not, is a stunningly talented prose writer, whose marvelous *I Know Why the Caged Bird Sings* has quite properly become a contemporary classic. Why should it be necessary, then, for her to represent herself publicly as the author of such an embarrassing tangle as

> I'd touched your features inchly
> heard love and dared the cost.
> The scented spiel reeled me unreal
> and found my senses lost.

And why, instead of encouraging Angelou, didn't some friendly editor Block (as *The New Yorker* would say) the following Metaphor:

> A day
> drunk with the nectar of
> nowness
> weaves its way between
> the years
> to find itself at the flophouse
> of night. . . .

To be fair, not all the verse in *Oh Pray . . .* is quite as bad as these two examples. A few of the colloquial pieces—"Pickin Em Up and Layin Em Down" or "Come. And Be My Baby"—have the slangy, unpretentious vitality of good ballads. "The Pusher" ("He bad / O he bad"), with its echoes of Brooks's "We real cool", achieves genuine scariness. And "John J." might be a portrait in verse of Bailey, the handsome brother Angelou renders so beautifully in *I Know Why. . . .* But these are only four or five poems out of the thirty-six in this collection. And most of the others, when they're not awkward or stilted, are simply corny. The writer whose unsentimental wit and passionate accuracy gave us such a fresh account of growing up black and female really doesn't need to publish "No one knows / my lonely heart / when we're apart" or "No lady cookinger than my Mommy / smell that pie / see I don't lie / No lady cookinger than my Mommy" (from "Little Girl Speakings"). Angelou can hardly be accused of self-parody: for one thing, most of the poetry here is too unself-conscious, too thoughtless, to be in any sense parodic. But, for whatever reason, the wings of song certainly don't seem to fit her very well right now.

Sandra M. Gilbert, "A Platoon of Poets," *Poetry* 128, No. 5 (August 1976): 296–97

EUGENE REDMOND   A multi-tiered ballet-symphony conceived and directed by writer-director Maya Angelou, *And Still I Rise!* was exuberantly received by full houses during four August weekends at the Oakland Ensemble Theatre. ⟨. . .⟩

Black-based, with dramatic tentacles and sub-themes that are global (indeed, galaxial!), *And Still I Rise!* is an admirable adaptation of subtle, poignant and humorous verse-songs from a rich cross-spread of Afro-American poets. Household names such as Paul Laurence Dunbar, Gwendolyn Brooks, Langston Hughes and Nikki Giovanni, are mixed with an ample sprinkling of lesser known bards—Frank Horne, Richard A. Long, Joyce Carol Thomas and Ray Garfiend Dandridge. Spices from the "traditional" song-book (those "black and unknown bards") and Miss Angelou's own volumes make up the remainder of this tasty drama. These items form a histrionic bridge between Africa and the New World via six sub-themes (Childhood, Youth, Love, Work, Religion, and The Old Souls) that evoke nostalgia, fear, humor and pride. ⟨. . .⟩

As a dramatic exploration of black survival and endurance, *And Still I Rise!* is coincidentally an enormous praise-song, a totemic tribute to those gone souls and a challenge to those living and unborn. Maya Angelou has brought years of formidable experience, research and travel to bear on her serious interest in the black cultural legacy. *And Still I Rise!* congeals a substantial body of her own portfolio as writer-actress-dancer-singer-director into relentless drama. And we are all the better for it.

Eugene Redmond, [Review of *And Still I Rise!*], *Black Scholar* 8, No. 1 (September 1976): 50–51

UNSIGNED   *Black Scholar*: Can you comment a bit on the importance of endurance in black writers?

Maya Angelou: Endurance is one thing. I think endurance with output, endurance with productivity is the issue. If one has the fortune, good or bad, to stay alive one endures, but to continue to write the books and get them out—that's the productivity and I think that is important to link with the endurance.

I find myself taking issue with the term minor poet, minor writer of the 18th century, minor writer of the 19th century; but I do understand what people mean by that. Generally they mean that the writer, the poet who only wrote one book of poetry or one novel, or two, is considered a minor poet or a minor writer because of his or her output, its scarcity. I can't argue with that. I do believe that it is important to get work done, seen, read, published, and *given* to an audience. One has enjoyed oneself, one has done what one has been put here to do, to write. Another thing is that one has given a legacy of some quantity to generations to come. Whether they like it or not, whether the writer values the next generation, or values the work or not, at least there is something, there is a body of work to examine and to respond to, to react to.

I know a number of people who do work very slowly but I don't believe, although I have friends who write slowly, in taking five years to write one book. Now I think they have psyched themselves into believing they cannot work more quickly, that hence because they work slowly their work is of more value. They also believe—they have bought that American baloney, the masterpiece theory—everything you write must be a masterpiece, each painting you paint must be a masterpiece.

Black Scholar: I want to talk to you more about that. I think any artist in this society is inhibited in many ways because it is not an aesthetic society.

Maya Angelou: Materialistic.

Black Scholar: I think the black writer has even more difficulty because his vision is antagonistic, it's a racist society, his whole stuff is different. Do you think that the masterpiece syndrome further inhibits the output of black writers?

Maya Angelou: To me that inhibits *all* artists. Every artist in this society is affected by it. I don't say he or she is inhibited, he or she might work against it and make that work for them, as I hope I do, but we are affected by it.

It is in reaction to that dictate from a larger society that spurs my output, makes me do all sorts of things, write movies and direct them, write plays, write music and write articles. That's because I don't believe in the inhibition of my work; I am obliged, I am compulsive, I will work against it. If necessary I will go to work on a dictionary, you understand, just to prove that that is a lot of bullshit.

So every artist in the society has to deal with that dictate. Some are crippled by it, others, I believe, are made more healthy. Because they are made more strong, and become more ready to struggle against it.

Black Scholar: More vigilant.

Maya Angelou: Absolutely. But the black writer or black artist—I include every type, from graphics to entertainment—has generally further to come from than his or her white counterpart unless the artist is an entertainer. Often this black artist is the first in his family and possibly in his environment to strive to write a book, to strive to paint a painting, to sculpt, to make being an artist a life work. So the black writer, the black artist probably has to convince family and friends that what he or she is about is worthwhile.

Now that is damned difficult when one comes from a family, an environment, a neighborhood or group of friends who have never met a writer, who have only heard of writers, maybe read some poetry in school.

But try to explain to a middle-aged black that the life of art one wants to lead is a worthwhile one and can hopefully improve life, the quality of life for all people, that's already a chore.

Because, like most people anywhere, the middle-aged black American that comes from a poor background for the most part wants to see concrete evidence of success. So they want things. If you are really going to be a success go and become a nurse, be a doctor, be a mortician, but a *writer?* So there are obstacles to overcome, to be either done or else just given up on.

Unsigned, "The *Black Scholar* Interviews: Maya Angelou," *Black Scholar* 8, No. 4 (January 1977): 44–45

ANTAR SUDAN KATARA MBERI   Well, she's back and smoking with another bombshell under her belt. Maya Angelou, the author of five highly acclaimed works of lasting literary quality, has done it again. She sings with the evocative and sometimes provocative cadence of the blues master. In her world, language serves content. Characteristic depth of meaning blossoms and pollinates her work. She is a vintage craftswoman plying her artistic tools with polished economy and confidence.

Like the blues player she is, her lyrics bubble and brim over. She paces us through her snapshots of the Afro-American community, its women and their problems, which become ours as well; through love and its triumphs and defeats; and through shared personal experiences and outlooks that draw you further out of yourself and into her world. This is the power and the magic of *And Still I Rise.* ⟨. . .⟩

It is a book of instructiveness, love, joy, pain, but always *shared* optimism. And in a country with so many anti-human, self-negating values, it is like a cool glass of water finally received, to read Ms. Angelou's work. After doing so, we know one thing for sure—we are not going to "Diiie" of thirst. Do yourself a favor, and quench your thirst. Buy it.

Antar Sudan Katara Mberi, "Like a Cool Glass of Water," *Freedomways* 19, No. 2 (Second Quarter 1979): 109–10

ROBERT B. STEPTO   *And Still I Rise* is Angelou's third volume of verse, and most of its thirty-two poems are as slight as those which dominated the pages of the first two books. Stanzas such as this one,

> In every town and village,
> In every city square,
> In crowded places
> I search the faces
> Hoping to find
> Someone to care.

or the following,

> Then you rose into my life,
> Like a promised sunrise.
> Brightening my days with the light in your eyes.
> I've never been so strong,
> Now I'm where I belong.

cannot but make lesser-known talents grieve all the more about how this thin stuff finds its way to the rosters of a major New York house while their stronger, more inventive lines seem to be relegated to low-budget (or no-budget) journals and presses. On the other hand, a good Angelou poem has what we call "possibilities." One soon discovers that she is on her surest ground when she "borrows" various folk idioms and forms and thereby buttresses her poems by evoking aspects of a culture's written and unwritten heritage. "One More Round," for example, gains most of its energy from "work songs" and "protest songs" that have come before. In this eight-stanza poem, the even-number stanzas constitute a refrain—obviously, a "work song" refrain:

> One more round
> And let's heave it down.
> One more round
> And let's heave it down.

At the heart of the odd-number stanzas are variations upon the familiar "protest" couplet "But before I'll be a slave / I'll be buried in my grave," such as the following: "I was born to work up to my grave / But I was not born / To be a slave." The idea of somehow binding "work" and "protest" forms to create a new art is absolutely first rate, but the mere alternation of "work" and "protest" stanzas does not, in this instance, carry the idea very far. ⟨. . .⟩

Up to a point, "Still I Rise," Angelou's title poem, reminds us of Brown's famous "Strong Men," and it is the discovery of that point which helps us define Angelou's particular presence and success in contemporary letters and, if we may say so, in publishing. The poetic and visual rhythms created by the repetition of "Still I rise" and its variants clearly revoice that of Brown's "strong men . . . strong men gittin' stronger." But the "I" of Angelou's refrain is obviously female and, in this instance, a woman forthright about the sexual nuances of personal and social struggle:

> Does my sexiness upset you?
> Does it come as a surprise
> That I dance like I've got diamonds
> At the meeting of my thighs?

Needless to say, the woman "rising" from these lines is largely unaccounted for in the earlier verse of men and women poets alike. Most certainly, this "phenomenal woman," as she terms herself in another poem, is not likely to appear, except perhaps in a negative way, in the feminist verse of our time. Where she *does* appear is in Angelou's own marvelous autobiographies, *I Know Why the Caged Bird Sings* and *Gather Together in My Name*. In short, Angelou's poems are often woefully thin as poems but they nevertheless work their way into contemporary literary history. In their celebration of a particularly defined "phenomenal woman," they serve as ancillary, supporting texts for Angelou's more adeptly rendered self-portraits, and even guide the reader to (or back to) the autobiographies. With this achieved, Angelou's "phenomenal woman," as persona *and* self-portrait, assumes a posture in our literature that would not be available if she were the product of Angelou's prose or verse alone.

> Robert B. Stepto, "The Phenomenal Woman and the Severed Daughter," *Parnassus: Poetry in Review* 8, No. 1 (Fall–Winter, 1979): 313–15

CAROLYN KIZER   It is as if Maya Angelou was born knowing how to write, and how to do a great many other things well, with seeming effortlessness: act, compose, direct, edit, make a film or a baby, and much much more. She rhymes with ease and assurance and there's the rub. If writing poems is easy, it's apt to seem that way to the reader as well. It can collapse into near-doggerel, like the following:

> Life is too busy, wearying me.
> Questions and answers and heavy thought.
> I've subtracted and added and multiplied,
> and all my figuring has come to naught.
> Today I'll give up living.

Her verse is not all like this, though too often it is. ⟨. . .⟩ there is a wonderful ballad, of just 10 lines, that Auden, if he were here, might memorize, recite and anthologize, "Contemporary Announcement":

> Ring the big bells,
> cook the cow,
> put on your silver locket.
> The landlord is knocking at the door
> and I've got the rent in my pocket.
>
> Douse the lights
> Hold your breath,
> take my heart in your hand.

> I lost my job two weeks ago
> and rent day's here again.

More like these, please, Ms. Angelou! But if you don't have time, we will understand.

> Carolyn Kizer, [Review of *Shaker, Why Don't You Sing?*], *Washington Post Book World*, 26 June 1983, p. 8

CANDELARIA SILVA   Maya Angelou's poetry is easily accessible, relying often on rhythm for its success. The poems are pared down with a sculptor's precision to simple yet elegant lines. She writes about love, beauty, the South, the human struggle for freedom and the incredible dignity black people have maintained against all odds. Her perceptive vision is emphatic and clear. Angelou is best in her poems which rhyme, like "Weekend Glory" and "Impeccable Conception." Her rhymes never seem awkwardly constructed or contrived. (She is less successful when she uses other methods for they don't seem to come from her natural voice.) Her sense of music in language, her heritage from her Southern black roots, is not utilized as much as in other volumes, notably *And Still I Rise*; however, Angelou writes poems which are very appropriate for junior high and high-school students.

> Candelaria Silva, [Review of *Shaker, Why Don't You Sing?*], *School Library Journal* 30, No. 1 (September 1983): 143

CAROL E. NEUBAUER   Within four years of the publication of *Just Give Me a Cool Drink 'Fore I Diiie*, Maya Angelou completed a second volume of poetry, *Oh Pray My Wings Are Gonna Fit Me Well* (1975). By the time of its release, her reputation as a poet who transforms much of the pain and disappointment of life into lively verse had been established. During the 1970s, her reading public grew accustomed to seeing her poems printed in *Cosmopolitan*. Angelou had become recognized not only as a spokesperson for blacks and women, but also for all people who are committed to raising the moral standards of living in the United States. The poems collected in *My Wings*, indeed, appear at the end of the Vietnam era and in some important ways exceed the scope of her first volume. Many question traditional American values and urge people to make an honest appraisal of the demoralizing rift between the ideal and the real. Along with poems about love and the oppression of black people, the poet adds several that directly challenge Americans to reexamine their lives and to strive to reach the potential richness that has been compromised by self-interest since the beginnings of the country.

One of the most moving poems in My Wings is entitled "Alone," in which carefully measured verses describe the general alienation of people in the twentieth century. "Alone" is not directed at any one particular sector of society but rather is focused on the human condition in general. No one, the poet cautions, can live in this world alone. This message punctuates the end of the three major stanzas and also serves as a separate refrain between each and at the close of the poem:

> Alone, all alone
> Nobody, but nobody
> Can make it out here alone.

Angelou begins by looking within herself and discovering that her soul is without a home. Moving from an inward glimpse to an outward sweep, she recognizes that even millionaires suffer from this modern malaise and live lonely lives with "hearts of stone." Finally, she warns her readers to listen carefully and change the direction of their lives:

> Storm clouds are gathering
> The wind is gonna blow
> The race of man is suffering.

For its own survival, the human race must break down barriers and rescue one from loneliness. The only cure, the poet predicts, is to acknowledge common interests and work toward common goals. ⟨. . .⟩

In one poem, "Southern Arkansia," the poet shifts her attention from the general condition of humanity to the plight of black people in America. The setting of this tightly structured poem is the locale where Angelou spent most of her childhood. At the end of the three stanzas, she poses a question concerning the responsibility and guilt involved in the exploitation of the slaves. Presumably, the white men most immediately involved have never answered for their inhumane treatment of "bartered flesh and broken bones." The poet doubts that they have ever even paused to "ponder" or "wonder" about their proclivity to value profit more than human life.

Carol E. Neubauer, "Maya Angelou: Self and Song of Freedom in the Southern Tradition," Southern Women Writers: The New Generation, ed. Tonette Bond Inge (Tuscaloosa: University of Alabama Press, 1990), pp. 134–35

GLORIA T. HULL   *I Shall Not Be Moved* is Maya Angelou's fifth book of poetry. Because of who she is as actress, activist, woman of letters, and acclaimed autobiographer (*I Know Why the Caged Bird Sings* and succeeding volumes), she is able to command our ear. As I listen, what I hear in her open, colloquial poems is racial wit and earthy wisdom, honest black female pain and strength, humor, passion, and rhetorical force. What I miss—probably because of my academic training and my own predilections as reader and practicing poet—is verbal ingenuity, honed craft, intellectual surprise, and flawless rhythms. Each of her books has at least one striking poem that stands as a centerpiece. Here, it is the title-inspiring work, "Our Grandmothers," which begins:

> She lay, skin down on the moist dirt,
> the canebrake rustling
> with the whispers of leaves, and
> loud longing of hounds and
> the ransack of hunters crackling the near branches.
>
> She muttered, lifting her head a nod toward freedom,
> I shall not, I
> shall not be
> moved.

With slavery figuring so prominently in recent African American women's writings, it is not surprising that this keystone poem of Angelou's mines that tenacious reality.

Gloria T. Hull, "Covering Ground," *Belles Lettres* 6, No. 3 (Spring 1991): 1–2

▦ *Bibliography*

I Know Why the Caged Bird Sings. 1969.
Just Give Me a Cool Drink of Water 'Fore I Diiie: The Poetry of Maya Angelou.
        1971, 1988 (with *Oh Pray My Wings Are Gonna Fit Me Well*).
Gather Together in My Name. 1974, 1985.
Oh Pray My Wings Are Gonna Fit Me Well. 1975.
Singin' and Swingin' and Gettin' Merry Like Christmas. 1976.
And Still I Rise. 1978.
Weekend Glory. 198-.
The Heart of a Woman. 1981.

Poems. 1981, 1986.

Shaker, Why Don't You Sing? 1983.

All God's Children Need Traveling Shoes. 1986.

Now Sheba Sings the Songs. 1986.

Conversations with Maya Angelou. Ed. Jeffrey M. Elliot. 1989.

I Shall Not Be Moved. 1990.

Maya Angelou Omnibus. 1991.

On the Pulse of Morning. 1993.

Soul Looks Back in Wonder. 1993.

Lessons in Living. 1993.

Life Doesn't Frighten Me. 1993.

Wouldn't Take Nothing for My Journey Now. 1993.

I Love the Look of Words. 1993.

And My Best Friend Is Chicken. 1994.

⊞ ⊞ ⊞

Gwendolyn Brooks
b. 1917

GWENDOLYN ELIZABETH BROOKS was born on June 7, 1917, in Topeka, Kansas, but grew up in Chicago. At the age of seven she began to write poetry, and her first poem was published when she was thirteen. Some of these poems were sent to James Weldon Johnson and Langston Hughes, who encouraged her work. As Willard Motley had done before her, Brooks began a weekly column for the *Chicago Defender* when she was sixteen. After graduation in 1936 from Wilson Junior College, she worked as publicity director for the NAACP Youth Council in Chicago. Brooks married Henry Lowington Blakely II in 1939; they have two children.

Brooks's career was launched in 1945 with the publication of her first book of poems, *A Street in Bronzeville*. Its acclaim was immediate; Brooks received a grant from the National Institute of Arts and Letters the next year, as well as a Guggenheim Fellowship. Her next book, *Annie Allen* (1949), won her the Pulitzer Prize for poetry: she was the first black American ever to receive the Pulitzer Prize. More poems followed, as well a book of poems for children (*Bronzeville Boys and Girls*, 1956), frequent book reviews, and the novel *Maud Martha* (1953).

In 1967 Brooks attended the Second Fisk University Writers' Conference and as a result became increasingly concerned with black issues. She left Harper & Row, her longtime publisher, for the black-owned Broadside Press, submitted her poetry to black-edited journals only, edited the magazine *Black Position*, and wrote introductions to several anthologies of work by young black writers. In May 1967 she formed a poetry workshop in Chicago for teenage gang members, eventually encountering Don L. Lee (Haki R. Madhubuti) and Carolyn M. Rodgers, who would go on to become distinguished poets in their own right. Brooks's anthology, *Jump Bad* (1971), collects poems written at this workshop. In 1968 she was named Poet Laureate of the State of Illinois.

By the time she was fifty Gwendolyn Brooks had already become an institution. The Gwendolyn Brooks Cultural Center opened at Western

Illinois University (Macomb, Illinois) in 1970. The next year a large anthology, *The World of Gwendolyn Brooks*, appeared, collecting several of her previous books. Between 1969 and 1973 she was separated from her husband, but they reconciled and in 1974 traveled to Ghana, England, and France. In 1976 Brooks became the first black woman elected to the National Institute of Arts and Letters.

Honors continued to accrue during the 1980s. On January 3, 1980, she recited a poem at the White House. In 1981 the Gwendolyn Brooks Junior High School opened in Chicago. She became the first black woman to serve as Consultant in Poetry at the Library of Congress in 1985–86. Although health problems in the 1970s reduced her output, she continues to write poems, poetry manuals for children (*Young Poet's Primer*, 1980; *Very Young Poets*, 1983), and articles for major magazines. A second omnibus of her work, *Blacks*, appeared in 1987.

Brooks has taught at City College, the University of Wisconsin at Madison, Northeastern Illinois University, Elmhurst College, and Columbia College in Illinois. She has received honorary degrees from nearly fifty universities. The first volume of her autobiography, *Report from Part One*, appeared in 1972; a second volume is in progress. Gwendolyn Brooks presently lives in Chicago.

▓ *Critical Extracts*

STANLEY KUNITZ   If only a single poem could be saved out of this book ⟨*Annie Allen*⟩, I should speak up for the one entitled (from a witty line by Edward Young) "Pygmies Are Pygmies Still, Though Percht on Alps":

> But can see better there, and laughing there
> Pity the giants wallowing on the plain.
> Giants who bleat and chafe in their small grass,
> Seldom to spread the palm; to spit; come clean.
>
> Pygmies expand in cold impossible air,
> Cry fie on giantshine, poor glory which
> Pounds breast-bone punily, screeches, and has
> Reached no Alps: or knows no Alps to reach.

I should vote for this brief poem because of the exquisite rightness of its scale; because, knowing its own limits, it is cleanly and truly separated from the jungle of conception and sensibility that constitutes the not-poem; because the imagery is sharp, the rhythm supple, the word-choice and word-play agreeably inventive; because the small and sequent pleasures of the verse are continually linked and at the last resolved, made one, and magnified. The concluding line is obviously triumphant in its massive concentration; among the other details that please me are the effective manipulation of the off-rhyme, the wallowing and bleating of the giants, the teasing ambiguity of "come clean"; the magical connotations of "giantshine"; the explosive irony in context of the adverb "punily."

How right Gwendolyn Brooks can be, as in projecting the crystalline neatness of—"Pleasant custards sit behind / The white Venetian blind"; or in arriving at the studied casualness of—"Chicken, she chided early, should not wait / Under the cranberries in after-dinner state. / Who had been beaking about the yard of late"; or in producing on occasion the flat, slapping image—"stupid, like a street / That beats into a dead end"; or in distilling her irony into—"We never did learn how / To find white in the Bible"; or in raising her voice without shrillness to the pitch of—"What shall I give my children? who are poor, / Who are adjudged the leastwise of the land, / Who are my sweetest lepers . . ."; or in achieving the beautiful and passionate rhetoric of the lines that close her book—"Rise. / Let us combine. There are no magics or elves / Or timely godmothers to guide us. We are lost, must / Wizard a track through our own screaming weed."

These are as many kinds of rightness, scattered though they be, as are tentatively possessed by any poet of her generation. To make the possession absolute and unique is the task that remains.

Stanley Kunitz, "Bronze by Gold," *Poetry* 76, No. 1 (April 1950): 55–56

HUBERT CREEKMORE   "She was learning to love moments. To love moments for themselves." And this tale of Maud Martha Brown's youth, marriage and motherhood is made up of the moments she loved. With a few exceptions when straightforward narrative takes over, it is presented in flashes, almost gasps, of sensitive lightness—distillations of the significance of each incident—and reminds of Imagist poems or clusters of ideograms from which one recreates connected experience. Miss Brooks' prose style here embodies the finer qualities of insight and rhythm that were notable in her two earlier books of poetry (her *Annie Allen* received the Pulitzer Prize), and gives a freshness, a warm cheerfulness as well as depth of implication to her first novel. In technique and impression it stands virtually alone of its kind.

Hubert Creekmore, "Daydreams in Flight," *New York Times Book Review*, 4 October 1953, p. 4

ARTHUR P. DAVIS   The range of color in the Negro community is fascinating; but, unfortunately, it tends to create a problem *within* the group similar to that between colored and white America. The *inside* color line has never been as definitely prescribed or as harshly drawn as the outside; nevertheless, the problem *has* existed, and it *has* caused friction, misunderstanding and on occasion heartache and tragedy. For obvious reasons, this color difference within the group has made things particularly difficult for the dark girl. ⟨. . .⟩

Miss Brooks uses again and again some variant of a black-and-tan symbol, often that of a dark girl in love with a tan boy who rejects her. But she is always aware of the larger implications of the theme. Her characters, we feel, are not just poor, lost black girls in an inhospitable world; they are poor, lost humans in a modern world of other rejections equally as foolish as those based on color.

Gwendolyn Brooks has published three works: *A Street in Bronzeville* (1945), a volume which ranks with ⟨Countee Cullen's⟩ *Color* and ⟨Langston Hughes's⟩ *The Weary Blues* as a significant first work; *Annie Allen* (1949), which won for her the Pulitzer Prize in Poetry; and the *Bean Eaters* (1960), her latest work. It is not my intention to deal with all of the poems in these works. I am concerned only with those which either directly or by implication involve the black-and-tan symbol. It is my belief that an understanding of Miss Brooks's use of this symbol will give added meaning and significance to all of her works.

The scene on which Miss Brooks places her characters is always "a street in Bronzeville," and Bronzeville is not just Southside Chicago. It is also Harlem, South Philadelphia, and every other black ghetto in the North. Life in these various Bronzeville streets is seldom gay or happy or satisfying. The Bronzeville world is a world of run-down tenements, or funeral homes, or beauty parlors, of old roomers growing older without graciousness, or "cool" young hoodlums headed for trouble, of young girls having abortions. Unlike the South, it is not a place of racial violence, but in other respects it is worse than the South. It is a drab, impersonalized "corner" of the metropolitan area into which the Negro—rootless and alone—has been pushed. A sombre cloud of futility lies over Bronzeville, and nowhere is its presence more tragically felt than in its black-and-tan situations. ⟨. . .⟩

From the time of Phillis Wheatley on down to the present, practically every Negro poet has protested the color proscription in America. Perhaps it is what every sensitive and honest Negro poet *has* to do if he is to retain his self-respect. Gwendolyn Brooks has followed the tradition, but she has written poetry and not polemic.

> Arthur P. Davis, "The Black-And-Tan Motif in the Poetry of Gwendolyn Brooks," *CLA Journal* 6, No. 2 (December 1962): 90–92, 97

DAVID LITTLEJOHN   What she seems to have done is to have chosen, as her handle on the "real" (often the horribly real), the other reality of craftsmanship, of technique. With this she has created a highly stylized screen of imagery and diction and sound—fastidiously exact images, crisp Mandarin diction, ice-perfect sound—to stand between the reader and the subject; to stand often so glittering and sure that all he can ever focus on is the screen. The "subjects"—racial discrimination, mother love, suffering—are dehumanized into *manerismo* figurines, dancing her meters. It is *her* intelligence, *her* imagination, *her* brilliant wit and wordplay that entrap the attention. Always, the subjects are held at arm's length away. Whoever the persona—and she is often forced to make the speakers fastidious, alienated creatures like herself—it is always her mind and her style we are dwelling in.

This can (to a reader still concerned with "subjects") run to excess, when all "idea" is honed away in overcontrol, when all that is left, it seems, is wordplay and allusion and technique: crisp, brisk phrases and images like the taps of steel spike heels, going nowhere. In many of her early poems (especially the *Annie Allen* poems) Mrs. Brooks appears only to pretend to talk of things and of people; her real love is words. The inlay work of words, the *précieux* sonics, the lapidary insets of jeweled images (like those of Gerard

Manley Hopkins) can, in excess, squeeze out life and impact altogether, and all but give the lie to the passions professed in the verbs.

The style itself cannot be described briefly. There is enough new-bought diction and shivery tonic phrasing and rhythmic play to fascinate a university seminar in modern poetics for months. She has learned her art superbly. The words, lines, and arrangements have been worked and worked again into poised exactness: the unexpected apt metaphor, the mock-colloquial asides amid jeweled phrases, the half-ironic repetitions—she knows it all. The stylistic critic could only, at his most keen, fault the rare missed stitch of accent, the off-semitone of allusion.

David Littlejohn, <i>Black on White: A Critical Survey of Writing by American Negroes</i> (New York: Grossman Publishers, 1966), pp. 90–91

MARGARET T. G. BURROUGHS

Will she be remembered because of a limited vocabulary filled with sensational and titillating four letter words used and excused on the basis of relevancy? I think not.

Will she be remembered because her poetry is filled with rage, hate and violence, that hate which is the antithesis of creativity, that hate which corrupts, destroys, and thwarts creativity? I think not.

Will she be remembered because she has mastered the dexterity to embroider cute designs on the page with a typewriter? I think not.

Miss Brooks and her poetry will be remembered and will speak to generations yet to come because in the first instance she is a creative human being who is concerned with all humanity. She will be remembered because she speaks from the deep wellsprings of her own black experience which shares common universals with all downtrodden and oppressed peoples, black, brown, red, white and yellow.

However above all, there is this fact which should be of great import to all younger poets who would seek to emulate Miss Brooks; Miss Brooks is a student and scholar of poetry and writing. She has done and continues to do her homework, that meticulous dedication which is necessary to produce a meaningful and lasting work of art. Miss Brooks has thoroughly mastered her craft. She knows it inside and out and in all of its aspects. She does not resort to fads, tricks or gimmicks of the moment.

Margaret T. G. Burroughs, " 'She'll Speak to Generations Yet to Come,' " <i>To Gwen with Love: An Anthology Dedicated to Gwendolyn Brooks</i>, ed. Patricia L. Brown, Don L. Lee, and Francis Ward (Chicago: Johnson Publishing Co., 1971), pp. 129–30

TONI CADE BAMBARA   Like the younger black poets, Gwen Brooks since the late Sixties has been struggling for a cadence, style, idiom and content that will politicize and mobilize. Like the young black poets, her recent work is moving more toward gesture, sound, intonation, attitude and other characteristics that depend on oral presentation rather than private eyeballing. It is important to have the poet herself assess these moves in her own way so as to establish the ground for future critical biographies. But "change" and "shift" may be too heavy-handed, somewhat misleading; for in rereading the bulk of her work, which *Report ⟨from Part One⟩* does prompt one to do, we see a continuum.

Gwen Brooks's works have also been very much of their times. Prior to the late Sixties, black writers invariably brought up the rear, so to speak, having to prove competence in techniques already laid down by mainstream critics. Jim Crow esthetics decreed that writing "negro" was not enough, not valid—not universal. In these times, however, black writers and critics are the vanguard. Black works of the Thirties and Forties reflect the "social consciousness" of the times. There was a drastic reduction in race themes as compared with the Twenties and an adoption of a "global" perspective; concern about European War II or whatever. The works of the Forties and Fifties gave credence to the shaky premise on which "protest" literature rests—that the oppressor simply needed information about grievances to awaken the dormant conscience. The works of these times, on the other hand, reflect quite another sensibility.

As Gwen Brooks says, "I knew there were injustices, and I wrote about them, but I didn't know what was behind them. I didn't know what kind of society we live in. I didn't know it was all organized." Or, assessing her appeal-to-the-Christian-heart period: "But then, I wasn't reading the books I should have read when I was young. If I'd been reading W. E. B. Du Bois, I would have known." Or, "I thought I was happy, and I saw myself going on like that for the rest of my days, I thought it was the way to live. I wrote . . . But it was white writing, the different trends among whites. Today I am conscious of the fact that my people are black people: it is to them that I appeal for understanding."

> Toni Cade Bambara, [Review of *Report from Part One*], *New York Times Book Review,*
> 7 January 1973, p. 1

GLORIA T. HULL   Verbal economy ⟨. . .⟩ is accomplished more easily in an imperative or declarative mood. Consequently, these moods predominate in Miss Brooks's poetry and, combined with her short lines and generalizing statements, produce gnomic saws and aphorisms. The whole of her famous sonnet, "First fight. Then fiddle," is a classic instance of her speaking in this mode. She adopts the same tone in her later "Second Sermon on the Warpland," part two of which begins: "Salve salvage in the spin. / Endorse the splendor splashes" (*Mecca*). Her penchant for simple declaratives is illustrated by these Eliotic lines:

> The only sanity is a cup of tea.
> The music is in minors.
> (*Mecca*)

Her prediliction for raw statement often results in a string of one-word modifiers appended to a declaration she has just made:

> Peanut is
> Richard—a Ranger and a gentleman.
> A signature. A Herald. And a Span.

Such a juxtaposition of phrases without supplying the grammatical, logical, or emotional links leaves this rich but potentially-difficult creative task to the reader and holds her overt statement of her idea down to its minimum length.

This second set of qualities comprising the economical use of language almost totally characterizes Miss Brooks's *Annie Allen*, the book for which she won the Pulitzer Prize and which, ironically, is generally least liked—particularly by young blacks who reject it for reasons which directly relate to its rugged, intellectual style. Don L. Lee's reaction is typical:

> *Annie Allen* (1949), important? Yes. Read by blacks? No. *Annie Allen* more so than *A Street in Bronzeville* seems to have been written for whites. . . . This poem ("The Anniad") is probably earth-shaking to some, but leaves me completely dry.

Miss Brooks says that when she wrote "The Anniad," she "was fascinated by what words might do there in the poem," and calls it "labored, a poem that's very interested in the mysteries and magic of technique" (*Report from Part One*).

Finally, Miss Brooks has a characteristic way of handling three minor devices. First, her alliteration is often heavy and unsubtle—as a glance back through the quotations will show. Second, she uses rhyme and quick rhyme to integrate her free verse ("In the Mecca," for instance). And last, she sometimes personifies abstractions and non-human entities—a practice which may reflect her animistic beliefs, and certainly contributes to her quaint, colloquial tone. Examples occur plentifully in her poetry: "clawing the suffering dust," "the sick and influential stair," and "The ground springs up; / hits you with gnarls and rust."

In isolation, these peculiarities of style identified in Miss Brooks's poetry seem to be stilted and artificial. Yet it is obvious that she is able to make them work for her, with relatively few lapses or outright failures. She has taken definitive techniques of diction, verbal economy, and sound which are the shared tools of every poet and used them in an individual way to give herself a recognizably distinctive poetic voice.

Gloria T. Hull, "A Note on the Poetic Technique of Gwendolyn Brooks," CLA Journal 19, No. 2 (December 1975): 283–85

HORTENSE J. SPILLERS   For over three decades now, Gwendolyn Brooks has been writing poetry which reflects a particular historical order, often close to the heart of the public event, but the dialectic that is engendered between the event and her reception of it is, perhaps, one of the more subtle confrontations of criticism. We cannot always say with grace or ease that there is a direct correspondence between the issues of her poetry and her race and sex, nor does she make the assertion necessary at every step of our reading. Black and female are basic and inherent in her poetry. The critical question is *how* they are said. Here is what the poet has to say about her own work:

> My aim, in my next future, is to write poems that will somehow successfully "call" all black people: black people in taverns, black people in alleys, black people in gutters, schools, offices, factories, prisons, the consulate; I wish to reach black people in mines, on farms, on thrones; *not* always to "teach"—I shall wish often to entertain, to illumine [emphasis Brooks]. My newish voice will not be an imitation of the contemporary young black voice, which I so admire, but an extending adaptation of today's G. B. voice.

Today's G. B. voice is one of the most complex on the American scene precisely because Brooks refuses to make easy judgments. In fact, her disposition to reserve judgment is directly mirrored in a poetry of cunning, laconic surprise. Any descriptive catalog can be stretched and strained in her case: I have tried "uncluttered," "clean," "robust," "ingenious," "unorthodox," and in each case a handful of poems will fit. This method of grading and cataloguing, however, is essentially busywork, and we are still left with the main business: What in this poetry is stunning and evasive?

To begin with, one of Brooks's most faithfully anthologized poems, "We Real Cool," illustrates the wealth of implication that the poet can achieve in a very spare poem:

> We real cool. We
> Left school. We
> Lurk late. We
> Strike straight. We
> Sing sin. We
> Thin gin. We
> Jazz June. We
> Die soon.

The simplicity of the poem is stark to the point of elaborateness. Less then lean, it is virtually coded. Made up entirely of monosyllables and end-stops, the poem is no non-sense at all. Gathered in eight units of three-beat lines, it does not necessarily invite inflection, but its persistent bump on "we" suggests waltz time to my ear. If the reader chooses to render the poem that way, she runs out of breath, or trips her tongue, but it seems that such "breathlessness" is exactly required of dudes hastening toward their death. Deliberately subverting the romance of sociological pathos, Brooks presents the pool players—"seven in the golden shovel"—in their own time. They make no excuse for themselves and apparently invite no one else to do so. The poem is their situation as *they* see it. In eight (could be nonstop) lines, here is their total destiny. Perhaps comic geniuses, they could well drink to this poem, making it a drinking/revelry song.

Hortense J. Spillers, "Gwendolyn the Terrible: Propositions on Eleven Poems," *Shakespeare's Sisters: Feminist Essays on Women Poets*, ed. Sandra M. Gilbert and Susan Gubar (Bloomington: University of Indiana Press, 1979), pp. 233–34

HARRY B. SHAW   Perhaps the most important technique that Miss Brooks uses in developing her social themes is her masterful control of artful ambiguity. Demanding a great deal of creative response from the reader, her poems are all the more an embodiment of the black experience because the technique of indirection which is vital to black survival is so prevalent in them. Using the black experience and the condition of oppression at the hands of the white man as the underlying social theme of virtually all her poetry, Miss Brooks records the black man's anguish, protest, pride, and hope in his thralldom with the artful ambiguity characteristic of black United States folk poetry. The general approach of her poetry to the life around her reflects the tradition of the black spirituals, black secular slave songs, and blues ballads with their double and triple meanings that hide the underlying and sometimes subliminal meaning that was a form of unoffensive, inconspicuous, or even invisible protest.

As an extension of the intuitive beauty of ambiguity in art used to vent the pent-up feelings of a people whose survival has demanded acquiescence, Miss Brooks's poetry often couches the predominant social themes in such ostensibly displayed conventional themes as death, religion, war, sexual and Platonic love, and peace, to name a few. She also uses many commonplace concrete subjects, such as movies, pool players, old age, apartment dwellings, and physical deformity, that are so innocent or asocial in appearance that they may beguile the unperceptive reader into a superficial reading and, therefore, perhaps a superficial appreciation, missing the heart of the poetry's black message.

Miss Brooks's ability to use the tangible to explain the intangible to reveal the tangible in its proper perspective along with her continuous complexity and subtlety are assets in the overall efficacy of her poetry in conveying social messages. Her poetry is aligned with the black tradition of artful ambiguity and indirection and therefore communicates with a subconscious sophistication that is not possible with expression made solely on the conscious level.

Harry B. Shaw, *Gwendolyn Brooks* (Boston: Twayne, 1980), pp. 182–83

R. BAXTER MILLER   The simple plot and structure of "In the Mecca" (the poem) present an urban setting. For convenience one can divide the narrative into three sections. Part I sets forth the return home from work of Mrs. Sallie Smith, mother of nine. The focus here is on the neighbors that she encounters and on the characterizations of her children. In the second part, the shortest, the woman notices that Pepita, one of her girls, is missing. This prompts the first search through the tenement and allows for further characterization and biblical parody. Part II also concerns the paradox of American myth. The longest section is Part III, which constitutes almost half of the verse. Here the police retrace the Smiths' search. Because of its themes and styles, Part III is probably the richest. The following contribute to its power: militant declarations, interracial lovemaking, rhetorical questions, and Christian myth. The poem ends with the discovery of Pepita's corpse under the bed of Jamaican Edward.

"In the Mecca" represents opposite strains of the Anglo-American tradition. One finds a naturalistic version of Walt Whitman, by way of the industrial age, and the redemptive, if frustrated, potential that characterizes the world of T. S. Eliot. But these influences work so that the peculiarities of the Black American experience transform them into a new and creative vision. By adapting to the social forces of the sixties, the poet uses a new milieu. Her canvas is a most demanding time in American history. For this and other times, Gwendolyn Brooks holds to light the soundness of body and mind against the decline of courage and assurance, a lapse which emerged with modernity and the shadow of the holocaust. She continues to believe that imaginative and verbal power challenge and balance finally the danger which posits the insignificance of human life and the indifference to human extinction. For her generation, the defining emblem is ultimately the whirlwind, the collapse of self-confidence, the failure to transform social ill once more into epic victory and to reclaim from the time before the holocaust, and the later accusation of "reverse discrimination" in the United States, the heroic and bluesesque will of Black hope. Whereas for Margaret Walker, cleansing has been the metaphor for the perspective which woman takes on historical and cosmic evil, the depth here every bit as great as Melville's "mystery of iniquity," for Brooks the sign is medication. The artistic process itself plays out the action of healing, while the poem serves as both epic quest and sacramental liberation.

R. Baxter Miller, " 'Define . . . the Whirlwind': Gwendolyn Brooks' Epic Sign for a Generation," *Black American Poets Between Worlds, 1940–1960*, ed. R. Baxter Miller (Knoxville: University of Tennessee Press, 1986), pp. 162–63

D. H. MELHEM   "Bronzeville," Brooks remarks, was a name invented by the *Chicago Defender*. She described it to ⟨Elizabeth⟩ Lawrence as a South Side area of about forty blocks, running north and south from 29th to 69th Streets, and east and west about thirteen blocks from Cottage Grove to State Street (Sept. 28, 1944). An anatomy of Bronzeville appears in the important sociological study *Black Metropolis*, by St. Clair Drake and Horace R. Clayton. These authors analyze the nature and consequences of segregated black life and call for integration to combat its evils. In "Bronzeville 1961," a new chapter for the 1962 edition, Drake and Clayton find that their foci of investigation or "axes of life" remain what they had been in 1945 when the study was first made. The categories are " 'staying alive,' 'getting ahead,' 'having fun,' 'praising god,' and 'advancing the Race.' " In some respects these topics gloss *A Street in Bronzeville*, although skepticism tinges "praising god" and irony touches the "Race Hero" who is "advancing the Race."

A corollary aspect of "advancing the Race" by individual achievement or through social action is "the demand for solidarity" (Drake). This long-standing desire roots Brooks's later concern, most marked in *Beckonings* and "In Montgomery." It partly explains the early sources of her interest and the depth of her later chagrin at the erosion of unity.

Brooks initially planned *A Street in Bronzeville* to portray a personality, event, or idea representing each of thirty houses on a street in the vicinity. The sequence of twenty poems in the first section, "A Street in Bronzeville," is close in tone and milieu to the following five, grouped here as "Five Portraits." All the poems give humanistic and compassionate glimpses of black life. The first section focuses on common existence; the middle one, except for "Hattie Scott," offers longer poems that probe distinct and dramatic characters. The third and last section, "Gay Chaps at the Bar," comprises the sonnet sequence. Thematically, the volume is largely structured around two units: local/black and national/multiracial. Brooks exposes their interrelationships—personal, social, and national. The theme of entrapment, by community norms, socioeconomic forces, and personal psychology, underlies the whole.

D. H. Melhem, *Gwendolyn Brooks* (Lexington: University Press of Kentucky, 1987), pp. 19–20

GLADYS WILLIAMS   Brooks has been an innovative poet. She is also an artist in whom the forces of tradition and continuity have enriched her craft. She has written carefully disciplined and well-wrought sonnets in the tradition of Shakespeare. Metrical craft and poetic form have been as much a consideration for Brooks as they have been in her antecedents Yeats and Frost. The metaphysical wit of Eliot, Pound, Frost, and the younger Robert Lowell have exerted a significant influence on the poet. The basic and central free-verse tradition that comes to Brooks through Walt Whitman, James Weldon Johnson, Sterling Brown, William Carlos Williams, and her beloved Langston Hughes is especially strong. Certain features of her art originate in the black folk art forms—the blues, the ballads, the folk tales, the sermons Brooks grew up with—as well as in the works of Shakespeare, Frost, Dickinson, et al. The poet's penchant for understatement, her wry and ironic humor, her terseness, her skill in giving her poetry the sound of the human voice, and the ethnotropic metaphor she creates are brilliantly present in her ballads as they are in the folk ballad antecedents. The Brooks ballad reveals one stream of the multiple literary influences that flow through her poetry.

> Gladys Williams, "The Ballads of Gwendolyn Brooks," A *Life Distilled: Gwendolyn Brooks, Her Poetry and Fiction*, ed. Maria K. Mootry and Gary Smith (Urbana: University of Illinois Press, 1987), pp. 222–23

GEORGE E. KENT   Actually, *Annie Allen* challenges not so much by its particularism as by its craft and its universality—further developments of the resources and approaches present in *A Street in Bronzeville*. The poems in *A Street* offer a deceptively full realistic surface and make use of well-known devices from the conventions and techniques of poetic realism. There are abrupt beginnings in *A Street* and some elliptical syntax, which demand that the reader drop everything and attend closely, but neither is developed to the extent manifested in *Annie Allen*.

One major difference between the two works is that the reader of *Annie Allen* is more openly confronted with the necessity to read actively. Although people and their life stories appear in plots sharply outlined, presenting easily recognized issues from the daily round of existence, and move to definite climaxes and decisive conclusions, there are frequent signals of the presence of more than one perspective—additional comments upon the human condition available beneath the poems' realistic surface, representing engagement with the contradictoriness and complexity of experience.

The opening poems of the two works illustrate the difference. A *Street* opens with "the old-marrieds": "But in the crowding darkness not a word did they say. / Though the pretty-coated birds had piped so lightly all the day." Except for the abrupt beginning with "but," there is nothing to discomfit the reader. The syntax is regular except for punctuation of a clause as a full sentence in the second line—certainly no radical break with established practice.

Annie Allen, proper, on the other hand, opens with "the birth in a narrow room": "Weeps out of Western country something new. / Blurred and stupendous. Wanted and unplanned." Whereas in "the old-marrieds" the issue and perhaps the mystery of the story are almost immediately suggested, "the birth" requires careful and repeated readings to grasp the theme: the slow absorption of "reality" by infant life and the creative experiences awaiting the infant between the stages of unreflecting confrontation with existence and realization of its limitations. The poem demands greater reader participation and creativity: an acceptance of the elliptical syntax in the first stanza and grasp of images with mythic functions—not merely of day-to-day "reality." The infant's first movement into time is an almost passive survey of artifacts, with the last image foreshadowing something of the magic of the childhood world: "the milk-glass fruit bowl, iron pot, / The bashful china child tripping forever / Yellow apron and spilling pretty cherries." The second stanza mixes images of reality with expressions and gestures connoting the transforming power of early childhood imagination:

> But prances nevertheless with gods and fairies
> Blithely about the pump and then beneath
> The elms and grapevines, then in darling endeavor
> By privy foyer, where the screenings stand
> And where the bugs buzz by in private cars
> Across old peach cans and old jelly jars.

George E. Kent, *A Life of Gwendolyn Brooks* (Lexington: University Press of Kentucky, 1990), pp. 80–81

◈ Bibliography

A Street in Bronzeville. 1945.
Annie Allen. 1949.

Maud Martha. 1953.

Bronzeville Boys and Girls. 1956.

We Real Cool. 1959.

The Bean Eaters. 1960.

Selected Poems. 1963.

In the Time of Detachment, in the Time of Cold. 1965.

The Wall. 1967.

In the Mecca. 1968.

Martin Luther King, Jr. 1968.

For Illinois 1968: A Sesquicentennial Poem. 1968.

Riot. 1969.

Family Pictures. 1970.

Aloneness. 1971.

The World of Gwendolyn Brooks. 1971.

Elegy in a Rainbow: A Love Poem. 1971.

A Broadside Treasury 1965–1970 (editor). 1971.

Black Steel: Joe Frazier and Muhammad Ali. 1971.

Jump Bad: A New Chicago Anthology (editor). 1971.

Aurora. 1972.

Report from Part One. 1972.

The Tiger Who Wore White Gloves; or, What You Are You Are. 1974.

Beckonings. 1975.

A Capsule Course in Black Poetry Writing (with Keorapetse Kgositsile, Haki R. Madhubuti, and Dudley Randall). 1975.

Other Music. 1976.

The Mother. 1978.

Primer for Blacks. 1980.

Young Poet's Primer. 1980.

To Disembark. 1981.

Black Love. 1982.

The Progress. 1982.

Mayor Harold Washington and Chicago, the I Will City. 1983.

Very Young Poets. 1983.

The Near-Johannesburg Boy and Other Poems. 1986.

Blacks. 1987.

Winnie. 1988.

The Second Sermon on the Warpland. 1988.

Gottschalk and the Grande Tarantelle. 1988.

Jane Addams: September 6, 1860–May 21, 1935. 1990.
Children Coming Home. 1991.
Christmas Morning Comes Too Soon. 1992.

Alice Childress
1920–1994

ALICE CHILDRESS was born in Charleston, South Carolina, on October 12, 1920. She was raised in Harlem in New York City by her grandmother, Eliza Campbell. Although her education extended only to the fifth grade, Campbell was a great storyteller; according to Childress, however, "she was not fond of remembering her mother's account of slavery and the mockery of so-called freedom" in the Reconstruction South. Childress dropped out of high school after two years, but was a voracious reader and continued her education at the public library. She became interested in acting after hearing Laura Bowman recite scenes from Shakespeare and, in 1941, joined the American Negro Theatre in Harlem, going on to perform in some of ANT's biggest hits, such as *On Strivers' Row* and *Anna Lucasta*.

In 1949 Childress wrote her first play, a one-act piece entitled *Florence*. The play (purportedly written in one night) was a moderate success and proved typical of Childress's work in its exploration of contemporary racial issues. *Florence* was followed by *Just a Little Simple* (1950), an adaptation of Langston Hughes's novel *Simple Speaks His Mind*, and by *Gold through the Trees* (1952), a play about Harriet Tubman that was the first play by a black woman to be professionally produced in the United States. In 1955 Childress wrote *Trouble in Mind*, a critically and financially successful play about a group of black actors who, while rehearsing a lynching melodrama written and directed by whites entitled *Chaos in Belleville*, protest the offensive stereotyping of the play's black characters. Childress published the play in Lindsay Patterson's *Black Theatre* in 1971, deleting a final act in which the director agrees to a rewrite of *Chaos*. Plays following *Trouble in Mind* include *Wedding Band: A Love/Hate Story in Black and White* (produced 1966; published 1973), a play about an interracial couple in Charleston in 1918; *Wine in the Wilderness* (1969), a television play about the insensitivity of "revolutionary" black nationalists toward less educated, older, and less politically correct black Americans; the one-act *String* (produced 1969; published, with *Mojo*, 1971), an adaptation of Guy de Maupassant's short story "A Piece of String"; and most recently *Moms* (1989), a biographical drama about the black vaudeville comedienne Jackie "Moms" Mabley.

In addition to plays, Childress wrote a book based on her conversations with black domestic workers, *Like One of the Family* (1956). She wrote a variety of works, including theatricals and novels, for children. Her first young adult novel, *A Hero Ain't Nothin' But a Sandwich* (1973), about a fourteen-year-old heroin addict, was adapted by the author into a critically successful film produced in 1977. Other young adult novels include *A Short Walk* (1979), *Rainbow Jordan* (1981), and *Those Other People* (1989). She also published two plays for children, *When the Rattlesnake Sounds* (1975) and *Let's Hear It for the Queen* (1976).

Childress was married twice, but information on her first husband is unavailable; from this marriage she had one daughter. She married musician Nathan Woodard in 1957. Alice Childress died on August 14, 1994.

⊠ *Critical Extracts*

A. G.   A fresh, lively and cutting satire called *Trouble in Mind* is being played downtown by an inter-racial group of Equity members. ⟨. . .⟩

Their play's setting is backstage at a Broadway theatre during the first rehearsal of a tawdry melodrama dealing with a Negro lynching in the South. The author of *Trouble in Mind* is Alice Childress, a writer with a quick eye for the foibles and crotches, the humor and pathos of backstage life in the type of Broadway production that utilizes a predominantly Negro cast.

Miss Childress, who was a member of the original company of *Anna Lucasta*, has some witty and penetrating things to say about the dearth of roles for Negro actors in the contemporary theatre, the cut-throat competition for these parts and the fact that Negro actors often find themselves playing stereotyped roles in which they cannot bring themselves to believe.

She also has some sharp comments to make about the jumpy state of nerves in the much-investigated entertainment media. But it is all done with good humor and, except for the last ten or fifteen minutes, manages to avoid any impassioned sermonizing.

A. G., "Play in Village Is Well Worth the Trip," *New York Times*, 5 Novemeber 1955, p. 23

DORIS E. ABRAMSON   *Trouble in Mind* has interesting characters
and dialogue, though both tend to ring false whenever they are saturated
with sermonizing. The setting, the stage of a theatre during rehearsals,
invites an audience to participate in a ritual usually forbidden them and
therefore tantalizing. The plot amounts to very little—a group of actors
rehearse a play, quarrel about interpretation, get the director to agree to
ask the playwright to make changes in the script. What lends the play
significance is that the cast is predominantly Negro. As attitudes in the
company are modified, people's lives are affected, and this play about a
rehearsal makes a comment on life itself.

And yet, too much of *Trouble in Mind* is willed—what the French call
voulu. A reader of the script is very much aware of the author pulling strings,
putting her own words into a number of mouths. This is not, however, to
deny the theatrical effectiveness of the play in production. One critic's
description of the audience participation suggests a very direct involvement:

> The satirical scenes rocked and moved the audience until it
> became part of the action on the stage. Many members of the
> audience were so moved that they vocally expressed dislike or
> approval of the actions and speeches of the characters on stage. I
> have not seen anything like it since I was a boy and sat in the
> gallery with other kids watching Wild West melodramas.

Brooks Atkinson found the play "well worth a trip downtown" and praised
Miss Childress for writing a "fresh, lively and cutting satire" without sermonizing until the last ten or fifteen minutes.

To read the play is to be much more aware than these critics were—
they were under the spell of what was reportedly a good production—of
the extent to which Miss Childress loaded the play with Negro problems.
True, she makes us understand her need to write about her people when
she says:

> Many of us would rather be writers than Negro writers, and when
> I get that urge, I look about for the kind of white writer—which
> is what we mean when we say "just a writer"—that I would
> emulate. I come up with Sean O'Casey. Immediately, I am a
> problem writer. O'Casey writes about the people he knows best
> and I must.

It would be better if she did not assault race prejudice at every turn, for
she sometimes sacrifices depth of character in the process.

What a critic once said of Mildred, the heroine of Miss Childress' collection of stories, *Like One of the Family*, could be said of characters in her
play, especially of Wiletta:

> One longs for the shock (so often encountered in life) of an
> unexpected taste or point of view. One longs also to penetrate
> beyond the "typical" view we are given . . . to the private agony
> and unique courage of such a woman.

The characters need a humanizing complexity to keep them from ever
becoming the stereotypes featured in *Chaos in Belleville*.

Doris E. Abramson, *Negro Playwrights in the American Theatre 1925–1959* (New York:
Columbia University Press, 1967), pp. 203–4

ELBERT R. HILL   The important differences between novels and
films become particularly apparent when the same author treats a story in
both media, as Alice Childress did when she wrote the screenplay for *A
Hero Ain't Nothin' But a Sandwich* (1978), based on a novel she had published
five years earlier. ⟨. . .⟩

⟨. . .⟩ the movie ⟨*A Hero Ain't Nothin' But a Sandwich*⟩ never makes it
sufficiently clear how or why Benjie becomes addicted to drugs. To show
that Benjie is becoming hooked, the filmmaker resorts to the device of
repetitive scenes showing him using the drugs and earning money for this
habit by delivering drugs. In the movie, the whole time lapse from Benjie's
first use of marijuana to when we know that he is, in fact, unable to
quit heroin, seems altogether too brief and unrealistically sudden. And the
question of *why* Benjie takes drugs remains quite puzzling. Though bothered
by the fact that he does not know where his real father is, he appears to
have no other problem. Because of the shift in setting and some other
changes as well, Benjie's environment seems neither hostile nor threatening.
At home, he is surrounded by people who care about him, even though
they have their own needs and preoccupations too. And in school he even
seems to be something of a star. There is a scene in Nigeria's class in which
Benjie is able to amaze the whole class, teacher included, with his knowledge
about a particular black leader. And in Bernard Cohen's class, he is asked
to read aloud a composition for which he is publicly praised and given an
"A".

The scene is apparently used to show two things: first, assigned to write about a member of his family, Benjie has selected his mother, thus revealing her importance to him as his only remaining parent. Second, when as part of his praise Cohen says, "Keep this up and some day you'll be somebody," Benjie replies, "I'm somebody now." We are confronted with a common adolescent problem: the feeling that adults don't give them credit for being someone *now*, and focus too much on what they *may* grow up to be. The scene thus fulfills some valid functions in the movie, but combined with the scene in Nigeria's class it also suggests that Benjie's school provides a generally supportive atmosphere. In the book, the praise Benjie receives for the paper about his mother is said to be something that happened years before the time of the book, and it is not typical of his school career. There is no equivalent in the book of the scene in Nigeria's class.

In addition, the Benjie of the novel tells us several times that one of his problems is that he feels betrayed by Nigeria Greene, who, along with Cohen, has turned him in for drug use. Though the movie does show the two teachers taking him out of class when he is obviously stoned, it does not emphasize for us the importance that this betrayal has for Benjie because it has not made sufficiently clear how he has idolized Nigeria.

A time shift that is even more troublesome ⟨. . .⟩ concerns the change in the relationship between Benjie and Butler. In the book, after Butler has saved his life, Benjie writes "Butler is my father" one hundred times. This indicates that Benjie finally realizes that Butler does indeed care for him, and suggests to the reader that the boy is accepting Butler's role in his life. ⟨. . .⟩ In the movie, Benjie writes "Butler is my father" much earlier, *before* Butler has saved his life—and so far as we know Butler never sees the piece of writing. Thus, the movie Benjie's motivation for trying to get off drugs— like his motivation for getting on them—is not fully clear ⟨. . .⟩

The ending of the movie is revealing of the overall differences between the two forms. In the movie, when Butler waits for Benjie at the Rehab Center, the boy actually appears; in the book Butler only waits and hopes. The movie ending is weaker in consequence ⟨. . .⟩ The reader was led to believe that Benjie will appear, because this would be the logical result of his realization of Butler's love for him and of his acceptance of the older man as his hero. But since moviegoers have not had this clear motivation for Benjie to change, they need to be shown that the boy does indeed intend to change.

Elbert R. Hill, "A *Hero* for the Movies," *Children's Novels and the Movies*, ed. Douglas Street (New York: Frederick Ungar, 1983), pp. 236, 240–42

ALICE CHILDRESS   I try to bend my writing form to most truth-fully express content; to move beyond the either/or of "artistic" and politi-cally imposed limitations. I never planned to become a writer. Early writing was done almost against my will. Grandmother Eliza gently urged, "Why not write that thought down on a piece of paper? It's worth keeping." Writing was jotting things down. The bits and pieces became stories. Writing was a way of reminding myself to go on with thoughts, to take the next step. Jottings became forms after I discovered the public library and attempted to read two books a day. Reading and evaluating form, I taught myself to know the difference of structure in plays, books, short stories, teleplays, motion picture scenarios, and so forth. Knowledge of such form and much content taught me to break rules and follow my own thought and structure patterns with failure and success. I acquired a measure of self-discipline, to make myself write against my will in the face of a limited market. ⟨. . .⟩

My books tend to read somewhat like plays because theater heavily influenced my writing. I think mainly in terms of visual, staged scenes and live actors in performance—even in a novel. The novel and film allow for more wandering and changing of "setting." The stage play, confined to one area, taxes the imagination more than other forms. It is the greatest challenge because it also depends heavily on the cooperation of many other individuals with several approaches to creative expression—the director, the producer, set, scene and lighting people, costumer etc. ⟨. . .⟩

While one is creating a character there are glad moments of divorce from one's own conscious theories and beliefs. We can be taken over by a charac-ter. I was tempted to remove "The Pusher" from *A Hero Ain't Nothin' But a Sandwich*: the villain was too persuasive, too good at self-defense, too winning in his sinning; however, he is the toughest form of street temptation, so I let him live. The book was banned from the Island Trees School Library, case still pending along with several others after going through two courts. It was also the first book banned from a Savannah, Georgia, school library since *Catcher in the Rye* was banned during the fifties. Writing is indeed exciting and the joy of creation, though tedious at times, is the highest form of compensation. Well, I can't find a thought to better this old one. . . .

Alice Childress, "A Candle in a Gale Wind," *Black Women Writers (1950–1980): A Critical Evaluation*, ed. Mari Evans (Garden City, NY: Anchor Press/Doubleday, 1984), pp. 114–16

SAMUEL A. HAY   In two ways, *Florence* is typical of Alice
Childress's seventeen plays: (a) Childress in interested in a well-crafted
situation about an essentially good person who is hurt by Blacks or whites
because the person mistakes (false) signs for (true) symbols; and (b) Childress
changes her dramatic structure according to whether a Black or a white
person creates the hurt. The first typicality places Childress in the William
Wells Brown tradition of writing well-structured plays which aim to show
how things ought to be, or where they have gone wrong. ⟨. . .⟩

What sets Childress apart is the second typicality. Childress switches the
protagonist-antagonist functions and creates several other revolutionary
changes in order to support her political and ethical concerns. ⟨. . .⟩

Childress can be classified as a traditionalist in structure because she (a)
treats her episodes as the building blocks of her play, (b) distinguishes one
episode from another by the appearance of a new character or by a principal
character's leaving the scene or retiring from participation in the action, and
(c) avoids improvisational and experimental structural devices altogether.
Nevertheless, Childress designs her episodes for quite different purposes
than the usual psychological characterization popularized by Eugene O'Neill
during the forties and fifties, and adopted by such newcomers in the fifties
as Tennessee Williams and Arthur Miller. Instead, Childress keeps the
traditional beginning, middle, and end, and she substitutes theme for character. The substitution strains the traditional structure because Childress does
not reveal the theme through characterization but through argumentation.
Therefore, each episode develops not only the usually slim Childress story
but, more importantly, the Main Idea. Because the constituent ideas simply
repeat the Main Idea, the purpose of each episode, then, is to represent
another "circumstantial detail" of the Main Idea. Elder Olson explains:

> If I remark that the news of the day includes a murder, a robbery,
> a fire, a suicide, a bank failure, and a divorce, you respond with
> simple ideas of these; but if I go into circumstantial detail, you
> frame very complex ones. By "circumstances," I mean the doer of
> the action, the act, the purpose, the instrument with which it was
> done, the manner in which it was done, the person or object to
> which it was done, the result, the time, the place, and all similar
> matters.

To understand fully the substitutions of the idea for character and of circumstantial detail for the Main Idea development, the concerns must be to
identify which circumstantial detail develops which constituent idea of the

Main Idea. For example, the Main Idea in *Florence* is: "Black people—not white liberals—must struggle if there is to be real political and economic equality."

Samuel A. Hay, "Alice Childress's Dramatic Structure," *Black Women Writers (1950– 1980): A Critical Evaluation*, ed. Mari Evans (Garden City, NY: Anchor Press/Double-day, 1984), pp. 118–19

GAYLE AUSTIN ⟨Childress's⟩ plays themselves ⟨. . .⟩ break down ⟨. . .⟩ binary oppositions. Stage one deals with the images of women composed by men, with woman as object. Stage two deals with women as artists, with women as subjects, actively telling their own stories. Stage three is still somewhat undefined but deals more with women as critics, with textual conventions and the ways women tell their stories.

Many of the characters and ideas in *Trouble in Mind* are as fresh as and perhaps more generally recognizable than they were thirty years ago. Both the character, Wiletta, and author Childress are actively protesting the few and false images of black women written by white men with "blind spots." ⟨. . .⟩ Childress, in writing the roles of Wiletta and Millie, has provided some alternative images of black women, three dimensional characters with weaknesses and strengths.

In terms of the second stage, Wiletta becomes a critic/artist of the play she is performing, changing from passive object to active subject in front of our eyes ⟨. . .⟩ Wiletta's argument against the character she is trying to "act" builds in act two ⟨. . .⟩ She asks, "Why we sendin' him out into the teeth of a lynch mob? I'm his mother and I'm sendin' him to his death. This is a lie. . . . The writer wants the damn white man to be the hero— and I'm the villain." ⟨. . .⟩ Wiletta's criticism reshapes some other cast members' ideas of the play, and her challenge to Manners that he is a racist rewrites Wiletta's career story, making her an unemployed subject rather than employable object. That situation will only change when the entire system changes, the difficulty of which is put into the mouth of the director during his tirade:

> MANNERS: . . . Get wise, there's damned few of us interested in putting on a colored show at all, much less one that's going to say anything. . . . Do you think I can stick my neck out by telling the truth about you? There are billions of things that *can't be said.* . . .

Where the hell do you think I can raise a hundred thousand
dollars to tell the unvarnished truth? (*Picks up the script and waves
it.*) So maybe it's a lie . . . but it's one of the finest lies you'll
come across for a damned long time! . . . The American public is
not ready to see you the way you want to be seen because, one,
they don't believe it, two, they don't want to believe it, and
three, they're convinced they're superior—and that, my friend, is
why Carrie and Renard [white characters] have to carry the ball!
Get it? Now you wise up and aim for the soft spot in that
American heart, let 'em pity you, make 'em weep buckets, be
helpless, make 'em feel so damned sorry for you that they'll lend a
hand in easing up the pressure.

That is a most concise and accurate statement of the dynamic of both black
and female cultural images in this country, and it comes from a white male
character who both knows the score and helps perpetuate the game. But
he does not get the final word in this play, and Wiletta's continuing presence
on stage is something new and potentially powerful. ⟨. . .⟩

Inserting women's *presence* into a story is an even more powerful weapon
⟨. . .⟩ and that is the one chosen by Childress in this play. She also uses
some theatrical devices in ways that help to write women into the script.
Her play-within-a-play structure allows her to demonstrate the way male
images portray black women and show both the actor's true and false feelings
about those images. ⟨. . .⟩ She also uses Wiletta's singing of a song in *Chaos
in Belleville*, first in a manner of "despair" and then in "strength and anger"
to show Wiletta's growing rebellion, Manners' dissatisfaction with the latter
interpretation, and the double-edged weapon art can become. Overlapping
dialogue more than once conveys chaos in both the rehearsal situation and
Wiletta's mind. In bending conventional tools to her use as well as "speaking
the unspoken" Childress helped fill the absence of role models for black
women playwrights (this was four years before Lorraine Hansberry wrote *A
Raisin in the Sun*) and the lack of substantial roles for black actresses.

Gayle Austin, "Alice Childress: Black Woman Playwright as Feminist Critic," *Southern Quarterly* 25, No. 30 (Spring 1987): 56–59

SANDRA Y. GOVAN   ⟨. . .⟩ moving readers, and demonstrating
that her characters are indeed human and not mere symbols, statistics,

images, or stones, is clearly a part of Childress's multi-layered strategy, part of the function of her art.

And when we examine ⟨Rainbow Jordan . . .⟩ we see Childress being attentive not only to function but to the other considerations of the Black Aesthetic as well. If, for instance, the function of Black art is to accent racial identity—who we are and where we are going; or if it is to make myths and render the ordinary extraordinary—Childress achieves this "function" and yet accomplishes this in her own singular fashion. Unlike a Mildred Taylor or a Toni Cade Bambara, writers known for their creation of sassy or tough young female protagonists, in Rainbow Jordan Childress makes her heroine, and each of her other characters, walk the high wire in a solo balancing act, alone and unsteady until they learn first to reach inward for self-validation and strength, then outward to touch others who themselves are authentic and thus willing to reach out.

The usual or traditional community support structures typically illustrative of Afro-American life and culture play virtually no role in Rainbow. The Black church, a staple symbol in much Afro-American literature, is notable by its absence. In fact, Josephine's Quaker neighbor teaches Rainbow the Quaker concept of "centering down" rather than prayer to help face a problem. The strong nurturing community with neighbor helping neighbor, a recurring motif in much Afro-American literature, especially that set in the South, is also absent. Rather, Childress unabashedly depicts the divisive, splintered, often antagonistic communities which are, regretfully, a truism of contemporary urban living.

Rainbow's awkward family situation stands as ironic counterpoint to the dominant Afro-American literary tradition that paints a strong cohesive family, either nuclear or extended, as central element in the formation of character. Here we have a portrait of family disintegration, again an all too frequent truism of modern urban life. Authentic female bonding among peers, such as that which occurs in Toni Morrison's Sula (1973) or Paule Marshall's Brown Girl, Brownstones (1959), is also missing. Of course, Rainbow and Josephine "bond" but 14 and 57 is hardly the same peer group. Instead, Rainbow painfully learns the wisdom of that deathless folk pronouncement, "Everybody who say they your friend, ain't." Intriguingly, the one remaining traditional symbol or cultural ritual which Childress permits is a very subtle bow to the blues. Both Rainbow and Josephine suffer from heartache; and heartaches are, as every mature reader knows, a staple of the blues. Even Kathie has heartaches, but she is essentially a "good time girl," another kind of staple blues figure. Heartaches, of course, don't last always and by novel's end, Rainbow and Josephine have hardened their will, left the "low-down" men in their lives behind, and walked away. They suffer still, but they've experienced the catharsis the blues afford.

Because of the skill with which they are invoked, both Rainbow (and certainly the name is weighted with obvious symbolic intent) and Josephine become, despite any intent to the contrary, symbols of survival. They are also powerful images of what it can mean to "hold fast" to one's dreams, as Langston Hughes has said, and to live with integrity and dignity. Childress's commitment to depicting the lives of people within the working class and middle class Black communities provides us with, as Trudier Harris says, a "sensitive readable book which entertains quietly and teaches without being overly didactic."

> Sandra Y. Govan, "Alice Childress's *Rainbow Jordan:* The Black Aesthetic Returns Dressed in Adolescent Fiction," *Children's Literary Association Quarterly* 13, No. 1 (Summer 1988): 73

CATHERINE WILEY   Julia's problem throughout the play ⟨*Wedding Band*⟩ is less her white lover than her reluctance to see herself as a member of the black community. Although a mostly white theater audience would see her as a different sort of heroine because of race, her black neighbors perceive her as different from them for issues more complex than skin color. She assumes that her racial transgression with Herman will make her unwelcome among the women she wishes to confide in, but her aloofness from their day-to-day interests also serves as a protective shield. In this, Julia is similar to Lutie Johnson in Ann Petry's *The Street*, written in 1946. Both characters are ostensibly defined by their unequal relations with men, but their potential for salvation lies in the larger community that depends on the stability of its women. ⟨. . .⟩ Neither poor nor uneducated, Julia finds herself defying the black community by asserting her right to love a white man, but this self-assertion is, in a larger sense, a more dangerous defiance of the white community. She wants her love story to be one of individual commitment and sacrifice, but it is that only in part. Julia's refinement in manners, education, and financial independence, which are middle-class, traditionally white attributes, make her and Herman available to each other.

But theirs is, as the subtitle insists, a "love/hate" story, in which interracial love cannot be divorced from centuries of racial hate. ⟨. . .⟩

The first white character to appear in the play is the Bell Man, a foil to Herman, who pedals dime-store merchandise in the poor neighborhood using the insidious installment system, "fifty cent a week and one long, sweet year to pay." Recognizing Julia from another neighborhood, he comments sardonically that she moves a lot, invites himself into her bedroom, and bounces on the bed. "But seriously, what is race and color?" he asks. "Put a paper bag over your head and who'd know the difference." When Julia chases him out with a wooden hanger, he calls her a "sick-minded bitch" because she refuses to play the historical role of the master's sexual toy, already bought and paid for on the slave market. Like the landlady, who also has pushed herself unwanted into Julia's rented room, the Bell Man objectifies Julia into a representative of her race. If for Fanny the proper black woman is to be asexual, for the salesman she is to be a body with a paper bag over her head, hiding not only her race but her existence as an individual with a face and a name. Fanny's attitude constitutes one legitimate response to centuries of white men's sexual abuse of black women. Julia's relationship with Herman should not leave her open to the insults of a traveling salesman, but in his eyes, and perhaps in Fanny's, that relationship makes her another black woman who "prefers" white men.

This scene points to the inseparability of racism and sexism, an issue that cannot be isolated from the historical relationship of the civil rights and women's movements. ⟨. . .⟩ The signal white women's liberationists ⟨of the 1960s⟩ sent to black women echoed the one suffragists had sent to their abolitionist sisters a century earlier: your race matters less than your gender. ⟨. . .⟩ If a black woman is to be a feminist, it appears she must cease to be black. Julia's treatment by Fanny and the salesman effects the opposite but equally insidious contradiction: she can be a member of the black race, but as such she cannot be an individual woman.

Catherine Wiley, "Whose Name, Whose Protection: Reading Alice Childress's *Wedding Band*," *Modern American Drama: The Female Canon*, ed. June Schlueter (Rutherford, NJ: Fairleigh Dickinson University Press, 1990), pp. 188–90

❖ *Bibliography*

Like One of the Family: Conversations from a Domestic's Life. 1956.

Wine in the Wilderness: A Comedy-Drama. 1969.

Black Scenes (editor). 1971.

Mojo and String. 1971.

A Hero Ain't Nothin' But a Sandwich. 1973.

Wedding Band: A Love/Hate Story in Black and White. 1973.

When the Rattlesnake Sounds. 1975.

Let's Hear It for the Queen. 1976.

A Short Walk. 1979.

Rainbow Jordan. 1981.

Many Closets. 1987.

Those Other People. 1989.

Lucille Clifton
b. 1936

LUCILLE CLIFTON was born Thelma Lucille Sayles on June 27, 1936, in Depew, New York. She was named Lucille after her great-grandmother, who was the first black woman legally hanged in Virginia (she shot and killed the white man who impregnated her, but her mother's standing in the community was such that she was not lynched). Lucille Sayles's parents were estranged and her family quite poor; nevertheless, she grew up in a nurturing and supportive environment filled with stories of her family's history, all of which she missed a great deal when she attended Howard University in Washington, D.C., from 1953 to 1955. After two years at Howard, she attended Fredonia State Teachers College (now State University of New York College at Fredonia) for a year. She married educator, writer, and artist Fred James Clifton in 1958; they would eventually have six children. Her family figures prominently in Clifton's work.

Clifton's first job was as a claims clerk for the New York State Division of Employment in Buffalo, New York. After working there for two years (1958–60), she gave up her career to stay home and raise her children. She took to writing only in her early thirties, by which time she also resumed employment, this time in the academic community: she was a literature assistant for the Central Atlantic Regional Educational Laboratory from 1969 to 1971 and poet in residence at Coppin State College in Baltimore from 1971 to 1974.

Clifton's first book of poetry, *Good Times*, was published in 1969 to critical acclaim, being cited as one of the year's ten best books by the *New York Times*. This volume was followed by several other books of poetry: *Good News about the Earth: New Poems* (1972), *An Ordinary Woman* (1974), *Two-Headed Woman* (1980), the retrospective *Good Woman: Poems and a Memoir 1969–1980* (1987), *Next: New Poems* (1987), and *Quilting: Poems 1987–1990* (1991). Clifton's poems discuss racial issues, celebrate her blackness and her womanhood, and explore her spiritual experiences. Clifton

45

also has examined her family's history in America in the prose volume *Generations: A Memoir* (1976) as well as in her poetry.

In addition to her adult books, Clifton has been a prolific writer of children's books specifically aimed at black juvenile readers. These take the form of highly accessible poems accompanied by illustrations. Her children's books include *The Black BC's* (1970), *The Boy Who Didn't Belive in Spring* (1973), and the Everett Anderson stories, which revolve around the life and adventures of a young urban black boy.

Clifton has in recent years been a visiting writer at a number of colleges and universities, including Columbia and George Washington. She made her family home in Baltimore, becoming Poet Laureate of the State of Maryland in 1979, a position she held until 1982. Clifton was widowed in 1984 and moved to Santa Cruz, where since 1985 she has been professor of literature and creative writing at the University of California at Santa Cruz.

◈ Critical Extracts

JANE O'REILLY   *Everett Anderson's Christmas Coming* is for modern urban celebrators. Everett Anderson, black and boyish, is glimpsed, rather than explained through poems about him, written by Lucille Clifton. White middle-class parents will want answers to certain questions. For example, on Dec. 22 Everett thinks about "If Daddy was here," but where Daddy is, is never explained. It doesn't really have to be and city children know that. The joys of living in Apt. 14A are perfectly clear, and I really liked Dec. 15:

> Boys with lots
> of boxes
> smiles Everett Anderson
> spend all day Christmas
> opening
> and never have much fun.

which appears with a picture of Everett holding the world's most splendid guinea pig, labeled "Merry Christmas."

Jane O'Reilly, "For Young Readers: 'Tis the Season," *New York Times Book Review*, 5 December 1971, p. 90

LUCILLE CLIFTON   I write the way I write because I am the kind
of person that I am. My styles and my content stem from my experience.
I grew up a well-loved child in a loving family and so I have always known
that being very poor, which we were, had nothing to do with lovingness
or familyness or character or any of that. ⟨. . .⟩ We were/are quite sure that
we were/are among the best of people and not having any money had
nothing to do with that. Other people's opinions didn't influence us about
that. We were quite sure. When I write, especially for children, I try to get
that across, that being poor or whatever your circumstance, you are capable
of being the best of people and that best, as a human, does not come from
the outside in, it comes from the inside out.

I use a simple language. I have never believed that for anything to be
valid or true or intellectual or "deep" it had to first be complex. I deliberately
use the language that I use. Sometimes people have asked me when I was
going to try something hard or difficult, as if my work sprang from my
ignorance. I like to think that I write from my knowledge not my lack,
from my strength and not my weakness. I am not interested if anyone knows
whether or not I am familiar with big words, I am interested in being
understood not admired. I wish to celebrate and not be celebrated (though
a little celebration is a lot of fun).

I am a woman and I write from that experience. I am a Black woman
and I write from that experience. I do not feel inhibited or bound by what
I am. That does not mean that I have never had bad scenes relating to
being Black and/or a woman, it means that other people's craziness has not
managed to make me crazy. At least not in their way because I try very
hard not to close my eye to my own craziness nor to my family's, my sex's,
nor my race's. I don't believe that I should only talk about the beauty and
strength and goodness of my people but I do believe that if we talk about
our room for improvement we should do it privately. I don't believe in
public family fights. But I do think sometimes a good fight is cleansing. We
are not perfect people. There are no perfect people. ⟨. . .⟩

When my first book was published I was thirty-three years old and had
six children under ten years old. I was too busy to take it terribly seriously.
I was very happy and proud of course, but had plenty of other things to
think about. It was published by Random House and that seemed to bother
some of my friends. At first my feelings were a little hurt that anyone would
even be concerned about it but I got over that. I decided that if something
doesn't matter, it really doesn't matter. Sometimes I think that the most

anger comes from ones who were late in discovering that when the world said nigger it meant them too. I grew up knowing that the world meant me too but that was the world's insanity and not mine. I have been treated in publishing very much like other poets are treated, that is, not really very well. I continue to write since my life as a human only includes my life as a poet, it doesn't depend on it. ⟨. . .⟩

My family tends to be a spiritual and even perhaps a mystical one. That certainly influences my life and my work. I write in the kitchen or wherever I happen to be though I do have a study. I write on a typewriter rather than in longhand. My children think of me as a moody person; I am shy and much less sunny than I am pictured. I draw my own conclusions and do not believe everything I am told. I am not easily fooled. I do the best I can. I try.

> Lucille Clifton, "A Simple Language," in *Black Women Writers* (*1950–1980*): *A Critical Evaluation*, ed. Mari Evans (Garden City, NY: Anchor Press/Doubleday, 1984), pp. 137–38

AUDREY T. McCLUSKEY   ⟨Clifton's⟩ children's books are her most prolific literary product, and no analysis of her work could ignore their overall importance. Her books for children introduce themes, ideas and points of view that may sometimes find their way into her poetry. It is important to note that she does not greatly alter her style as she moves from one genre to another. Her language remains direct, economical, and simply stated. She does not patronize the children for whom she writes. She gives them credit for being intelligent human beings who do not deserve to be treated differently because of their age. Being the mother of six children must certainly give her material for her books, but it is her respect for children as people and her finely tuned instincts about what is important to them—their fears, their joys—that make her a successful writer of children's literature. ⟨. . .⟩

Clifton is very cognizant of the fears that are ignited by a child's imagination. Her books are written to help give reassurance. She delicately treats both the pains and joys of childhood in order to help children accept both emotions as part of the unique experience of being who they are. In Clifton's books for children, self-love, and self-acceptance is the message. An example of this message is summarized in *The Black BC's*, a collection of rhymes depicting Black history and the Black experience.

> N is for natural
> or real or true
> the you of yourself
> and the self in you

In her poetry, Clifton continues to advocate that Black children be taught self-worth and encouraged to develop the mental and spiritual toughness that they will require to survive in a society that is hostile to their development. In the following poem, the children are called upon to make decisions for themselves and to begin to take control of their lives. They must become socially responsible—for they will someday lead.

> Come home from the movies
> Black girls and boys.
> The picture be over and the screen
> be cold as our neighborhood.
> Come home from the show,
> don't be the show . . .
> Show our fathers how to walk like men,
> they already know how to dance.

The movies serve as a metaphor for the fantasies and falseness in society that stunt our children's growth. She believes that what is important in life is found, not in the movies but in the values that are passed through generations.

> we have always love each other
> children   all ways
> Pass it on.

Clifton's view of herself as a writer is based, in part, upon her belief that "things don't fall apart. Things hold. Lines connect in ways that last and last and lives become generations made out of pictures and words just kept." She is interested in the continuity of experience and the writer's unique ability to connect generations of people and to remind them who they are and from whence they came.

Audrey T. McCluskey, "Tell the Good News: A View of the Works of Lucille Clifton," in *Black Women Writers (1950–1980): A Critical Evaluation*, ed. Mari Evans (Garden City, NY: Anchor Press/Doubleday, 1984), pp. 140–42

ANDREA BENTON RUSHING   Clifton's early verse clearly
indicates the influence of the Black Arts movement. In accord with its
dictates about how poetry should raise the cultural and political consciousness of "the Black community," Clifton dedicates *Good News about the Earth*
to those killed in student uprisings at Orangeburg, South Carolina, and
Jackson, Mississippi. ⟨. . .⟩ The volume also features verse to Angela Davis,
Eldridge Cleaver, and Bobby Seale. In addition to treating these political
subjects, Clifton mirrors the tenets of the Black Arts movement by directing
herself to a general African-American audience using the grammar, vocabulary, and rhythm of idiomatic African-American speech. Interestingly, none
of Clifton's verse on these vivid figures parallels so many of the tributes to
them in relying on typographical quirks, like capitalized words and slashes,
or haranguing either African-American or Euro-American readers.

In light of Clifton's later poetry, it is crucial to indicate the ways in
which her early work diverges from the creations of her contemporaries.
Many of the women poets who came to prominence during the sixties and
seventies shocked readers. Despite their slight stature and (in a few cases)
bourgeois upbringing, they mirrored the strident stance, profane language,
and violent imagery of urban, male poetry. Part of my interest in Clifton's
lyrical verse arises from my admiration for the acumen with which she found
her own voice during a turbulent period when so many poets sounded the
same chords of outrage and militancy. ⟨. . .⟩ Furthermore, while other poets
have tended to focus on historical figures such as Harriet Tubman, Sojourner
Truth, Frederick Douglass, and Malcolm X, Clifton anticipated Alex Haley's
Roots in personalizing history and using her own natal family as a symbol
of the anguish and triumph of the African-American experience. Moreover,
in an era when many African-American nationalists were harshly critical
of their accommodating "Uncle Tom" and "Aunt Jemima" elders, the "opi-
ate" of African-American Christianity, and the Anglo-Saxon proper names
which are a living legacy of chattel slavery and cultural assimilation, Clifton
wrote in a different key. While others complained of their elders' failures,
she celebrated her ancestors, while others converted to Islam, she wrote
about the life-giving power of African-American religion; and, though others
assumed African and Arabic names, Clifton justified her own.

> light
> on my mother's tongue
> breaks through her soft
> extravagant hip

into life.
Lucille
she calls the light,
which was the name
of the grandmother
who waited by the crossroads
in Virginia
and shot the whiteman off his horse,
. . . .
mine already is
an Afrikan name.

Beginning with an allusion to the origins of the name "Lucille" in the Latin
for "bright light," Clifton goes on to affirm a throbbing connection between
Africa, the slave experience, and her own twentieth-century life.

Andrea Benton Rushing, "Lucille Clifton: A Changing Voice for Changing Times,"
Coming to Light: American Women Poets in the Twentieth Century, ed. Diane Wood
Middlebrook and Marilyn Yalom (Ann Arbor: University of Michigan Press, 1985),
pp. 215–17

E. K. LAING   Clifton's poems have an internal brilliance ⟨. . .⟩
Chanting, droning, humming, her poems almost always work something
out.

With Clifton, nothing is reckless—neither her multifaceted use of "i,"
nor the absence of titles on most poems, nor the lack of punctuation. Each
poem appears as a meditation on power; what it means to control, withhold,
or relinquish power as an ultimate demonstration of mastery.

Unadorned, Clifton's gemlike forms are resplendent, refracting the
author's themes of family, the grace that can mean survival, the environment,
and perhaps most of all, individual responsibility for the future. ⟨. . .⟩

Black and white on the page, black and white in society, Clifton's poems
do not equivocate. If ever they are gray, it is because they are as exacting
as a steel blade cutting to central issues. They say a lot about black being
white in America. "I grieve my whiteful ways," she says. But this is not the
limit of her scope. She uses her experience as black, woman, mother, and
child to describe relationships more far-reaching than those labels would
admit. ⟨. . .⟩

Her words reveal not a victim, but a visionary. In the witness tradition
of Brooks and Baldwin, Whitman and Wheatley, Clifton eagerly takes up
arms in the struggle to salvage what grace in life remains.

E. K. Laing, "Lucille Clifton's Poetry: The Voice of a Visionary, Not a Victim,"
Christian Science Monitor, 5 February 1988, p. 83

DIANNE JOHNSON   Fortunately for the world of young people's
literature, there are those authors who broaden our realms of experience by
representing and exploring African-American culture. Lucille Clifton is one
of the most prolific and accomplished of this number. In this context, her
work is especially impressive when viewed as an entire oeuvre. Each book
works in concert with the others to illuminate aspects of the communities,
largely African-American, in which the characters live their lives. Everett
Anderson's is one of the lives which is documented through a series of
books. An examination of the Everett Anderson stories reveals the range
and richness of this youngster's life and of the series book itself. This is
especially true when examined within the context of the secondary function
(intentional or not) of Clifton's telling of story: the exploration of Afro-
American community and consciousness.

Everett Anderson is, in fact, the character most readily identified with
Lucille Clifton. His story is both powerful and accessible precisely because
of its inclusivity. It records not only memorable events such as births, but
also the everyday. Everett Anderson can make any Wednesday afternoon
into an adventure:

> Who's black
> and runs
> and loves to hop?
> Everett does.
>
> Who's black
> and was lost
> in the candy shop?
> Everett Anderson was.
>
> Who's black
> and noticed the
> peppermint flowers?
> Everett Anderson did.

Who's black
and was lost for
hours and hours?
Everett Anderson

Hid!

Considered carefully, these verses from *Some of the Days of Everett Anderson* are not as simplistic as they might appear upon cursory examination. They are complicated—communicating more than a child's adventure—by the one recurring line, "Who's black."

A negative reaction to the line might include the argument that its prominent placement (not to mention its mere presence) is somewhat exclamatory and unjustifiable. What, after all, does being Black have to do with a trip to the candy store or playing hide and seek? This line of reasoning, however, obscures the more germane questions: Why is this particular detail included along with the unremarkable? One obvious answer is that this fact too should be unremarkable—unremarkable in the sense that it is so integral and organic a part of the character of Everett Anderson that it would be even more conspicuous in its absence.

Certainly the words "Who's black" are not called upon literally or blatantly in every episode that Clifton relates. But they are present in a spiritual and fundamental way. The point is that Everett is Black, as are many of his fellow characters. They are. And it is a condition of their being. This fact is simultaneously neither remarkable nor ignorable. It is for this reason that the boys share a brotherhood. When their blackness deserves or demands special attention, then it is accorded. When it deems no particular attention, it is left so. Everett's maturation process, like that of his peers, consists partly of learning how to mediate between the two levels of consciousness.

Dianne Johnson, "The Chronicling of an African-American Life and Consciousness: Lucille Clifton's Everett Anderson Series," *Children's Literary Association Quarterly* 14, No. 4 (Winter 1989): 174–75

HANK LAZER   As both her poetry and *All Us Come Cross the Water* illustrate, ownership is linked to language and to naming. Telling the story, choosing the dialect, and picking the name are acts of power with direct consequences in terms of dignity and autonomy. Clifton's acts of naming are *not* the transcendental "perfect fits" imagined by Ralph Waldo Emerson, whose Adam-poet gives the "true" and "original" names to the creatures of the earth. It seems to me that Emerson's ideal is imaginable *only* from a position of power and privilege, not from within a family and a race where names are imposed as a brand and an exercise of power by someone else. Clifton's position as namer gets written in "the making of poems":

> the reason why i do it
> though i fail and fail
> in the giving of true names
> is i am adam and his mother
> and these failures are my job.

But Lucille Clifton's failure is her success. That is, Clifton affirms most effectively when she fuses limitation and grace ⟨. . .⟩

In her newest poems, Clifton's revisionary history focuses more insistently on women. In one poem, she rewrites woman's power relationship to God, concluding "i am the good daughter who stays at home / singing and sewing. / when i whisper He strains to hear me and / He does whatever i say." Earlier in her writing, Clifton found herself "turning out of the / white cage, turning out of the / lady cage"; now, the poem she writes goes by the title "female" and affirms

> there is an amazon in us.
> she is the secret we do not
> have to learn.
> the strength that opens us
> beyond ourselves.
> birth is our birthright.
> we smile our mysterious smile.

Thus, her newest poems continue her work in defining and affirming "us."

The other equally effective affirmation in Clifton's poetry is akin to a power of the blues, what Houston Baker hears as the blues' "powers at the junctures of American experience—its power to wed quotidian rituals of everyday American experience to the lusters of a distinctively American expressive firmament." For Clifton, that wedding is accomplished in poems such as "homage to my hips," "homage to my hair," and "what the mirror said" ⟨. . .⟩

If, as many readers and writers of poetry are aware, a dominant feature of poetry in our time is its diversity, the absolute fragmentation of audience and the decentralization of its production and distribution, then many important consequences ensue from Ron Silliman's conclusion that "the result has been a decentralization in which any pretense, whether from the 'center' or elsewhere, or a coherent sense as to the nature of the whole of American poetry is now patently obvious as just so much aggressive fakery." It especially matters that white male readers, writers, and professors reach out and resist the drawing of xenophobic boundaries so that they can begin to live in the fullness of the present moment, so that we might have, as Gertrude Stein had wished, "all of our contemporaries for our contemporaries." In so doing, we can begin to undo one of the most damaging, lingering, and conservative goals of high modernist poetry. Instead of seeking to "purify the language of the tribe," we can begin to acknowledge with and through Lucille Clifton's writing, and the poetry of many other African-American poets, that "there are / too many languages for / one mortal tongue." What we need is not a purification of the language of the tribe, but an attentiveness to the languages of the many tribes constituting American expression.

Hank Lazer, "Blackness Blessed: The Writings of Lucille Clifton," *Southern Review* 25, No. 3 (Summer 1989): 768–70

JEAN ANAPORTE-EASTON   Last summer I gave a reading to a class of women in a prison for young drug offenders. I had read poems by a few other poets before I got to Clifton's "homage to my hips." The polite smiling audience sat up a little, looked at each other and grinned; there was even some noise. So I read "homage to my hair," and when I got to, "i'm talking about my nappy hair," the class burst into startled laughter. If big hips that are free and magical return to women some of our true identity, nappy hair was an even bigger shot of oxygen. There is no more political statement than saying to one deprived of self-esteem, "Take who you are and flaunt it."

"Nappy hair" is a point of contact between Clifton and her audience and also between Clifton and her truth-telling power. The touchstone for her truth-telling is the body and physical experience from a Black woman's perspective. Daily existence is the medium through which Clifton examines ethical and spiritual issues. The voice and rhythm emerge from the style of folk tales and the gutsy, here-and-now texture of Black vernacular. The imagery begins with brief, sometimes fragmentary observations about things ranging from hair and hips to the death of someone's son, and move inward where it is transformed by Clifton's particular brand of social and spiritual awareness.

Look at "homage to my hair." Not only the rhythm and sounds but the imagery is physical. The hair "jumps" and "dances" to suggest music. The pattern linking these images further energizes them:

> when i feel her jump up and dance
> i hear the music! my God
> i'm talking about my nappy hair!
> she is a challenge to your hand
> black man,
> she is as tasty on your tongue as good greens
> black man,
> she can touch your mind
> with her electric fingers and
> the grayer she do get, good God,
> the blacker she do be!

The spondee of "jump up" followed by the stressed "dance" at the end of the line creates a rising energy that lands on "hear" in the next line. The stresses in "nappy hair" are so close together as to have the impact of another spondee shooting electricity back to "jump up" and forward to "good greens." The spondees and the line breaks inject the rhythm with stops and flourishes so that the abstract "challenge" is given concrete meaning. Most of the lines contain three or two stresses. When extra stresses are added to lines one, six, and ten, those lines rush ahead with added impetus which is gathered and released deliberately in a slower beat in lines two and eleven—"i hear the music! my God" and "the blacker she do be!" The short two stress lines, "black man," hold up a rolling motion to deliver a challenge and give it time to sink in. The entire poem, in fact, is a challenge, an outrageous boast on the powers not only of dethroned nappy hair but grey hair.

Clifton's poetry specifically addresses Black people, but speaks to all who consider themselves ordinary. However, on Clifton's tongue, ordinary can be quite extraordinary so long as it is part of daily human experience. Since dailiness is global and cyclical, all varieties of human experience are admitted, including what is peculiar, excluded, or painful—womanhood, motherhood, Blackness, six-fingered hands, young boys dragging wagons to a riot. Acceptance is celebrations: Sing your nappy hair, your twelve fingers, your fear of being without a man, the cruelty and numbness of fear, the despair and violence in people's isolation. Sing these details of our lives until they become our mysteries and our magic, our means of transformation.

Jean Anaporte-Easton, " 'She Has Made Herself Again': The Maternal Impulse as Poetry," *13th Moon* 9, Nos. 1 & 2 (1991): 116–17

◈ *Bibliography*

Good Times. 1969.

Some of the Days of Everett Anderson. 1969.

The Black BC's. 1970.

Everett Anderson's Christmas Coming. 1971.

Good News about the Earth: New Poems. 1972.

All Us Come Cross the Water. 1973.

Don't You Remember? 1973.

Good, Says Jerome. 1973.

The Boy Who Didn't Believe in Spring. 1973.

An Ordinary Woman. 1974.

Everett Anderson's Year. 1974.

All of Us Are All of Us. 1974.

The Times They Used to Be. 1974.

My Brother Fine with Me. 1975.

Three Wishes. 1976.

Everett Anderson's Friend. 1976.

Generations: A Memoir. 1976.

Amifika. 1977.

Everett Anderson's 1 2 3. 1977.

Everett Anderson's Nine Month Long. 1978.

The Lucky Stone. 1979.

My Friend Jacob (with Thomas DiGrazia). 1980.

Two-Headed Woman. 1980.

Sonora Beautiful. 1981.

Everett Anderson's Goodbye. 1983.

Good Woman: Poems and a Memoir 1969–1980. 1987.

Next: New Poems. 1987.

Why Some People Be Mad at Me Sometimes. 1988.

Ten Oxherding Pictures. c. 1988.
Quilting: Poems 1987–1990. 1991.
The Book of Light. 1993.

🔷 🔷 🔷

Rita Dove

b. 1952

RITA FRANCES DOVE was born on August 28, 1952, in Akron, Ohio, to Ray A. Dove and Elvira Elizabeth Hord. Dove was a precocious child who ranked among the top one hundred high school seniors in the country and was therefore invited to the White House as a "Presidential Scholar." After graduating from high school, Dove entered Miami University at Oxford, Ohio. In 1973 she graduated *summa cum laude*, then entered Tübingen University in what was then West Germany on a Fulbright scholarship. While in Germany, Dove actively sought out Afro-Germans in an attempt to understand their circumstances. Dove discovered that many Afro-German women suffered from the same feelings of rejection and isolation that Dove had felt in the United States. Somewhat optimistically, she wrote about the possibility of unified action among black communities worldwide— action that would inspire a revolution in world consciousness. In 1979 Dove married a German writer, Fred Viebahn, with whom she had one child.

Upon returning from Germany, Dove entered the Iowa Writers Workshop, where she received an M.F.A. in 1977. She worked principally on her poetry, which thereafter increasingly appeared in magazines and journals. In 1977 *Ten Poems*, Dove's first book of verse, appeared. It reveals her interest in the revolutionary politics of the 1960s as well as the influence of other black revolutionary poets on her work, such as Don L. Lee (Haki R. Madhubuti) and LeRoi Jones (Amiri Baraka). Many of the poems in this first small volume were reprinted along with new verses in her first full-length collection, *The Yellow House on the Corner* (1980). For the most part, the collection was poorly received. Not until the publication of *Museum* (1983) and *Thomas and Beulah* (1986) did Dove receive considerable critical praise. The latter volume also won her a Pulitzer Prize, making her only the second black poet to have won a Pulitzer Prize for poetry (the first was Gwendolyn Brooks). *Thomas and Beulah* is a long narrative poem telling the story of her family from two points of view, her grandfather's and her

59

grandmother's. A chronology at the end of the volume provides a guide to the sometimes confusing overlap of the two stories.

More recently, Dove has published *The Other Side of the House* (1988), a set of poems to accompany photographs by Tamarra Kaida, and *Grace Notes* (1989). Her *Selected Poems* appeared in 1993. She has also written a novel, *Through the Ivory Gate* (1992), and a play, *The Darker Face of the Earth* (1994).

Dove began her teaching career as a professor of English at Arizona State University in 1981. In 1989 she became a professor of English at the University of Virginia. She was a writer in residence at the Tuskegee Institute in 1982 and has served as a member of the literature panel of the National Endowment for the Arts. Since 1987 she has been commissioner of the Schomburg Center for the Preservation of Black Culture at the New York Public Library. In 1993 she became the first black American to be appointed the United States Poet Laureate.

Critical Extracts

PETER STITT   "Shakespeare Say" ⟨in *Museum*⟩ is linear and narrative. The moment of telling occurs during an evening when "Champion Jack Dupree, black American blues singer" (as he is identified in the note to the poem) is performing in a Munich nightclub. The mode of narration is not limited to this single period of time, however; to portray the singer's state of mind, the speaker recounts several events in sequential order, first returning to "That afternoon" when "two students / from the Akademie / showed him the town." Later in the poem, we are presented with a generalized description of the evening in question ("And tonight // every song he sings / is written by Shakespeare"), while still later we learn what happens as Champion Jack is "going down / for the third set / past the stragglers / at the bar."

The quality of this poem is evident in Dove's accuracy of description and in how she interlaces Champion Jack's songs with her narrative to flesh out his portrait:

> Champion Jack in love
> and in debt,

in a tan walking suit
with a flag on the pocket,
with a red eye
for women, with a
diamond-studded
ear, with sand
in a mouthful of mush—
poor me
poor me
I keep on drifting
like a ship out
on the sea.

In line with the imagery in the song he sings, Jack is described variously as looking like a ship ("a flag on the pocket"), as looking like a pirate (the "red eye" and the earring), and as sounding like an inverted Demosthenes (whereas the Greek orator, according to legend, filled his mouth with pebbles and declaimed to the sea in an effort to strengthen his voice, Jack seems to have filled his mouth with "sand," so great is his sense of sorrow).

In contrast to the narrative and linear structure of "Shakespeare Say," "The Copper Beech" is a descriptive poem in circular form (description in poetry is almost always static with regard to time). Though the poem contains twenty-five lines arranged into nine stanzas, it takes its form not from these distinguishing external features but from the progression inherent in its five sentences. The first sentence establishes setting, character, and theme: "Aristocrat among patriarchs, this / noble mutation is the best / specimen of Rococo // in the park of the castle / at Erpenberg." The second sentence delves into the past to tell how a Baroness brought the tree from South America, and the next sentence furthers interpretation: "This trailing beech became Erpenberg's / tree of grief, their // melancholy individualist, / the park philosopher."

The fourth sentence furthers the description, while the concluding provides a final description/interpretation that unites the whole:

The aesthetic principles
of the period: branches

pruned late to heal
into knots, proud flesh ascending
the trunk:

living architecture.

The movement of the poem is not narrative, not progressive through time, but accretive around an instance of perception; the form is therefore circular rather than linear. Rita Dove is a poet of considerable skill and promise. The poems in *Museum* are as intellectually interesting as they are attractive in rhythm and image.

Peter Stitt, "The Circle of the Meditative Moment," *Georgia Review* 38, No. 2 (Summer 1984): 403–4

LINDA GREGERSON   In *Museum*, as its title and its cover art-work announce, the author has advanced to full prominence ⟨her⟩ preoccupations with displacement and multiple frames for point of view, frames that are rather superimposed than synthesized. The book is structured and conceived with great deliberation and coherence, from its section titles and sequencing epigraphs, its attributions and its dedication: *"for nobody,"* reads a page at the front, *"who made us possible."* The book's recurrent thematics are those of light and shade, the exotic and the domestic, reticence (with its furthest limit a nearly Delphic impenetrability, like the hush in a museum) and disclosure ⟨. . .⟩ On both geographical and temporal coordinates, the sweep of the book is large: from Argos to Erpenberg to the poet's native Ohio, from the Western Han Dynasty to the nuclear age. Nor are these distances a species of lush window dressing: Dove believes in history and is capable of mining it for the lucid intersections of imagination and prag-matic ways-and-means, for the junctures where solitary virtuosity finds both its intractable limits (as Catherine of Alexandria was "deprived of learning and / the chance to travel") and its most urgent motives. And according to that other perspective on history, as captured in books or museums, Dove is concerned to render the altered status of a subject when it has been set aside for special delectation, like the fish in the archeologist's stone or like Fiammetta in Boccaccio's mind: the creature lifted to visibility by the pressure of a gaze is also partly stranded there, unsponsored even while it is wholly possessed. In technical terms—their use of the luminous image, their eco-nomics of plotting and musical phrase, their reliable modulations of syntax and levels of diction—these poems continue the same expert craftsmanship that marked Dove's earlier work. In their collective argument—and it is a profound one—they go much further.

Linda Gregerson, [Review of *The Yellow House on the Corner* and *Museum*], *Poetry* 145, No. 1 (October 1984): 47–48

HELEN VENDLER   *Thomas and Beulah* manages to keep intact the intensity of the drama and inexplicability of life and marriage. The mutual criticism of Dove's Akron couple, their enterprise and defeat, while specified to a degree that is satisfying as fiction, will remind readers of analogous episodes in the years 1900–1969 undergone by their own parents or grandparents. Dove does not suggest that black experience is identical with white experience, but neither does she suggest that it is always different. Beulah's experience of motherhood—her terror of doing it wrong, the exhaustion of having no privacy, her irritation at the grown girls—is universal. But Beulah's anger when her daughters take her to the Goodyear company picnic after Thomas's death will be personally familiar only to black readers:

> Now this *act of mercy:* four daughters
> dragging her to their husbands' company picnic,
> white families on one side and them
> on the other, unpacking the same
> squeeze bottles of Heinz, the same
> waxy beef patties and Salem potato chip bags.

Over the segregated picnickers floats the Goodyear company symbol—"a white foot / sprouting two small wings." Beulah's interior monologue, here as elsewhere, has the naturalness and accuracy of art concealing art. Dove has planed away unnecessary matter: pure shapes, her poems exhibit the thrift that Yeats called the sign of a perfected manner.

Helen Vendler, "In the Zoo of the New," *New York Review of Books*, 23 October 1986, pp. 51–52

ARNOLD RAMPERSAD   ⟨. . .⟩ with the consistently accomplished work of thirty-three year old Rita Dove, there is at least one clear sign if not of a coming renaissance of poetry, then at least of the emergence of an unusually strong new figure who might provide leadership by brilliant example. Thus far, Rita Dove has produced a remarkable record of publications in a wide range of respected poetry and other literary journals. Two books of verse, *The Yellow House on the Corner* (1980) and *Museum* (1983), have appeared from Carnegie-Mellon University Press. A third book-length manuscript of poetry, "Thomas and Beulah," is scheduled to be published early in 1986 by the same house. Clearly Rita Dove has both the energy and the sense of professionalism required to lead other writers. Most importantly—even a first reading of her two books makes it clear that she also possesses the talent to do so. Dove is surely one of the three or four most gifted young black American poets to appear since LeRoi Jones ambled with deceptive nonchalance onto the scene in the late nineteen fifties, and perhaps the most disciplined and technically accomplished black poet to arrive since Gwendolyn Brooks began her remarkable career in the nineteen forties.

These references to the sixties and early seventies are pointed. Rita Dove's work shows a keen awareness of this period—but mainly as a point of radical departure for her in the development of her own aesthetic. In many ways, her poems are exactly the opposite of those that have come to be considered quintessentially black verse in recent years. Instead of looseness of structure, one finds in her poems remarkably tight control; instead of a reliance on reckless inspiration, one recognizes discipline and practice, and long, taxing hours in competitive university poetry workshops and in her study; instead of a range of reference limited to personal confession, one finds personal reference disciplined by a measuring of distance and a prizing objectivity; instead of an obsession with the theme of race, one finds an eagerness, perhaps even an anxiety, to transcend—if not actually to repudiate—black cultural nationalism in the name of a more inclusive sensibility. Hers is a brilliant mind, reinforced by what appears to be very wide reading, that seeks for itself the widest possible play, an ever expanding range of reference, the most acute distinctions, and the most subtle shadings of meaning. ⟨. . .⟩

As a poet, Dove is well aware of black history. One of the five sections of *The Yellow House* is devoted entirely to poems on the theme of slavery and freedom. These pieces are inspired by nameless but strongly representative victims of the "peculiar institution," as well as by more famous heroic figures (who may be seen as fellow black writers, most of them) such as Solomon Northrup, abducted out of Northern freedom on a visit to Washington ("I remember how the windows rattled with each report. / Then the wine, like a pink lake, tipped. / I was lifted—the sky swivelled, clicked into place"), and the revolutionary David Walker ("Compass needles, / eloquent as tuning forks, shivered, pointing north. / Evenings, the ceiling fan sputtered like a second pulse. / *Oh Heaven! I am full!! I can hardly move my pen!!!*"). In these works and others such as "Banneker" in the later volume, *Museum*, Dove shows both a willingness and a fine ability to evoke, through deft vignettes, the psychological terror of slavery. She is certainly adept at recreating graphically the starched idioms of the eighteenth and early nineteenth centuries, at breathing life into the monumental or sometimes only arthritic rhythms of that vanished and yet still echoing age. Her poems in this style and area are hardly less moving than those of Robert Hayden, who made the period poem (the period being slavery) virtually his own invention among black poets. Dove's special empathy as a historical poet seems to be with the most sensitive, most eloquent blacks, individuals of ductile intelligence made neurotic by pain, especially the pain of not being understood and of not being able to express themselves.

Arnold Rampersad, "The Poems of Rita Dove," *Callaloo* 9, No. 1 (Winter 1986): 52–54

PETER HARRIS   Rita Dove's *Thomas and Beulah*, winner of the 1987 Pulitzer Prize, has a distinctive, ambitiously unified design. It traces the history of two blacks who separately move North, to Ohio, meet and get married in the 1920's, and go on to raise four girls, enduring many vicissitudes before their deaths in the 1960's. Arranged serially and accompanied by an almost essential chronology, the poems, we are told in a note beforehand, are meant to be read in order. Much as Michael Ondaatje has done in his poem-like novel, *Coming through Slaughter*, Dove reconstructs the past through a series of discontinuous vignettes which enter freely into the psyches of the two main characters.

It is important that the poems are arranged chronologically because we often need all the help we can get in clarifying many of the references. Even with chronology as a guide, the poems sometimes seem unnecessarily obscure and cryptic. More often, however, the difficulty of the work is justifiable because the insights are exactly as subtle as they are oblique. In exploiting the virtues of ellipsis, Dove evidently has faith we will have gumption enough to stare a hole in the page until our minds leap with hers across the gaps. For example, in the opening poem, "The Event," Thomas dares his drunken friend, Lem, to jump off a riverboat and swim to a nearby island. Lem jumps and drowns. Later in the volume, we find out that Thomas is haunted by Lem's death for the rest of his life. But in the opening poem, the aftershock goes unmentioned:

> Thomas, dry
> on deck, saw the green crown shake
> as the island slipped

under, dissolved
in the thickening stream.
At his feet

a stinking circle of rags,
the half-shell mandolin.
Where the wheel turned the water

gently shirred.

Given Dove's reticent lyricism, we can't be completely sure from this description that Lem had drowned; we can only guess. That leaves us uncertain
and, therefore, vulnerable, which is quite appropriate because the world we
are entering with Thomas is fraught with deceptive beauty and danger. Even
the shirring of roiled water can indicate death. ⟨. . .⟩

⟨. . .⟩ The psychic cost of suffering makes itself keenly felt in *Thomas and
Beulah*, a blues book that aims, through music and sympathy, to reach an
affirmative answer to the question posed by Melvin B. Tolson, which Dove
includes as the epigraph to the volume:

> Black Boy, O Black Boy,
> is the port worth the cruise?

Peter Harris, "Poetry Chronicle: Four Salvers Salvaging: New Work by Voigt, Olds,
Dove, and McHugh," *Virginia Quarterly Review* 64, No. 2 (Spring 1988): 270–73

STEVEN SCHNEIDER   SS: How does it feel to be the first black
woman poet since Gwendolyn Brooks to win the Pulitzer Prize?

RD: My first reaction was quite simply disbelief. Disbelief that first of all
there hasn't been another black person since Gwendolyn Brooks in 1950
to win the Pulitzer Prize in poetry, though there certainly have been some
outstanding black poets in that period. On a public level, it says something
about the nature of cultural politics of this country. It's a shame actually.
On a personal level, it's overwhelming.

SS: Did you feel you had written something special when you completed
Thomas and Beulah?

RD: I felt I had written something larger than myself, larger than what
I had hoped for it to be. I did not begin this sequence as a book; it began
as a poem. The book grew poem by poem, and it wasn't until I was about
a third of the way through that I realized it would have to be a book. So

I grew with it and I had to rise to it. I started with the Thomas poems because I wanted to understand my grandfather more—what he was like as a young man, how he grew up and became the man I knew. To do that though, I realized pretty early on that I could rely neither on my memories of him nor on the memories of my mother or her sisters or brothers, but I had to get to know the town he lived in. What was Akron, Ohio like in the '20s and '30s? It was different from the Akron I knew. That meant I had to go to the library and read a whole bunch of stuff I never counted on researching to try to get a sense of that period of time in the industrial Midwest. On other levels, I had to enter male consciousness in a way which was—well, I knew I could do it for one or two poems but this was an extended effort. I was really, at a certain point, very very driven to be as honest as I could possibly be. Also, I didn't want to impose my language or my sensibility upon their lives. And things got—

SS: Things got very complicated?

RD: That's right.

SS: Did you have a different kind of satisfaction about finishing this book than your other two books?

RD: It was different. I am not going to say I was more satisfied; I don't think I have a favorite book of mine. But there was a feeling of relief because I had made it through.

Steven Schneider, "Coming Home: An Interview with Rita Dove," *Iowa Review* 19, No. 3 (Fall 1989): 112–13

ROBERT McDOWELL   Rita Dove has always possessed a storyteller's instinct. In *The Yellow House on the Corner* (1980), *Museum* (1983), and *Thomas and Beulah* (1985), this instinct has found expression in a synthesis of striking imagery, myth, magic, fable, wit, humor, political comment, and a sure knowledge of history. Many contemporaries share Dove's mastery of some of these, but few succeed in bringing them together to create a point of view that, by its breadth and force, stands apart. She has not worked her way into this enviable position among poets without fierce commitment.

Passing through a graduate writing program (Iowa) in the mid-1970s, Dove and her peers were schooled in the importance of sensation and its representation through manipulation of The Image. The standard lesson plan, devised to reflect the ascendancy of Wallace Stevens and a corrupt revision of T. S. Eliot's objective correlative, instructed young writers to renounce realistic depiction and offer it up to the province of prose; it promoted subjectivity and imagination-as-image; it strangled a generation of poems.

How and why this came to pass is less important, really, than admitting that it is so. Literary magazines are gorged with poems devoid of shapeliness and scope. Imagistic, cramped, and confessional, they exist for the predictably surprising, climactic phrase. A historically conscious reader, aware of literary tradition, might understandably perceive an enormous cultural amnesia as the dubiously distinguishing feature of such poems. Such a reader will rue the fact that the writing and interpretation of poetry has diminished to a trivial pursuit, a pronouncement of personal instinct. If this is the dominant direction of a discouraging Moment, then Rita Dove distinguishes herself by resolutely heading the other way.

Unlike the dissembling spirit indicated above, Dove is an assembler who gathers the various facts of this life and presents them in ways that jar our lazy assumptions. She gives voice to many positions and many characters. Like the speaker/writer of classic argumentation, she shows again and again that she understands the opposing sides of conflicts she deals with. She tells all sides of the story. Consider the titles of her books, their symbolic weight. The personal turning point *House on the Corner* evolves, becoming the public Museum (symbol of preserved chronology); that, in turn, gives way to the names of two characters whose lives combine and illustrate the implicit meanings of the personal House and the public Museum.

Robert McDowell, "The Assembling Vision of Rita Dove," *Conversant Essays: Contemporary Poets on Poetry*, ed. James McCorkle (Detroit: Wayne State University Press, 1990), p. 294

JOHN SHOPTAW   At the beginning of Rita Dove's arresting new volume of poetry ⟨*Thomas and Beulah*⟩, we are given directions for reading that turn out to be true but impossible to follow: "These poems tell two sides of a story and are meant to be read in sequence." The impossibility is not physical, as in the instructions prefacing John Ashbery's long double-columned poem, *Litany*, which tell us that the columns "are meant to be read as simultaneous but independent monologues"; rather, the impossibility in reading the two sides of Rita Dove's book—Thomas's side (I. "Mandolin," 23 poems) followed by Beulah's side (II. "Canary in Bloom," 21 poems)— is biographical and historical. The lives of Thomas and Beulah, whether considered together or individually, lack what would integrate them into a single story. The events in *Thomas and Beulah* are narrated in strict chrono-logical order, which is detailed in the appended chronology. The subjection of story time to historical time, unusual in modern narratives, gives Dove's sequence a tragic linearity, a growing sense that what is done cannot be undone and that what is not done but only regretted or deferred cannot be redeemed in the telling. The narrative runs from Thomas's riverboat life (1919) to his arrival in Akron (1921) and marriage to Beulah (1924), to their children's births, his jobs at Goodyear, his stroke (1960) and death (1963). Then the narrative begins again with Beulah: her father's flirtations, Thomas's flirtations and courtship (1923), their marriage (1924), a preg-nancy (1931), her millinery work (1950), a family reunion (1964), and death (1969). In the background, the Depression and the March on Wash-ington mark respectively the trials of the couple's and their children's genera-tion.

The sequence of *Thomas and Beulah* resembles fiction more than it does poetic sequence—Faulkner's family chronicles in particular. Dove's modern-ist narrator stands back paring her fingernails like an unobtrusive master or God. The cover shows a snapshot, of Thomas and Beulah presumably, and the volume may be considered as a photo album, or two albums, with only the date and place printed underneath each picture. Thomas and Beulah are probably Rita Dove's grandparents; the book is dedicated to her mother, Elvira Elizabeth, and the third child born to Thomas and Beulah is identified in the chronology as Liza. But whether the couple is actually Rita Dove's grandparents is less important than the fact that all evidence of their relation has been removed. Any choice of genre involves an economy of gains and losses. Objective, dramatic narration—showing rather than telling—has the advantage of letting the events speak for themselves and the disadvantage of dispensing with the problematics of narrative distortion and a camera-eye or God's eye view. *Thomas and Beulah* tells it like it is and assumes it is like it tells us.

John Shoptaw, "Segregated Lives: Rita Dove's *Thomas and Beulah*," *Reading Black, Reading Feminist: A Critical Anthology*, ed. Henry Louis Gates, Jr. (New York: Meridian, 1990), pp. 374–75

BONNIE COSTELLO   The discipline of writing *Thomas and Beulah*, a family epic in lyric form, required Rita Dove to focus, as never before, her talent for compression. How to get years of her grandparents' joy and anguish into spare lines without presuming to sum up for them; how to telescope distances of place, background, dreams, without narrating—these were some of the problems she solved so brilliantly in that book. The past shed its patina as bits of voice and image shone through to bespeak whole epochs and regions. The book moved us by its understatement, the major ally of compression, and by its sympathetic imagination, that refused to make Thomas and Beulah stereotypes, the mere objects of our pity or nostalgia.

In *Grace Notes* Dove returns to the range of subjects and settings that characterized her first two books (she is remarkably broad in the scope of her references without ever being showy). All the features we have grown to appreciate in this poet arise here in their finest form: descriptive precision, tonal control, metaphoric reach within uncompromising realism. Moreover, she had brought these talents to bear upon a new intimacy and moral depth, served by memory and imagination working together.

The first poem of *Grace Notes*, set off as a kind of prologue, establishes the tone and terms of the volume. "Summit Beach, 1921" presents a girl of courtship age, refusing to join in the festive abandon of young dancers on the beach and choosing to sit by the fire instead. Within 25 lines we learn the history of this girl's stance and come to know her motives and desires even while we never know her name or her relation to the poet. A scar on her knee is the consequence of her childhood fantasy of flying off "Papa's shed." Yet she still "refused / to cut the wing," advised by her father to preserve angelic innocence ("you're all you've got") and waits, instead, for love's "music skittering up her calf." The dreams of this young woman, her "parasol and invisible wings" are in one sense betrayed by the reality around her, the limits imposed because of gender and race—this is a "Negro beach"—and more universally because of gravity and mortality. The winking scar on her knee is the constant reminder of the real world's pull. Yet the poet clearly admires the resilience of this dreamer and her spirit—scarred but winged—pervades the poems of *Grace Notes*. All of Dove's books have been marked by their thoughtful arrangement and *Grace Notes*, divided into five sections, marks out several distinctive areas of reflection, united by the dual images of wounds and wings, themes of pain and the will to resist one's limits, which she introduces in this first poem.

Bonnie Costello, "Scars and Wings: Rita Dove's *Grace Notes*," *Callaloo* 14, No. 2 (Spring 1991): 434–35

EKATERINI GEORGOUDAKI   Although conditions were more
hospitable for black women writers after the Black Power/Black Arts Movement of the 1960s and the Feminist Movement of the 1970s, the ideologies
of class, gender, and race still persisted in American society in the 1980s,
when Rita Dove started publishing her work. She therefore shares certain
dilemmas and concerns with previous Afro-American women poets, such
as their feelings of displacement, fragmentation, and isolation, and their
distaste for conventional stereotypes, hierarchies, divisions and boundaries.
She also continues their search for wholeness, balance, connection, continuity, reconciliation with the self and the world, as well as their efforts to
redefine the self and history, and to renew cultural values.

As a black person living in the predominantly white societies of the Old
and New World, having entered an inter-racial and inter-cultural marriage
(her husband is a German writer), and trying to forge an autonomous female
poetic voice against the background of a male dominated Euro- and Afro-
American literary tradition, Dove has often crossed social and literary boundaries, violated taboos, and experienced displacement, i.e. living "in two
different worlds, seeing things with double vision," wherever she has stayed
(USA, Germany, Israel). Talking to Judith Kitchen and Stan Sanvel Rubin
about her European experiences which inspired her second book, *Museum*
(1983), Dove admits that she had a sense of displacement while she was
in Europe, and that she expressed this sense through various characters
and situations in *Museum*. She remarks, however, that her stay in Europe
broadened her world view and contributed to her personal growth as a
person and an artist:

> When I went to Europe for the first time—that was in '74, way
> before I had thought of this book—it was mind boggling to see
> how blind I'd been in my own little world of America. It had
> never dawned on me that there was a world out there. It was
> really quite shocking to see that there was another way of looking
> at things. And when I went back in '80–81 to spend a lot of
> time, I got a different angle on the way things are, the way things
> happen in the world and the importance they take. Also as a
> *person* going to Europe I was treated differently because I was
> American. I was Black, but they treated me differently than
> people treat me here because I am Black. And in fact, I often felt
> a little like Fiammetta; I became an object. I was a Black
> American, and therefore I became a representative of all of that.
> And I sometimes felt like a ghost, I mean, people would ask me

questions, but I had a feeling that they weren't seeing *me*, but a
shell. So there was that sense of being there and not being there,
you know. Then because you are there you can see things a little
clearer sometimes. That certainly was something, I think, that
informed the spirit of *Museum*.

Dove's complex experiences in the USA and abroad (Europe, N. Africa,
Israel) have affected both her vision and her poetic method. Although she
deals with the problems of racism and sexism, she does not adopt the
polemical voice of either a black nationalist or a feminist poet, and therefore
she does not let indignation, anger, and protest control her verse. Although
she focuses on the black experience in many of her works she goes beyond
the definition of black literature which reflected the black ideal that pre-
vailed since the late 1960s: "Black literature BY blacks, ABOUT blacks,
directed TO blacks. ESSENTIAL black literature is the distillation of black
life."

> Ekaterini Georgoudaki, "Rita Dove: Crossing Boundaries," *Callaloo* 14, No. 2 (Spring
> 1991): 419–20

KIRKLAND C. JONES   In Dove's poems, dramatic monologue
and compressed narrative are the primary contexts through which the language of the people is presented. In her short stories, though they are often
very brief, the dialogues and musing of her characters are set forth in
authentic speech patterns. Moreover, Dove has a keen sense of history. She
links the past and the present through her characters' names and through
the appropriateness of their speech, revealing Dove's brilliant cross-cultural
perceptivity, as her characters' voices move in and out of the centuries,
simultaneously transcending the local and the mundane. "Catecorner," an
expression found in ⟨*Fifth Sunday*'s⟩ title story, is a folksy way of describing
the site of the church building, along with the phrase "let loose," meaning
to set free. And the language of the black church adds enough flavoring to
join the generations of worshippers with their inherited family and community traditions—"the junior ushers," "the junior choir," as they stand up to
sing, "their blue silk robes swaying slightly as they rocked to the beat." The
marching choir, the little-girl "gleaners," the fat officious women in white,
all fit the story's "Fifth Sunday" language, modern enough to be Methodist
and familiar enough to impart a quality of agedness and blackness.

Aunt Carrie, in the story that bears her name, speaks long dramatic monologues, and her speech is almost correct enough to match her assumed primness, allowing her to communicate with her young niece to whom she recounts more than one interesting story. Aunt Carrie is the type of matron who sprinkles her addresses with "dear." But she lapses occasionally into the remembered language of her parents and grandparents—"Don't go apologizing to me . . . makes me blush," she exclaims, and later in a much more relaxed, more confiding tone, she admits to her niece, "I didn't think about nothing at all." But on a whole, dialect is more subtle in the prose vignettes than in the author's most representative poems.

> Kirkland C. Jones, "Folk Idiom in the Literary Expression of Two African American Authors: Rita Dove and Yusef Komunyakaa," *Language and Literature in the African American Imagination*, ed. Carol Aisha Blackshire-Belay (Westport, CT: Greenwood Press, 1992), pp. 152–53

Bibliography

Ten Poems. 1977.

The Only Dark Spot in the Sky. 1980.

The Yellow House on the Corner. 1980.

Mandolin. 1982.

Museum. 1983.

Fifth Sunday. 1985.

Thomas and Beulah. 1986.

The Other Side of the House (with Tamarra Kaida). 1988.

Grace Notes. 1989.

Through the Ivory Gate. 1992.

Selected Poems. 1993.

The Darker Face of the Earth: A Verse Play in Fourteen Scenes. 1994.

Nikki Giovanni
b. 1943

NIKKI GIOVANNI was born Yolande Cornelia Giovanni, Jr., on June 7, 1943, in Knoxville, Tennessee. Her father, Jones Giovanni, was a social worker and her mother, Yolande Cornelia Watson, was an employee of the Welfare Department; they had one other child, Nikki's older sister Gary. Giovanni entered Fisk University in 1960, was tossed out, and re-entered in 1964, when she became serious not only about her studies but also the growing black political movements. She also began to write at this time. She attended the Fisk Writers Workshop directed by John Oliver Killens and graduated from Fisk *magna cum laude* in February 1967. In that same year, she participated in the Cincinnati Black Arts Festival. Giovanni continued her education at the University of Pennsylvania School of Social Work with the help of a Ford Foundation Grant and, later, a National Foundation for the Arts Grant.

At an early age, Giovanni expressed doubts about the traditional institution of marriage. Her alternative, independent, and politically active life led to her decision to become an unwed mother. In 1971 her son Tommy was born and she balanced her literary and political pursuits with an unfailing devotion to her son.

Giovanni's increasing interest in black identity and black history is revealed in her first two published books, *Black Feeling, Black Talk* (1968) and *Black Judgement* (1968). They are somewhat homogeneous in theme but varied in form, style, and tone (which ranges from militant to nostalgic). Many of the poems in these two collections touch upon political events, such as the assassinations of Martin Luther King, Jr., President Kennedy, and Malcolm X. These two books, initially published by a small press, were reissued in one volume in 1970.

A third collection of verse, *Re:Creation* (1970), continued along similar lines. But in 1971 Giovanni's first volume of children's verse appeared. *Spin a Soft Black Song: Poems for Children* is indeed much softer in tone, but much of her political vigor remains in these children's poems. She later published two more collections of children's verse: *Ego-Tripping and Other Poems for Young People* (1973) and *Vacation Time: Poems for Children* (1980). When she returned to writing for adults, Giovanni revealed a marked difference in theme and construction. Her next four collections of verse, *My House* (1972), *The Women and the Men* (1975), *Cotton Candy on a Rainy Day* (1978), and *Those Who Ride the Night Winds* (1983), show a greater interest in personal concerns and a broader, less militant, and more humanistic approach.

Giovanni experienced unexpected success with *Truth Is on Its Way* (1971), a sound recording on which she reads her poetry against a backdrop of gospel music. As a result, she found herself a celebrity attracting much public attention. She has issued several other recordings of her poetry readings. Giovanni has also written an autobiographical sketch entitled *Gemini: An Extended Autobiographical Statement on My First Twenty-five Years of Being a Black Poet* (1971), and a collection of essays, *Sacred Cows—and Other Edibles* (1988). Recently she has devoted attention to celebrating the intellectual and emotional heritage of the elderly, compiling the anthologies *Appalachian Elders* (1991; with Cathee Dennison) and *Grand Mothers* (1994).

Giovanni has taught and lectured at a variety of colleges and universities, including Queens College, Rutgers, and Ohio State; since 1987 she has been professor of English at Virginia Polytechnic Institute and State University in Blacksburg, Virginia.

▣ *Critical Extracts*

NIKKI GIOVANNI   I like all the militant poems that tell how we're going to kick the honkie's backside and purge our new system of all honkie things like white women, TV, voting and the rest of the ugly, bad things that have been oppressing us so long. I mean, I wrote a poem asking, "Nigger, can you kill?" because to want to live under President no-Dick Nixon is certainly to become a killer. Yet in listening to Smokey and the Miracles sing their *Greatest Hits* recently, I became aware again of the revolutionary quality of "You Can Depend on Me." And if you ask, "Who's Loving You?" just because I say he's not a honkie you should still want to know if I'm well laid. There is a tendency to look at the Black experience too narrowly.

The Maulana has pointed out rather accurately that "The blues is counter-revolutionary," but Aretha is a voice of the new Black experience. It's rather obvious that while "Think" was primarily directed toward white America, Ted White could have taken a hint from it. We must be aware of speaking on all levels. What we help to create we will not necessarily be able to control.

The rape of Newark in the 1968 election was criminal. If revolutionaries are going to involve themselves in politics, they should be successful. And while I'm sure poems are being written to explain the "success" of the Newark campaign, and essays and future speeches are being ground out on brand-new Scot tissues in living color blaming the Black community for not supporting the United Brothers, I would imagine the first problem the United Brothers encountered that they were unable to overcome is that they were not united. ⟨. . .⟩

Revolutionary politics has nothing to do with voting anyway. But if we enter electoral politics we should follow the simple formula that every Black person is a potential vote and must be welcomed and treated as such, with or without dashiki, with or without natural.

> Nikki Giovanni, "Black Poems, Poseurs and Power" (1969), Gemini: An Extended Autobiographical Statement on My First Twenty-five Years of Being a Black Poet (Indianapolis: Bobbs-Merrill, 1971), pp. 106–8

DON L. LEE   Nikki Giovanni has published two thin volumes of poetry, Black Feeling, Black Talk and Black Judgement, which reflect her awareness of the values of Black culture as well as her commitment to the · revolution. In "The True Import of Present Dialogue" she asks the Black male/warriors to "kill the nigger" in themselves, to let their "nigger mind die," to free their black hands and "learn to be Black men." Like many of us, Miss Giovanni is concerned that Black men have been sent out of the United States to kill other "colored" peoples of the world when the real enemy is here. She expresses this same concern in "Of Liberation," where she points out that there is an international bond between all peoples of color. Stress is placed on unity, the need to work together for mutual progress.

"Poem (No Name No. 3)" mentions leaders of the Black revolution who have been either silenced permanently or at least hampered seriously in their efforts to increase the awareness and involvement of our people and help them to effect a means to cast off the chains. Cautioning, warning the apathetic, Miss Giovanni states: "if the Black Revolution passes you bye its for damned sure / the white reaction to it won't."

In the autobiographical "My Poem," the poet tells us that she has been robbed, that because of her involvement in the movement she expects at any time a deliberate, planned attack on her very person. In spite of harassment and personal danger, however, she expresses her conviction that the killing/silencing of one revolutionary will not stop the onward movement of our people ⟨. . .⟩

Nikki writes about the familiar: what she knows, sees, experiences. It is clear why she conveys such urgency in expressing the need for Black awareness, unity, solidarity. She knows how it was. She knows how it is. She knows also that a change can be effected. ⟨. . .⟩

Nikki is at her best in the short, personal poem. She is definitely growing as a poet. Her effectiveness is in the area of the "fast rap." She says the right things at the right time. Orally this is cool, but it doesn't come across as printed poetry. We eagerly await her new book, Re: Creation, and hope that the sister has slowed down and tightened up her lines.

Don L. Lee, *Dynamite Voices: Black Poets of the 1960's* (Detroit: Broadside Press, 1971), pp. 68, 70, 74

PETER BAILEY   There are black artists—those in what is called "the black power literary establishment"—who are convinced that Nikki's emergence as a "star" will hinder her development as a *black* poet. Says one member of that group: "In the beginning I thought that Nikki was going to be one of the stabilizers in the black cultural scene; one who could be counted on to maintain her integrity. Unfortunately, she is off on an ego trip. That might be alright in and of itself, but her talent doesn't match her reputation. She needs to retire for a while and develop her talent rather than continue the quest to be a personality. What is happening to her happens to many committed black people when they get status, money and recognition. They start ego-tripping." The critic makes it clear that the success and acceptance of her album is important. "It is important because it reaches many new people. Black people respond to oral works and that makes it extremely important. That's why she must not get into the wrong bag." ⟨. . .⟩

Nikki listens carefully as these criticisms are related to her. Sometimes she smiles. Sometimes she blurts a four-letter comment. Sometimes there is no response at all. About the "black power literary establishment," she says its members are "as dumb and as decadent as their white counterparts." She accuses them of "trying to tell everyone what to do and telling people that 'if you do what we say, we will make you famous.' That's some s ." She blasts on: "Furthermore, there are only two black publishing houses and they mostly publish their friends and that's the god's truth. They select just who and what they will publish. I resent them always telling people what to do. They say, 'Don't publish with whitey; don't go on white TV shows,' yet everytime you look around there's one of them on the David Frost Show or something."

Nikki also rejects the notion that the black artist has a responsibility to provide possible solutions for black people in their liberation struggle; that black artists should not merely "tell it like it is" but also should tell it like it *can* and *should* be. "I'm not about telling people what they should do," she says. When asked if this is not an easy cop-out, an avoidance of responsibility, she replies: "Definitely not. People are going to do what they want to do. If a young brother came to me and told me that he had decided to go and have a rumble with a cop, I wouldn't try to stop him. I'd just ask him if he wanted to eat before he leaves." Even if he had only a brick and the cop had a gun? she is asked. "That's right. It's his decision to make."

Peter Bailey, " 'I Am Black, Female, Polite . . .' " (1972), *Conversations with Nikki Giovanni*, ed. Virginia C. Fowler (Jackson: University Press of Mississippi, 1992), pp. 35–37

JUNE JORDAN   One more essay ⟨in *Gemini*⟩ must be mentioned, her last: "Gemini—A Prolonged Autobiographical Statement on Why." This will prove particularly interesting to everyone familiar with the author's poems. When you compare the poetry with the ambivalence and wants expressed in this essay, it becomes clear that a transition is taking place inside the artist.

She has written in one poem: "Nigger / Can you kill. . . . Can we learn to kill WHITE for BLACK / Learn to kill niggers / Learn to be Black men." Now, in this final essay she is a woman writing: "I don't want my son to be a warrior. . . . I don't want my son to be a George or a Jonathan Jackson. . . . I didn't have a baby to see him be cannon fodder." Whatever the depth of the transition, the uncertainties are real and plainly spoken: "Perhaps Black people don't want Revolution at all. That too must be considered. I used to think the world needs what I need. But perhaps it doesn't." And, the final two lines of the book: "I really like to think a Black, beautiful, loving world is possible. I really do, I think."

To be sure, that is a puzzling conclusion. Is it the black part, or the beautiful, or the "loving world" part, that leaves her unsure—or all of them? Maybe that was the goal, to raise more questions about herself, at the age of 27, than she would or could answer. At 27, that might seem fair enough, and a lot less surprising than an honest-to-God autobiography.

June Jordan, [Review of *Gemini*], *New York Times Book Review*, 13 February 1972, p. 26

CLAUDIA TATE CLAUDIA TATE: The black revolutionary fervor of the sixties seems to be gone. We no longer even hear the rhetoric. Does this suggest that the revolution is over?

NIKKI GIOVANNI: I bought three new windows for my mother's basement. Have you ever bought windows for your mother's basement? It's revolutionary! It really is.

I have a problem I think I should share with you. For the most part this question is boring. We're looking at a phenomemon as if it were finished. Everyone says, "Well, what happened to the revolution?" If you want to deal with states [dialectical transitions] you have to deal with Marx. But I'm not into that. From where I am, I see a continuous black revolution going on for the last four hundred years in America. There has been a continuous revolution of black people for the last two thousand years. And it's not letting up.

When you look at the decade from 1954 to 1964, you're forced to say black Americans won their objectives. We didn't like the segregated buses. We didn't like the segregated schools. We didn't like the way we were treated in stores. We didn't like the housing patterns. We didn't like our lack of professionals. We won. But looking at the late seventies, there's no way you can consider the Bakke decision to be favorable. It was 5–4. It was really a bad decision. Close cases make bad law. There's no question Bakke should have come in 9–0 either way, if it's going to be definitive. Then you would have had a law. You don't have a law now.

I'm looking for a riot. I'm living in a city that kills cops like people kill flies. Cincinnati, Ohio is leading the nation in the number of policemen killed. We're number one. The black community seems to be saying, "Well, you can play Nazi, but we ain't playing Jew." And black folks have been shooting back. We're saying, "Wait a minute. Who do you think you're playing with?" Nobody's going back to 1954. No matter what the rollback is. It's not even going back to '64. No matter what "let's take the breather" is.

When people start to say "What happened to the sixties," we've got to remember, "Hey, this is the eighties and what are we going to do now?" Where are we going because it's going to continue. My generation didn't start the bus boycotts. But we decided where they should go. Now it's time again to decide on a direction. We weren't the first generation to say "This ain't right." But we were the first to know we had to fight in terms of our bodies. We recognized we were going to have to go to jail, and we were going to get beaten; our houses were going to get bombed. But we went on the line. I mean bodies, a lot of bodies. I'm not the first poet, neither is Carolyn Rogers nor Gwen Brooks, to say, "Hey, this is intolerable." Neither was Langston Hughes, nor Claude McKay. We're talking about a struggle for freedom that keeps going on and on. People are tending to approach the whole problem like, "Oh! Wow! It's all over. It's been done." This is not a movie!

Claudia Tate, "Nikki Giovanni," *Black Women Writers at Work* (New York: Continuum, 1983), pp. 61–62

JEAN GOULD   Nikki Giovanni forged her own identity painfully perhaps, but with great determination. She had left home with her infant son to set up her own household in New York City when she was offered a job as a consultant and contributing editor to *Encore* magazine by publisher-editor Ida Lewis, who became her close friend. The poet's success, once she had been launched, was phenomenal. In ten years she produced thirteen books—a variety of writing that includes poetry, autobiography, "raps" with James Baldwin and Margaret Walker (released also on records), besides extensive travel for readings and lectures. In all she did she took into consideration her son.

She early established a regime for herself that would be backbreaking for a far more robust body than hers appeared to be. When Tommy was small, she would be up in their three-bedroom apartment on the Upper West Side of Manhattan by six a.m., get him off to school nearby, do her household chores or shop until late morning, and then write most of the afternoon, at least until Tommy came home from school. After he went to bed she might work until dawn, depending on her deadlines. When she is on tour her son stays with a secretary, but from the time he was a small boy she took him with her to visit her parents, who had been aghast at the idea of their daughter, an "unwed mother," trying to bring up a child by herself, but they soon saw that she was entirely capable of parenthood as she had learned from them both the positive and negative aspects of it. One morning when she and Tommy were going toward the elevator, he stopped halfway there and said, "Carry me." Switching her constantly carried briefcase from her right arm to the left, Nikki picked him up. But she warned him, smiling, "If you aren't a good father, I'll brain you." Ida Lewis, who wrote the foreword to My House, Giovanni's second volume, noted that Nikki never said good husband or good provider, but "broke it down to a basic," as Ida wrote. Tommy had responded complacently by putting his thumb in his mouth; he was used to his mother's hyperbole; from infancy he had been given the security of her loving care. The two were partners in meeting life's challenge.

Jean Gould, "Nikki Giovanni," *Modern American Women Poets* (New York: Dodd, Mead, 1984), pp. 335–36

WILLIAM J. HARRIS   Giovanni is a frustrating poet. I can sympathize with her detractors, no matter what the motives for their discontent. She clearly has talent that she refuses to discipline. She just doesn't seem to try hard enough. In "Habits" she coyly declares:

> i sit writing
> a poem
> about my habits

which while it's not
a great poem
is mine

It isn't enough that the poem is hers; personality isn't enough, isn't a substitute for fully realized poems. Even though she has created a compelling persona on the page, she has been too dependent on it. Her ego has backfired. She has written a number of lively, sometimes humorous, sometimes tragic, often perceptive poems about the contemporary world. The best poems in her three strongest books, *Black Feeling, Black Talk, Black Judgement, Re:Creation*, and *Cotton Candy*, demonstrate that she can be a very good poet. However, her work also contains dross: too much unrealized abstraction (flabby abstraction at that!), too much "poetic" fantasy posing as poetry and too many moments verging on sentimentality. In the early seventies, after severely criticizing Giovanni's shortcomings, Haki Madhubuti said he eagerly awaited the publication of her new book, *Re:Creation;* he hoped that in it she would fulfill the promise of her early poetry. Even though it turned out to be one of Giovanni's better books, I find myself in a similar situation to Madhubuti's. I see that not only does Giovanni have promise, she already has written some good poems and continues to write them. Yet I am concerned about her development. I think it is time for her to stand back and take stock of herself, to take for herself the time for reflection, the vacation she says Aretha deserves for work well done. Nikki Giovanni is one of the most talented writers to come out of the Black sixties, and I don't want to lose her. I want her to write poems which grow out of that charming persona, not poems which are consumed by it. Giovanni must keep her charm and overcome her self-indulgence. She has the talent to create good, perhaps important, poetry, if only she has the will to discipline her craft.

William J. Harris, "Sweet Soft Essence of Possibility: The Poetry of Nikki Giovanni," *Black Women Writers (1950–1980): A Critical Evaluation*, ed. Mari Evans (New York: Anchor Books/Doubleday, 1984), p. 228

MARGARET B. McDOWELL   The most significant development in Giovanni's career has been her evolution from a strongly committed political consciousness prior to 1969 to a more inclusive consciousness which does not repudiate political concern and commitment, but which regards a revolutionary ethos as only one aspect of the totality of Black experience.

Her earlier political associates and favorable reviewers of the late 1960s often regarded her development after 1970 with consternation, as representing a repudiation of her racial roots and of political commitment, without perhaps fully understanding the basis for her widened concerns and interests. Giovanni's shift in interest from revolutionary politics and race as a collective matter towards love and race as they affect personal development and relationships brought strong reviewer reaction. (The shift to less favorable criticism, which is apparent in the reviews of My House, is also evident in the late notices of Gemini, Giovanni's most widely reviewed book.) The problems involved in studying the relationship between this shift in her poetry and the somewhat delayed shift from favorable to less favorable criticism, as her artistry grew, are complex. And they are further complicated by the fact that, at the very time the negative reviews of her poetry markedly increased, her popularity with readers surged dramatically ahead. Witness the late sales of Gemini (1971) and Black Feeling/Black Talk/Black Judgement (1970), the new sales of My House (1972), and the record-breaking sales of her two early albums of recorded poetry. Her audiences around the country grew markedly in size and enthusiasm in 1972, and feature articles and cover stories on "the Princess of Black Poetry" appeared in over a dozen popular magazines in 1972 and 1973.

Studying the relationships between the positive and negative reviews and between the opinions of reviewers and popular audiences is made more difficult by an anomaly presented by Giovanni's Black Feeling/Black Talk/ Black Judgement: two-thirds of the poems in this 1970 volume are brief, introspective lyrics which are political only in the most peripheral sense—that they mention a lover as someone the speaker met at a conference, for instance. The remaining third, poems which are strongly political and often militant, received practically all the attention of reviewers. Critics ignored almost completely the poems that foreshadow nearly all the poetry Giovanni was to write in the next thirteen years. In short, the wave of literary reviews that established Giovanni's national reputation as a poet also established her image as a radical. Yet, by the summer of 1970, when these reviews began to appear, Giovanni had been writing solely non-political, lyric poetry for a year. The label "the poet of the Black revolution" which characterized her in the popular media was already a misnomer in 1970, when it began to be popularly used.

Margaret B. McDowell, "Groundwork for a More Comprehensive Criticism of Nikki Giovanni," Studies in Black American Literature, ed. Joe Weixlmann and Chester J. Fontenot (Greenwood, FL: Penkevill Publishing Co., 1986), Vol. 2, pp. 143–44

MARITA GOLDEN   In *Sacred Cows and Other Edibles*, Nikki Giovanni—poet, personality, social critic, iconoclast and raconteur—exhibits
the best and the worst uses of the essay as a vehicle for expression, verbal
performance and exploration of the mundane and the special. ⟨. . .⟩
        The problem with *Sacred Cows and Other Edibles* ⟨. . .⟩ is that it falls short
precisely because Giovanni's glib, wise-cracking, overly conversational style
(which has made her poetry so popular) is ill-suited to the intellectual
requirements of the essay. These pieces mildly entertain more than they
probe; more often than not, the reader is merely reminded of what is obvious
rather than introduced to another way of seeing things.
        Giovanni is at her best in the selection titled "Reflections on My Profes-
sion" and "Four Introductions"—pieces dedicated to writers, among them
Paule Marshall and Mari Evans. In "An Answer to Some Questions on
How I Write" Giovanni asserts, "I don't have a lifestyle. I have a life,"
which made me want to cheer this hearty refutation of categories and
oversimplification of the human equation. And puncturing the vague pom-
posity of the current hot cliché, the "role model," Giovanni says: "When
people do not want to do what history requires, they say they have no role
models. I'm glad Phillis Wheatley did not know she had no role model and
wrote her poetry anyway." And she sums up the job of the writer with a
feisty confidence saying, "We write because we believe that the human
spirit cannot be tamed and should not be trained." This is Giovanni at her
best—sparkling *and* thoughtful.

> Marita Golden, "Tennis, Termites, Game Shows and the Art of Writing," *Washington
> Post Book World*, 14 February 1988, p. 3

MARTHA COOK   ⟨. . .⟩ Giovanni displays a new sense of herself
as a poet in *Those Who Ride the Night Winds*. In "A Song for New-Ark"
and also in "I Am She," Giovanni seems confident of the role she has
chosen for herself, secure in her place in society. As she says in the latter
poem, "I am she . . . who writes . . . the poems. . . ." Again the ellipses give
the sense of openness, of more to come from this poetic talent. While the
poems in this volume seem to reflect Giovanni's own feeling that she has
reached maturity as a poet, there are still indications of the necessity of
coping with the demands of modern life. She acknowledges the presence
of loneliness, not as she did through the poems in the volume *Cotton Candy*

on a Rainy Day, where loneliness seemed to be a problem for which she
could at the time see no solution, but in a way that indicates the strength
of her inner resources. In the poem, "The Room with the Tapestry Rug,"
she creates a persona who confronts loneliness by seeking out "the room
. . . where all who lived . . . knew her well. . . ." The room holds memories
of the past, symbolized by a garment created by a member of her family
who was important in her childhood, used in a literal and metaphorical
way to keep out the cold.

But Giovanni moves beyond this fairly traditional symbol, refusing to let
the room be only a place of confinement and protection from the larger
world; it becomes a place where she can also find comfort in the cool air
from outside, while luxuriating in the security of her own space:

> If it was cold . . . she would wrap herself . . . in the natted blue
> sweater . . . knitted by a grandmother . . . so many years ago . . . If
> warm . . . the windows were opened . . . to allow the wind . . . to
> partake of their pleasure . . .

The closing paragraph of the poem indicates the resources of the persona
beyond her memories of the past: "Her books . . . her secret life . . . in the
room with the tapestry rug. . . ." Here she shows not only the need for but
the fact of control over the places in her own life.

In the 1970s, such poems as "My House" conveyed an important theme
of the development of a strengthening identity as a single woman; in the
1980s, such poems as "The Room with the Tapestry Rug" and "I Am She"
illustrate not only the strength but also the depth and range of that identity.
It is appropriate that a volume that so strongly exhibits Giovanni's talents
as a writer should also attest to the importance of literature and art in her
life, an importance reflected as well in her continued involvement in efforts
to bring people and the arts together. ⟨. . .⟩

Looking at Giovanni's poetry in the context of Southern literature
expands rather than limits the possibilities for interpretation and analysis.
In fact, this approach reveals that within the body of her work lies a solid
core of poems that do not rely on political or personal situations for their
success. Rather, they develop universal themes, such as coming to terms
with the past and with the present so that one may move into the future—
again, themes that have been and continue to be of particular significance
in Southern poetry. These themes mark her work as a contribution to the
canon not just of Southern poetry, of black poetry, of feminist poetry, but

also of contemporary American poetry. However, Giovanni's response to
any generalization, any categorization, would probably echo the closing line
of her poem "Categories," from *My House*. Emphasizing her uniqueness as
an individual, she might well proclaim, "i'm bored with categories."

Martha Cook, "Nikki Giovanni: Place and Sense of Place in Her Poetry," *Southern
Women Writers: The New Generation*, ed. Tonette Bond Inge (Tuscaloosa: University
of Alabama Press, 1990), pp. 298–99

VIRGINIA C. FOWLER   As a poet who emerged during the 1960s
⟨. . .⟩ Giovanni has consistently believed in a connection between art and
action, a central impetus of the Black Arts Movement; in Larry Neal's
words, "It is a profound ethical sense that makes a Black artist question a
society in which art is one thing and the actions of men another. The Black
Arts Movement believes that your ethics and your aesthetics are one."
Although we have seen that Giovanni objected to the prescriptiveness that
eventually would destroy the Black Arts Movement, her poetry, both early
and late, reflects the kind of ethical concerns described by Neal. As she
goes on to explain to ⟨Claudia⟩ Tate, the "militant stance" prescribed by
adherents of a black aesthetic was as repugnant to her as any prescriptiveness;
but beyond this, it also lost its usefulness: "What are we going to do with
a stance? Literature is only as useful as it reflects reality." Ironically, prescrip-
tive assumptions of just this sort are evident in Tate's question. Had Giovanni's poetry continued to be "extroverted, militant, arrogant" (if one
accepts Tate's terms) in the 1970s and 1980s, it would have ceased to
"reflect reality." The "shift" to which Tate refers is not, Giovanni's answers
make clear, the result of a decision to write a different kind of poetry.
Instead, as the social and political realities of her world changed, both she—
who is "a part of the body politic"—and her poetry—which deliberately
attempts to "reflect" the world—also changed.

Elsewhere Giovanni identifies some of the changing realities that her
poetry reflects. "I started as a writer concerned about the black situation
in America and have grown to be a writer concerned about the black
situation in the world. I have come to realize that gender bias is a real
problem. It's difficult to be a woman, but being black and female produces
a double bind." In addition to this kind of expansion in her awareness and
focus, she points to the implications that space exploration has for human

beings: "A lot has happened. I don't want anybody to think it's just me. It's all of us. It has to do with the way we conceptualize the world. We are earthlings. When Viking II took off we became earthlings. Nobody knows what an earthling is, and how an earthling relates to other earthlings." Our world, in other words, looks very different now than it did in 1968 when Giovanni began her career as a poet. And her poetry will inevitably reflect those differences because they give shape to who she is.

Virginia C. Fowler, *Nikki Giovanni* (New York: Twayne, 1992), pp. 127–28

Bibliography

Black Feeling, Black Talk. 1968.

Black Judgement. 1968.

Black Feeling, Black Talk/Black Judgement. 1970.

Re:Creation. 1970.

All I Gotta Do. 1970.

Night Comes Softly: An Anthology of Black Female Voices (editor). 1970.

Poems of Angela Yvonne Davis. 1970.

Gemini: An Extended Autobiographical Statement on My First Twenty-five Years of Being a Black Poet. 1971.

Spin a Soft Black Song: Poems for Children. 1971.

My House. 1972.

A Dialogue (with James Baldwin). 1973.

Ego-Tripping and Other Poems for Young People. 1973.

A Poetic Equation: Conversations between Nikki Giovanni and Margaret Walker. 1974.

The Women and the Men. 1975.

Cotton Candy on a Rainy Day. 1978.

Vacation Time: Poems for Children. 1980.

Those Who Ride the Night Winds. 1983.

Sacred Cows—and Other Edibles. 1988.

Appalachian Elders: A Warm Hearth Sampler (editor; with Cathee Dennison). 1991.

Conversations with Nikki Giovanni. Ed. Virginia C. Fowler. 1992.

Grand Mothers: Poems, Reminiscences, and Short Stories about the Keepers of Our Traditions (editor). 1994.

Knoxville, Tennessee. 1994.

Racism 101. 1994.

◈ ◈ ◈

Lorraine Hansberry
1930–1965

LORRAINE VIVIAN HANSBERRY was born on May 19, 1930, in Chicago, Illinois, the youngest of four children of a well-to-do family. Her father, Carl Augustus Hansberry, the founder of his own real estate business, was a prominent figure in the black community in Chicago, and in her youth Hansberry encountered such distinguished figures as Paul Robeson and Duke Ellington. In 1938 her father bought a house in a white neighborhood and fought his case all the way to the Supreme Court for the right to live there. Even after his death in 1946, prominent black artists and politicians continued to be frequent guests to the Hansberry house.

Hansberry graduated from Englewood High School in Chicago in 1947. She studied art, English, and stage design at the University of Wisconsin but left in 1950 without taking a degree. Nevertheless, her urge to write was stimulated at Wisconsin, especially when she saw a production of Sean O'Casey's *Juno and the Paycock*. Moving to New York later that year, she began to write full-time for *Freedom* magazine, which was founded by Paul Robeson. Her articles on Africa and on civil rights issues affecting blacks, women, and the poor, and her speeches to civil rights and other groups, made her a prominent young spokeswoman for progressive causes. In 1952 she attended the Intercontinental Peace Congress in Montevideo, Uruguay, in place of Paul Robeson, whose passport had been removed by the U.S. government. After marrying Robert Barron Nemiroff, a Jewish man, in 1953, she devoted herself to writing while working at a variety of odd jobs, including a brief teaching stint at the Jefferson School of Social Science. The couple's financial worries were relieved when a song cowritten by Nemiroff became a hit, allowing Hansberry to quit her jobs and write full-time.

Hansberry's first play, A *Raisin in the Sun*, was begun in 1956 and completed in 1958. It is a starkly realistic play about the life of several generations of a black family on the South Side of Chicago, perhaps inspired in part by Arthur Miller's *Death of a Salesman*, although the title is taken from

Langston Hughes's celebrated poem "Harlem" ("What happens to a dream deferred . . . Does it dry up like a raisin in the sun . . . Or does it explode?"). It received tryouts in New Haven, Philadelphia, and Chicago before opening on Broadway in March 1959, starring Sidney Poitier, Ruby Dee, Lou Gossett, and others. The play received 530 performances in a nineteen-month run, and Hansberry became the first black American writer to win the New York Drama Critics Circle Award. In the screenplay she wrote for the film version, Hansberry added several scenes, but these were not filmed; nevertheless, the film was both a critical and popular success when it opened in 1961. Nemiroff's 1973 adaptation of A Raisin in the Sun as a musical won a Tony award. A made-for-television version of the play, which restored the omissions from the film version, aired in 1989. Hansberry's screenplay was published in 1992.

In 1960 Hansberry was commissioned by NBC to write a television play on slavery; the result was The Drinking Gourd, but NBC executives felt the play was too controversial and it was not produced. Her next play, The Sign in Sidney Brustein's Window, opened in October 1964, and in spite of mixed reviews was kept running by friends and admirers until the playwright's death of cancer at the age of thirty-four on January 12, 1965.

In spite of their divorce in 1964, Hansberry named Nemiroff her literary executor. His collection of excerpts from her plays, journals, speeches, and letters, To Be Young, Gifted and Black: Lorraine Hansberry in Her Own Words, was presented off-Broadway in 1969. He produced Les Blancs, a play set in Africa, in 1970. His edition of Les Blancs: The Collected Last Plays of Lorraine Hansberry, which includes The Drinking Gourd and What Use Are Flowers? as well as the title play, was published in 1972.

▨ Critical Extracts

HAROLD CLURMAN   A Raisin in the Sun is authentic: it is a portrait of the aspirations, anxieties, ambitions and contradictory pressures affecting humble Negro folk in an American big city—in this instance Chicago. It is not intended as an appeal to whites or as a preachment for Negroes. It is an honestly felt response to a situation that has been lived through, clearly understood and therefore simply and impressively stated.

Most important of all: having been written from a definite point of view
(that of a participant) with no eye toward meretricious possibilities in
showmanship and public relations, the play throws light on aspects of American life quite outside the area of race.

The importance of the production transcends its script. The play is organic
theatre: cast, text, direction are homogeneous in social orientation and in
quality of talent. Without the aid of an aesthetic program or bias of any kind
but through cultural and emotional consanguinity—a kind of spontaneous
combustion which occurs when individuals who share a common need find
each other under the proper circumstances—a genuine ensemble has been
achieved.

Harold Clurman, "Theatre," *Nation*, 4 April 1959, pp. 301–2

GERALD WEALES   Despite an incredible number of imperfections,
Raisin is a good play. Its basic strength lies in the character and the problem
of Walter Lee, which transcends his being a Negro. If the play were only
the Negro-white conflict that crops up when the family's proposed move
is about to take place, it would be an editorial, momentarily effective, and
nothing more. Walter Lee's difficulty, however, is that he has accepted the
American myth of success at its face value, that he is trapped, as Willy
Loman was trapped, by a false dream. In planting so indigenous an American
image at the center of her play, Miss Hansberry has come as close as possible
to what she intended—a play about Negroes which is not simply a Negro
play.

The play has other virtues. There are genuinely funny and touching
scenes throughout. Many of these catch believably the chatter of a family—
the resentments and the shared jokes—and the words have the ring of truth
that one found in Odets or Chayefsky before they began to sound like
parodies of themselves. In print, I suspect, the defects of *Raisin* will show
up more sharply, but on stage—where, after all, a play is supposed to be—
the impressive performances of the three leads (Poitier, Ruby Dee, and
Claudia McNeil) draw attention to the play's virtues.

Gerald Weales, "Thoughts on *A Raisin in the Sun*: A Critical Review," *Commentary*
27, No. 6 (June 1959): 529

ARNA BONTEMPS   Lorraine Hansberry, the exciting author of *Raisin in the Sun*, is in some very fundamental literary ways related to the sturdy author of *Native Son*, *Black Boy* and *Uncle Tom's Children*. Even the Hansberry-Wright link, however, which is by no means limited to the way in which they have drawn upon their common Chicago background for subject matter, is marked by notable differences. Miss Hansberry's star came up unheralded. Nothing from her typewriter had been published or produced prior to *Raisin in the Sun*. The critical and popular approval which followed this event made her famous, and the rejoicing this occasioned can only be compared to the kudos which followed Richard Wright's sunburst a little more than a decade earlier. But her recognition was based on a play. *Native Son* was a novel, *Black Boy* an autobiography, *Uncle Tom's Children* a collection of stories. And the two authors, though they had both spent crucial years of their lives in the Chicago jungle, if that's the word for the South Side of those days, were separated by more than just a span of time in their development.

Richard Wright's young manhood in Chicago was poverty ridden. Lorraine Hansberry's family was well-to-do by South Side standards. Her father was in the real estate business. He could, in a manner of speaking, have owned or managed the rental property in which Bigger Thomas killed the rat with the frying pan. How his perceptive daughter came to see the human turmoil in those substandard quarters through eyes of sympathy and deep understanding has not been told. Miss Hansberry's subsequent writing has consisted mainly of articles in periodicals. It has not tended toward autobiography.

A lesser writer, one imagines, particularly a lesser Negro writer in the United States, might have been in a hurry, given her talents and background, to give the world a picture of debutants' balls and gracious living to compensate for the ugliness Richard Wright had forced before the eyes of millions of readers, to the embarrassment of our favored few. She also avoided the equally unwise assumption that more of the same material that Wright had presented would prove to be equally arresting when presented by her, equally instructive. But it doesn't work that way without the addition of new elements, and the new Hansberry ingredient was *technique*.

In the theatre, a medium that demands a maximum of know-how, usually attained only after long and painful apprenticeship, years of heartbreaking trial and error, she showed up at first bow with complete control of her tools and her craft. This was little short of startling. Self-educated Richard

Wright had been a toiling, sometimes almost awkward manipulator of the devices of composition. He had won over this disadvantage by sheer power. In Lorraine Hansberry's case this particular shoe seemed to be on the other foot.

Arna Bontemps, "New Black Renaissance," *Negro Digest* 11, No. 1 (November 1961): 53–54

HAROLD CRUSE   *A Raisin in the Sun* demonstrated that the Negro playwright has lost the intellectual and, therefore, technical and creative, ability to deal with his own special ethnic group materials in dramatic form. The most glaring manifestation of this conceptual weakness is the constant slurring over, the blurring, and evasion of the internal facts of Negro ethnic life in terms of class and social caste divisions, institutional and psychological variations, political divisions, acculturation variables, clique variations, religious divisions, and so forth. Negro playwrights have never gone past their own subjectivity to explore the severe stress and strain of class conflict within the Negro group. Such class and clique rivalries and prejudices can be just as damaging, demoralizing and retarding as white prejudice. Negro playwrights have sedulously avoided dealing with the Negro middle class in all its varieties of social expression, basically because the Negro playwright has adopted the Negro middle-class morality. Therefore, art itself, especially the art of playwriting, has become a stepping stone to middle-class social status. As long as the morality of the Negro middle class must be upheld, defended, and emulated in social life *outside* the theater it can never be portrayed or criticized *inside* the theater à la Ibsen, or satirized à la Shaw. In this regard it becomes the better part of social and creative valor to do what Hansberry did—"Let us portay only the good, simple ordinary folk because this is what the audiences want, especially the white audiences; but let us give the whites the Negro middle-class ball to carry towards the goal of integration. Beyond that very functional use of the Negro in the theater, of what other value is this thing, the so-called Negro play? None at all, so let us banish it along with that other parochial idea 'The Negro Theater.' We don't like this 'Negro play' category in the American theater anyhow, and we don't like to be told that we must write it, but we'll *use* it (as a starter) and then we'll go on to better things; that is, we'll become what they call human and universal, which in the white folks' lexicon and cultural philosophy means 'universally white.' "

⟨. . .⟩ A *Raisin in the Sun* expressed through the medium of theatrical art that current, forced symbiosis in American interracial affairs wherein the Negro working class has been roped in and tied to the chariot of racial integration driven by the Negro middle class. In this drive for integration the Negro working class is being told in a thousand ways that it must give up its ethnicity and become human, universal, full-fledged American. Within the context of this forced alliance of class aims there is no room for Negro art (except when it pays off) or Negro art institutions (We middle-class Negroes ain't about to pay for that!), because all of this is self-segregation which hangs up "our" drive for integration. From all of this it can be seen how right E. Franklin Frazier was when he observed: "The new Negro middle class that has none of the spirit of service . . . attempts to dissociate itself as much as possible from identification with the Negro masses. . . . The lip service which they give to solidarity with the masses very often disguises their exploitation of the masses."

Harold Cruse, *The Crisis of the Negro Intellectual* (New York: William Morrow, 1967), pp. 281–83

JAMES BALDWIN   We really met ⟨. . .⟩ in Philadelphia, in 1959, when *A Raisin in the Sun* was at the beginning of its amazing career. Much has been written about this play; I personally feel that it will demand a far less guilty and constricted people than the present-day Americans to be able to assess it at all; as an historical achievement, anyway, no one can gainsay its importance. What is relevant here is that I had never in my life seen so many black people in the theatre. And the reason was that never in the history of the American theatre had so much of the truth of black people's lives been seen on the stage. Black people ignored the theatre because the theatre had always ignored them.

But, in *Raisin*, black people recognized that house and all the people in it— the mother, the son, the daughter and the daughter-in-law—and supplied the play with an interpretative element which could not be present in the minds of white people: a kind of claustrophobic terror, created not only by their knowledge of the house but by their knowledge of the streets. And when the curtain came down, Lorraine and I found ourselves in the backstage alley, where she was immediately mobbed. I produced a pen and Lorraine handed me her handbag and began signing autographs. "It only happens once," she said. I stood there and watched. I watched the people, who loved Lorraine for what she had brought to them; and watched Lorraine, who loved the people for what they brought to her. It was not, for her, a matter of being admired. She was being corroborated and confirmed. She was wise enough and honest enough to recognize that black American artists are in a very special case. One is not merely an artist and one is not judged merely as an artist: the black people crowding around Lorraine, whether or not they considered her an artist, assuredly considered her a witness. This country's concept of art and artists has the effect, scarcely worth mentioning by now, of isolating the artist from the people. One can see the effect of this in the irrelevance of so much of the work produced by celebrated white artists; but the effect of this isolation on a black artist is absolutely fatal. He *is*, already, as a black American citizen, isolated from most of his white countrymen. At the crucial hour, he can hardly look to his artistic peers for help, for they do not know enough about him to be able to correct him. To continue to grow, to remain in touch with himself, he needs the support of that community from which, however, all of the pressures of American life incessantly conspire to remove him. And when he is effectively removed, he falls silent—and the people have lost another hope.

Much of the strain under which Lorraine worked was produced by her knowledge of this reality, and her determined refusal to be destroyed by it.

James Baldwin, "Sweet Lorraine," *Esquire* 72, No. 5 (November 1969): 139

LLOYD W. BROWN   Ever since the sixties the reputation and significance of several established Black American writers have become issues in the running ethnopolitical debates on Black American literature. James Baldwin, Ralph Ellison, and LeRoi Jones, for example, have been at the center of confrontations between "militants" and "moderates," Black "extremists" and white "liberals," integrationists and Black nationalists, and so on. And it is increasingly evident that Lorraine Hansberry has joined this list of controversial writers, especially on the basis of her first play, *A Raisin in the Sun* (1959). On the anti-integrationist side, Harold Cruse ⟨in *The Crisis of the Negro Intellectual*, 1967⟩ deplores *Raisin* as "the artistic, aesthetic and class-inspired culmination of the efforts of the Harlem leftwing literary and cultural in-group to achieve integration of the Negro in the arts." In other words, it is a "most cleverly written piece of glorified soap opera," a "second-rate" play about working-class Blacks who "mouth middle class ideology." Moreover, the alleged shortcomings of Lorraine Hansberry's integrationist philosophy are linked, somehow, with her supposed inferiority as a dramatic artist: "*A Raisin in the Sun* demonstrated that the Negro playwright has lost the intellectual and, therefore, technical and creative, ability to deal with his own special ethnic group materials in dramatic form."

On the other side of the debate, both C. W. E. Bigsby ⟨in *Confrontation and Commitment: A Study of Contemporary American Drama 1959–1966*, 1967⟩ and Richard A. Duprey ⟨in "Today's Dramatists," *American Theatre*, 1967⟩ have praised Hansberry precisely because, in their view, she transcends those "special ethnic group materials." Thus, according to Duprey, *Raisin* is full of human insights that transcend any racial "concerns," and Bigsby praises her compassion and her understanding of the need to "transcend" history. In short, Hansberry's work has been caught up in the continuing conflict between the ethnic criteria of social protesters and the pro-integrationist's ethos of love and reconciliation. And when a critic such as Jordan Miller ⟨in "Lorraine Hansberry," *The Black American Writer*, Vol. 2, ed. C. W. E. Bigsby, 1971⟩ is confronted with this kind of debate he responds with the art-for-art's-sake thesis. He refuses to discuss Hansberry's work "on the basis of any form of racial consciousness" or "in any niche of social significance," and insists instead on the critic's "obligation" to judge the dramatist's work as "dramatic literature quite apart from other factors."

These three representative viewpoints need to be emphasized here because, taken together, they demonstrate a continuing problem in the study of Black literature: the tendency, for one reason or another, to isolate questions of structure or technique from those of social, or racial, significance.

Lloyd W. Brown, "Lorraine Hansberry as Ironist," *Journal of Black Studies* 4, No. 3 (March 1974): 237–38

ELLEN SCHIFF   A notably sensitive concept of the Jewish experience as archetypal furnishes the subtext of Lorraine Hansberry's *The Sign in Sidney Brustein's Window* (1965), at the same time illuminating one of the most successful characterizations of the Jew on the post-1945 stage. Brustein is the literary heir to the lineage established by Galsworthy's Ferdinand de Levis (*Loyalties*, 1922). He is the Jew who has found his niche in society and occupies it with the same aplomb with which he wears his identity.

In making Brustein the axis of her play and the magnet that attracts its other outsiders, Hansberry draws on the historical experience of the Jew. Her protagonist personifies an alien factor that has earned a degree of acceptance in society. Having accomplished that, he tends to regard race, creed and previous conditions of servitude largely as bothersome clichés and to devote himself to other pressing concerns. Hence Sidney, not unkindly, dismisses his black friend Alton's preoccupation with making a cause of his blackness: "Be a Martian if you wanna." He admonishes the homosexual David:

> If somebody insults you—sock 'em in the jaw. If you don't like
> the sex laws, attack 'em. I think they're silly. You wanna get up a
> petition? I'll sign one. Love little fishes if you want. *But*, David,
> please get over the notion that your particular sexuality is
> something that only the deepest, saddest, the most nobly tortured
> can know about. It ain't . . . it's just one kind of sex—that's all.
> And in my opinion . . . the universe turns regardless.

There is no question of Sidney Brustein's *becoming* assimilated. Married to "the only Greco-Gaelic-Indian hillbilly in captivity," preferring his bohemian life in Greenwich Village to the conventional security of his brother Manny's uptown office, removed enough to laugh with genuine amusement at his mother's carping, "*Not* that I have anything against the goyim, Sidney, she's a nice girl, but . . . ," he justifiably feels entitled to his past participle: "I'm assimilated," he declares.

Although he attributes his need for periodic retreats to an imaginary mountain top to a Jewish psyche "less discriminating than most," Brustein manifests distinctly Jewish traits. He loves life with the love of an idealist who prides himself on being true to his moral principles. An incurable optimist, at thirty-seven he refuses to be daunted by bad luck. For instance, the failure of his cabaret and his consequent indebtedness do not discourage him from investing in a small weekly newspaper. Even though he has sworn to put an end to his long career in the service of "every committee To Save, To Abolish, Prohibit, Preserve, Reserve and Conserve that ever was," Sidney is easily persuaded to support ward politician Wally O'Hara's campaign to clean up city government. Sidney is an incorrigible insurgent. "I *care!''* he explains to his gay friend David who writes plays about meaning-lessness and alienation, "I care about it all. It takes too much energy *not* to care."

Ellen Schiff, *From Stereotype to Metaphor: The Jew in Contemporary Drama* (Albany: State University of New York Press, 1982), pp. 156–57

ANNE CHENEY   Paul Robeson's influence on Lorraine Hansberry is difficult to assess. They constantly crossed paths in her lifetime. She loved his voice and the songs he sang. He was her first employer, at *Freedom*. Indirectly she learned through him and *Freedom* of the dire condition in which most blacks lived, and of the dangers of being an artist. He was an inspiration and, to some extent, a warning.

Langston Hughes's influence is much more obvious. He did not allow himself—especially in the McCarthy era—to become primarily involved in the political struggle for racial equality. His poetry reflects the lives of black people, frequently with humor, but he understates his sense of personal frustration or anger, or of impending danger to those who do not understand his poetry. Rather, he explains himself and others of his race. He did not hate those who chose to misunderstand; rather, he found them absurd. Of course, in "A Dream Deferred" Hughes does warn those who would thwart the lives of others, but it is a detached warning, an offering from a wise observer who is above all an artist.

Hansberry did not get her social consciousness primarily from Hughes. What she got from him instead was a consciousness of the poetic possibilities of her own race, an appreciation of the black American culture, and—because of Hughes himself—an awareness that, in spite of all obstacles, black people remain a dynamic, powerfully creative force in American society whose achievements must be celebrated in art.

From W. E. B. Du Bois she gained an admiration for the black intellectual, socialism, and black leadership. He spent most of his long life trying, with mixed success, to get a hearing for racial equality in America. Ironically, when the black population raised its collective voice and white people began to show signs of listening at last, he moved to Ghana, where he began to edit a multivolumed *Encyclopedia Africana*.

From Frederick Douglass, Hansberry learned about slavery and its psychol-ogy. This knowledge she would put to use in *The Drinking Gourd*, a play too outspoken to be broadcast on commercial television. From Douglass, too, she learned the invaluable lesson that the sufferings of a people may be presented truthfully in ways that rise above propaganda to the level of art. This lesson, perhaps, was the key to the synthesis of action and language toward which, in her own very different kind of writing, she was working.

These four men, among many people, particularly influenced Hansberry. But they could not, finally, answer the question she asked herself. Du Bois— even though he founded *Phylon* and edited *Crisis* to promote black art— and Douglass were not as deeply devoted to art for its own sake as were Robeson and Hughes. Rather, Du Bois and Douglass used their considerable rhetorical skills to illuminate and investigate the black conditions. They left behind books now considered works of art, but the creation of art was not their primary intention. Robeson sacrificed his musical career to pursue justice for members of his race and to become a revolutionary. Hughes pursued his art and—when forced to choose—left the struggle to others.

One month after she questioned her commitment to revolutionary activity, Hansberry wrote in her journal: "Have the feeling I should throw myself back into the movement. . . . But that very impulse is immediately flushed with a thousand vacillations and forbidding images. . . . *comfort* has come to be its own corruption. . . . *Comfort.* Apparently I have sold my soul for it. I think when I get my health back I shall go into the South to find out what kind of revolutionary I am. . . ." Hansberry died six months after writing of her intention to go South, where militants were being murdered, and as a result never answered her question. She died with her dilemma unresolved.

Anne Cheney, *Lorraine Hansberry* (Boston: Twayne, 1984), pp. 53–54

AMIRI BARAKA   *Raisin* first appeared in 1959, in the earlier stages of the civil rights movement. As a document reflecting the essence of those struggles, *Raisin* is unexcelled. For many of us it was—and remains—the quintessential civil rights play. It is probably also the most widely appreciated black play (particularly by Afro-Americans).

But Hansberry has done more than *document*, which is the most limited form of realism. She is a "critical realist," the way that Langston Hughes, Richard Wright and Margaret Walker are. That is, she analyzes and assesses reality and shapes her statement as an esthetically powerful and politically advanced work of art.

George Thompson in *Poetry and Marxism* points out that drama is the most expressive artistic form to emerge from great social transformation. Shakespeare is the artist of the destruction of feudalism—and the emergence of capitalism. The mad Macbeths, bestial Richard IIIs and other feudal worthies are shown, like the whole class, as degenerating. This is why Shakespeare deals with race (*Othello*), anti-Semitism (*The Merchant of Venice*) and feminism (*The Taming of the Shrew*).

Hansberry's play, too, was political agitation. It dealt with the same issues of democratic rights and equality that were being aired in the streets, but it dealt with them realistically, not as political abstraction. ⟨. . .⟩

We thought Hansberry's play belonged to the "passive resistance" part of the movement, which ended the minute Malcolm's penetrating eyes and words began to charge through the media with deadly force. We thought her play "middle class" in that its focus seemed to be on "moving in white folks' neighborhoods," when most blacks were just trying to pay their rent in ghetto shacks.

We missed the essence of the work: that Hansberry had created a family engaged in the same class and ideological struggles as existed in the movement—and within individuals. What is most telling about our ignorance is that Hansberry's play remains overwhelmingly popular and evocative of black and white reality; and the masses of black people saw it was true.

The next two explosions in black drama, Baldwin's *Blues for Mr. Charlie* and my own *Dutchman* (both 1964), raise up the militance and self-defense clamor of the movement as it evolved into the Malcolm era. But neither play is as much a statement from the majority of blacks as is *Raisin*. For one thing, both (regardless of their "power") are too concerned with white people.

Lorraine Hansberry's play, though it seems "conservative" in form and content to the radical petite bourgeoisie, is the accurate telling and stunning vision of the real struggle. The concerns I once dismissed as "middle class"—of buying a house and moving into "white folks' neighborhood"—actually reflect the essence of black will to defeat segregation, discrimination and oppression. The Younger family is our common ghetto Fanny Lou Hammers, Malcolm X's and Angela Davises, etc. And their burden surely will be lifted or one day it certainly will explode.

Amiri Baraka, "*Raisin in the Sun*'s Enduring Passion," *Washington Post*, 16 November 1986, pp. F1, 3

STEVEN R. CARTER   Hansberry's extensive use of parallels to *Hamlet* in *Les Blancs* is highly creative and she gained many advantages by it. First, it permitted her to make an indirect but glowing tribute to one of the finest products of English and European culture, thus indicating her keen awareness that Europe has created far more than colonialism and that much of what Europe has done remains immensely valuable to the whole world, including Africa. This appreciation is even stated explicitly in the play by Tshembe: "Europe—in spite of all her crimes—has been a great and glorious star in the night. Other stars shone before it—and will again with it." Tshembe also attests to the continuing relevance of *Hamlet* and other great European works when, upon being summoned to a meeting of resistance fighters, he explains that "it's an old problem, really . . . Orestes . . . Hamlet . . . the rest of them . . . We've really got so many things we'd rather be doing."

Second, having praised the highest ideals and achievements of European civilization, Hansberry could—so easily—point to the multitude of ways in which the European colonial powers and their offshoot, the United States, were currently failing to adhere to them. When Charlie Morris, an American journalist who has been seeking a dialogue with Tshembe, exposes his failure to understand the African's reference to the fierce woman spirit summoning him to fight for his people, Tshembe reminds this representative of Western culture that "when you knew her you called her Joan of Arc! Queen Esther! La Passionara! And you did know her once, you did know her! But now you call her nothing, because she is dead for you! She does not exist for you!" As Tshembe rightly implies, one of the great tragic ironies of history is that so many of the countries that had fought hard, bloody battles to establish the principles of liberty, equality and fraternity within their own boundaries then fought hard, bloody battles to suppress these principles in other countries solely to satisfy their greed and lust for power. An African nationalist upholding these values may thus be judged a truer heir to the mantle of Hamlet than European colonizers of their American counterparts. However, as Hansberry knew full well, this mantle does not belong only to the more idealistic African revolutionaries but may be donned by anyone who finds the strength and commitment to wear it. At the end, Charlie Morris himself, after many mistakes and vacillations, seems prepared to defy established authority at home and abroad for what he now knows to be the truth about the fight against colonialism in Zatembe. On the other hand, as the speaker of the truth about Tshembe and the resistance movement, perhaps Charlie qualifies more as Horatio, but Horatio too deserves respect.

Third, by paralleling the European drama of Hamlet with the African fable of the thinking hyena, Hansberry affirms that wisdom and folly are not the exclusive properties of any culture and that African culture is one of the "stars that shone before" European culture "and will again with it." Margaret B. Wilkerson, in her introduction to the New American Library edition of *Lorraine Hansberry: The Collected Last Plays*, has argued that while "the parallels to Hamlet are obvious . . . Hansberry, instinctively recognizing the inappropriateness of relying only on a Western literary reference point, provides Tshembe with another metaphor—from African lore—Modingo, the wise hyena who lived between the lands of the elephants and the hyenas." While Wilkerson's point is in general well taken, it seems more likely that what Hansberry did was deliberate rather than instinctive. In an interview with Patricia Marks for Radio Station WNYC in New York, Hansberry suggested that "perhaps we must take a more respectful view of the fact that African leaders today say that with regard to Europe and European traditions in the world we will take the best of what Europe has produced and the best of what we have produced and try to create a superior civilization out of the synthesis. I agree with them and I think that it commands respect for what will be inherently African in that contribution." Hansberry's *Les Blancs* provides an excellent example of how such a synthesis might be formed.

Steven R. Carter, "Colonialism and Culture in Lorraine Hansberry's *Les Blancs*," *MELUS* 15, No. 1 (Spring 1988): 30–31

J. CHARLES WASHINGTON   Viewers of *A Raisin in the Sun* can be moved by a tragic hero who is elevated by his growth from ignorance to knowledge, and deeply affected by a realistic hero whose transcendence involves a tremendous sacrifice—at the play's end, Walter and his family are as poor and powerless as they were before. The new house provides a "pinch of dignity" that allows them a bit more breathing and living space, but their lives are essentially unchanged. Without the greater financial rewards the business could have produced, they must all continue working at the same menial jobs in order to survive and pay for the house. In fact, they may be even worse off, since the birth of Ruth's second child will mean an extra mouth to feed. Walter and Ruth have made no substantive economic progress; their current life is a modern version of the life of Lena and Big Walter. The principal hope that Ruth and Walter have is the one Lena and Big Walter had and which people everywhere have always had— that some day in the future their children will be able to make their parents' dreams come true.

Considering that this sobering reality should provide a cause for despair would involve a serious misunderstanding of the author's intention and a grievous contradiction of her faith in the perfectibility of humanity based on her conviction that humankind will "do what the apes never will— *impose* the reason for life on life." Moreover, this small but significant hope, as well as the characters who embody it, offers perhaps the best example of the universal materials the play abounds in, giving Hansberry's art its distinguishing mark and enduring value. Illustrating her ability to see synthesis where others could only see dichotomy, Hansberry discovered the basis of this universal hope, indeed of her faith in humanity, in the Black experience: ". . . if blackness brought pain, it was also a source of strength, renewal and inspiration, a window on the potentials of the human race. For if Negroes could survive America, then there was hope for the human race indeed."

J. Charles Washington, "*A Raisin in the Sun* Revisited," *Black American Literature Forum* 22, No. 1 (Spring 1988): 123–24

MARGARET B. WILKERSON   Lorraine Hansberry, despite her bourgeois upbringing, had seen the fruit of racism and segregation in the struggles of her neighbors who came from all classes, since all blacks were confined to the Black Metropolis, Bronzeville, of Chicago. She had seen the personal toll on her father, and herself had been the near-victim of a mob protesting her family's move into a white neighborhood. Exactly when and how her sexual radicalization developed is less clear at this point, but what is obvious is that the usual generalizations about the black middle class simply were not borne out by a study of her early life. She was attracted to the theatre as a laboratory for manipulating and interpreting human experience, especially as it related to race, class, and gender; theatre as a persuasive and visible art form that allowed her to comment on the contradictions within the human personality; and the drama as the most attractive medium for, as she said, talking to people and sharing her vision of human potential. She found confirmation in the progressive left of Harlem—which she immediately joined upon moving to New York City—because it gave theatre and other cultural activities high priority, including them as a necessary extension and expression of ideas. Part of Hansberry's achievement in A *Raisin in the Sun* was to embody progressive ideas in the life and struggle of a black family (without resorting to the jargon of the left), and to build that family into a metaphor that whites and blacks, liberals, radicals, and even some conservatives could affirm, *while* winning one of the most prized awards of the theatre establishment. She managed it so well that the two FBI agents who saw the Broadway production and reported on its political import to the Bureau saw no revolutionary danger in the play. They, of course, did not realize that Walter Lee's sons and Mama's daughters would stride the boards in the next two decades, changing for good the image of blacks in the theatre and creating the artistic arm of the black nationalist movement. The line of Hansberry's influence stretches into and beyond the 1960s, but it begins in the 1930s and 1940s as she grew up in the peculiar crucible of segregation known as Chicago.

Margaret B. Wilkerson, "Excavating Our History: The Importance of Biographies of Women of Color," *Black American Literature Forum* 24, No. 1 (Spring 1990): 80–81

STEVEN R. CARTER   Hansberry's goal in all her work was realism—the truthful depiction, as she said, of "not only what is but what is possible . . . because that is part of reality too." A realism rooted, she hoped, in characters so truthfully and powerfully rendered that an audience could not but identify with them. But she did not think of realism as a specific form or genre, and strongly disagreed with those critics who saw it as limiting. As she told Studs Terkel, "I think that imagination has no bounds in realism—you can do anything which is permissible in terms of the truth of the characters. That's all you have to care about." She had a flair for significant, eye-and-mind-catching spectacle, as in Walter's imaginary spear-wielding table-top oratory and Iris Brustein's dance. *Les Blancs* in particular is filled with such spectacle, from the initial appearance of the woman warrior spirit with "cheeks painted for war," to Tshembe's elaborate ritual donning of ceremonial robes, to the gesture-filled oral storytelling of Peter/ Ntali, to the explosion and gunshot-packed climax. Her use of spectacle, moreover, was almost always symbolic, as in Tshembe's construction of a wall of cloth between Charlie Morris and himself representing the spiritual wall between them at the moment. Her "realistic" drama in such instances differed little from expressionism or poetic fantasy; she always chose the best means to express the whole truth about her characters, no matter whether critics would have deemed it appropriate to her form or not.

As a politically and socially committed writer, Hansberry strove to present a host of unpleasant and challenging truths in her work, although often with such wit and dramatic force that they no longer seemed unpalatable but inevitable. She was unquestionably a Marxist but in the largest sense of this frequently narrowed and abused term, as unhindered by doctrine and as open to new ideas as was Marx himself, and as complicated, wide-ranging, open-minded, and even at times ambivalent in her approach to esthetics as Henri Arvon has shown Marx to be. Keeping faith with her myriad commitments never precluded the portrayal of the full complexity of life as Hansberry saw it. Few writers in any genre have delineated so completely and strikingly the social dilemmas of our time, and none have surpassed—or are likely to surpass—her ability to point out the heights toward which we should soar.

> Steven R. Carter, *Hansberry's Drama: Commitment amid Complexity* (Urbana: University of Illinois Press, 1991), pp. 190–91

Bibliography

A Raisin in the Sun. 1959.

The Movement: Documentary of a Struggle for Equality. 1964.

The Sign in Sidney Brustein's Window. 1965.

To Be Young, Gifted and Black: Lorraine Hansberry in Her Own Words. Adapted by Robert Nemiroff. 1969.

Les Blancs. Adapted by Robert Nemiroff. 1972.

Les Blancs: The Collected Last Plays of Lorraine Hansberry. Ed. Robert Nemiroff. 1972.

A Raisin in the Sun: The Unfilmed Original Screenplay. Ed. Robert Nemiroff. 1992.

⬧ ⬧ ⬧

Frances E. W. Harper
c. 1825–1911

FRANCES ELLEN WATKINS HARPER, civil rights leader, abolitionist, suffragette, and poet, was born in Baltimore, Maryland, most probably in 1825, although some records indicate it may have been 1824. Although Maryland was a slave state at the time, Harper was born free to free parents. Her mother died when she was three or four years of age, and Harper moved in with her aunt, attending a school for free blacks owned by her uncle. Her formal education ended when she reached her teens, but she took a position in a Baltimore bookstore and used the opportunity to read widely.

Harper's first volume of poetry, *Forest Leaves*, was probably published in 1845. No copies of the book exist today, but it is thought that Harper republished the poems that appeared in it in later poetry collections. In 1850, wishing to move to a free state, Harper took a position at Union Seminary, a new school for free blacks founded by the African Methodist Episcopal Church and located near Columbus, Ohio. Harper did not enjoy teaching and wanted to be more directly involved in social activism. She moved to Little York, Pennsylvania, a town on the Underground Railroad, where she met and was deeply influenced by abolitionist and orator William Grant Still.

In 1853 Harper relinquished her teaching position, and in 1854 published her successful *Poems on Miscellaneous Subjects* (with a preface by William Lloyd Garrison) and gave her first abolitionist lecture. She became a professional lecturer for the abolitionist movement and was supported by various antislavery societies as she traveled from town to town, lecturing and reading her poems. Her poetry, not surprisingly, is written in an oral style and uses biblical themes and imagery familiar to her nineteenth-century audience. Harper created lyrical and emotional poems while maintaining the formal construction of the rhymed quatrain.

In 1860 she married Fenton Harper, a widower from Cincinnati, settled on a farm near Columbus, and had a daughter named Mary. Fenton Harper died in 1864, and Frances Harper resumed lecturing and toured the South twice between 1867 and 1871. She published *Moses: A Story of the Nile* in 1869, *Poems* in 1871, and *Sketches of Southern Life* in 1872. *Moses*, a blank verse biblical allegory without overt racial references, is considered by many critics to be her best work.

Harper became increasingly involved with the woman's suffrage movement and was especially concerned with the condition of newly freed black women in the Reconstruction South. In 1892 she published her only novel, *Iola Leroy; or, Shadows Uplifted*, a story about a mulatto and her family during and after the Civil War. The novel has recently attracted a great deal of critical attention, mostly focused on Harper's treatment of her title character, the mulatto Iola. Frances Harper died of heart failure on February 22, 1911.

◙ *Critical Extracts*

WILLIAM STILL   Fifty thousand copies at least of ⟨Harper's⟩ four small books have been sold to those who have listened to her eloquent lectures. One of those productions entitled *Moses* has been used to entertain audiences with evening readings in various parts of the country. With what effect may be seen from the two brief notices as follows:

> "Mrs. F. E. W. Harper delivered a poem upon 'Moses' in Wilbraham to a large and delighted audience. She is a woman of high moral tone, with superior native powers highly cultivated, and a captivating eloquence that holds her audience in rapt attention from the beginning to the close. She will delight any intelligent audience, and those who wish first-class lecturers cannot do better than to secure her services."—*Zion's Herald, Boston*
>
> "Mrs Frances E. W. Harper read her poem of 'Moses' last evening at Rev. Mr. Harrison's church to a good audience. It deals with the story of the Hebrew Moses from his finding in the wicker basket on the Nile to his death on Mount Nebo and his burial in an unknown grave; following closely the Scripture account. It contains about 700 lines, beginning with blank verse of the common measure, and changing to other measures, but always without rhyme; and is a pathetic and well-sustained piece. Mrs. Harper recited it with good effect, and it was well received.

She is a lady of much talent, and always speaks well, particularly when her subject related to the condition of her own people, in whose welfare, before and since the war, she has taken the deepest interest. As a lecturer Mrs. Harper is more effective than most of those who come before our lyceums; with a natural eloquence that is very moving."—*Galesburgh Register, Ill.*

Grace Greenwood, in the *Independent* in noticing a Course of Lectures in which Mrs. Harper spoke (in Philadelphia) pays this tribute to her:

Next on the course was Mrs Harper, a colored woman; about as colored as some of the Cuban belles I have met with at Saratoga. She has a noble head, this bronze muse; a strong face, with a shadowed glow upon it, indicative of thoughtful fervor, and of a nature most femininely sensitive, but not in the least morbid. Her form is delicate, her hands daintily small. She stands quietly beside her desk, and speaks without notes, with gestures few and fitting. Her manner is marked by dignity and composure. She is never assuming, never theatrical. In the first part of her lecture she was most impressive in her pleading for the race with whom her lot is cast. There was something touching in her attitude as their representative. The woe of two hundred years sighed through her tones. Every glance of her sad eyes was a mournful remonstrance against injustice and wrong. Feeling on her soul, as she must have felt it, the chilling weight of caste, she seemed to say:

I lift my heavy heart up solemnly,
As once Electra her sepulchral urn.

. . . As I listened to her, there swept over me, in a chill wave of horror, the realization that this noble woman had she not been rescued from her mother's condition, might have been sold on the auction-block, to the highest bidder—her intellect, fancy, eloquence, the flashing wit, that might make the delight of a Parisian saloon, and her pure, Christian character all thrown in— the recollection that women like her could be dragged out of public conveyances in our own city, or frowned out of fashionable churches by Anglo-Saxon saints.

William Still, "Frances Ellen Watkins Harper," *The Underground Rail Road*, rev. ed. (Philadelphia: People's Publishing, 1871), pp. 779–80

ROBERT T. KERLIN   Mrs. Harper attained to a greater popularity than any poet of her race prior to Dunbar. As many as ten thousand copies of some of her poems were in circulation in the middle of the last century. Her success was not unmerited. Many singers of no greater merit have enjoyed greater celebrity. She was thoroughly in the fashion of her times, as Phillis Wheatley was in the yet prevalent fashion of Pope, or, perhaps more accurately, Cowper. The models in the middle of the nineteenth century were Mrs. Hemans, Whittier, and Longfellow. It is in their manner she writes. A serene and beautiful Christian spirit tells a moral tale in fluent ballad stanzas, not without poetic phrasing. In all she beholds, in all she experiences, there is a lesson. There is no grief without consolation. Serene resignation breathes through all her poems—at least through those written after her freedom was achieved.

Robert T. Kerlin, "The Heritage of Song," *Negro Poets and Their Poems* (Washington, DC: Associated Publishers, 1923), pp. 26–27

VERNON LOGGINS   *Sketches of Southern Life*, originally published in 1872, and reprinted, each time with additions, in 1888 and 1896, presents in a connected series of poems two characters whom one remembers, Aunt Chloe and Uncle Jacob. Aunt Chloe is the narrator, and a very rambling one. While she does not speak in dialect, her idiom is true to the life of the primitive Negro. She says in "The Deliverance," in describing the conduct of the slaves on her plantation when they hear that they are free:

> We just laughed, and danced, and shouted,
> And prayed, and sang, and cried,
> And we thought dear Uncle Jacob
> Would fairly crack his side.

She has a homely Negro wit that sees straight through the farce of the black man in national politics, and her vigorous comment on Johnson and Grant is a charming display of honest common sense. One regrets that *Sketches of Southern Life* contains pieces, mainly on reform topics, in which Aunt Chloe is not the narrator and in which Uncle Jacob, a pleasing old mystic, is not on hand to warn and exhort. In creating these two characters Mrs. Harper perhaps did more than any other Negro poet before Dunbar in getting close to the reality of primitive Negro life.

However, in her most consistently even piece of work, that which shows her highest achievement as a versifier, she has nothing to say about the Negro. It is *Moses: a Story of the Nile*, published as early as 1869. The poem was obviously written to be read in public, and the opening hints that Mrs. Harper might have intended to make of it a drama. In a scene, the setting for which the reader is left to construct for himself, Moses discloses to the Princess who has reared him his determination to lead his people out of Egypt. She at first protests, but because she loves Moses as though he were her own child she finally agrees to his departure. After this opening the dramatic form is dropped, and the rest of the poem is a straight narrative of the life adventures of Moses. The verse, often metrically uneven, is the most natural which Mrs. Harper produced. In passages admitting of prettiness, as in the description of how angels come down from heaven and bury Moses, there is a delicate charm:

> And when the grave was finished,
> They trod with golden sandals
> Above the sacred spot,
> And the brightest, fairest flowers
> Sprang up beneath their tread.
> Nor broken turf, nor hillock,
> Did e'er reveal that grave,
> And truthful lips have never said,
> "We know where he is laid."

The poem is significant in Negro literature because one who reads it is not constantly aware of imitation. Mrs. Harper must yield place to Albery A. Whitman as the most talented Negro poet between Phillis Wheatley and Paul Laurence Dunbar. But of all Dunbar's predecessors who were not primitive and spontaneous singers Mrs. Harper came nearest to producing a fairly extensive body of verse which has a certain originality.

Vernon Loggins, *The Negro Author: His Development in America* (New York: Columbia University Press, 1931), pp. 343–44

J. SAUNDERS REDDING   In 1854, while Douglass was climbing in importance as the spokesman and ideal of the Negro race, there appeared in Philadelphia a thin volume called *Poems on Miscellaneous Subjects*, by Frances Ellen Watkins. The title is significant, for it indicates a different trend in the creative urge of the Negro. Except for Jupiter Hammon and

Phillis Wheatley, Negro writers up to this time were interested mainly in the one theme of slavery and in the one purpose of bringing about freedom. The treatment of their material was doctrinal, definitely conditioned to the ends of propaganda. A willful (and perhaps necessary) monopticism had blinded them to other treatment and to the possibilities in other subjects. It remained for Miss Watkins, with the implications in the title of her volume, to attempt a redirection. ⟨. . .⟩

In 1861 Mrs. Harper (Frances Ellen Watkins) wrote to Thomas Hamilton, the editor of the *Anglo-African*, a monthly journal that had been established the year before: "If our talents are to be recognized we must write less of issues that are particular and more of feelings that are general. We are blessed with hearts and brains that compass more than ourselves in our present plight. . . . We must look to the future which, God willing, will be better than the present or the past, and delve into the heart of the world." ⟨. . .⟩

To what degree Frances Ellen Watkins followed her own advice can be judged from her writings. In one sense she was a trail blazer, hacking, however ineffectually, at the dense forest of propaganda and striving to "write less of issues that were particular and more of feelings that were general." But she was seriously limited by the nature and method of her appeal. Immensely popular as a reader ("elocutionist"), the demands of her audience for the sentimental treatment of the old subjects sometimes overwhelmed her. On the occasions when she was free "to delve into the heart of the world" she was apt to gush with pathetic sentimentality over such subjects as wronged innocence, the evils of strong drink, and the blessed state of childhood. ⟨. . .⟩

Practically all the social evils from the double standard of sex morality to corruption in politics were lashed with the scourge of her resentment. Her treatment of these topics never varied: she traced the effects of the evil upon some innocent—a young and dying girl, as in "A Little Child Shall Lead Them," or a virtuous woman, as in "The Double Standard," or a sainted mother, as in "Nothing and Something." But her treating these evils at all entitles her to respect and gratitude as one who created other aims and provided new channels for the creative energies of Negro writers.

In some of Miss Watkins's verse one thing more is to be noted especially. In the volume called *Sketches of Southern Life* the language she puts in the mouths of Negro characters has a fine racy, colloquial tang. In these poems she managed to hurdle a barrier by which Dunbar was later to feel himself tripped. The language is not dialect. She retained the speech patterns of Negro dialect, thereby giving herself greater emotional scope (had she wished or had the power to use it) than the humorous and the pathetic to which it is generally acknowledged dialect limits one. In all of her verse Miss Watkins attempted to suit her language to her theme. In *Moses* she gives her language a certain solemnity and elevation of tone. In her pieces on slavery she employs short, teethy, angry monosyllables. Her use of dialectal patterns was no accident. She anticipated James Weldon Johnson.

J. Saunders Redding, *To Make a Poet Black* (Chapel Hill: University of North Carolina Press, 1939), pp. 38–43

PATRICIA LIGGINS HILL   Harper's popularity ⟨. . .⟩ is not based on conventional notions of poetic excellence. In her handling of poetic forms and her major subject matter—race (abolition in particular), religion, and women's rights—she is considered generally to be less a technician than either of her contemporary abolitionist poets, James Whitfield and George Moses Horton. ⟨. . .⟩ With the exception of *Moses: A Story of the Nile* (1869) and *Sketches of Southern Life* (1872), Harper's poetry varies little in form, language, and poetic technique.

Harper's fame as a poet, instead, rests on her excellent skills in oral poetry delivery. ⟨. . .⟩

Indeed, there are similarities between Frances Harper's poetry and the verse of the new black poets—Imamu Baraka (LeRoi Jones), Madhubuti (Don L. Lee), Nikki Giovanni, Lalia Mannan (Sonia Sanchez), and others. Just as these latter-day poets base their oral protest poetry primarily on direct imagery, simple diction, and the rhythmic language of the street to reach the masses of black people, Harper relies on vivid, striking imagery, simplistic language, and the musical quality and form of the ballad to appeal to large masses of people, black and white, for her social protest. Moreover, she, like the new black poets, embraces an "art for people's sake" aesthetic, rather than a Western Caucasian aesthetic assumption, "an art for art's sake" principle. In her poem "Songs for the People" which is her closest statement on aesthetics, Harper makes this point clear:

> Let me make the songs for the people,
>   Songs for the old and young;
> Songs to stir like a battle cry
>   Whenever they are sung.

Let me make the songs for the weary,
Amid life's fever and fret,
Till hearts shall relax their tension
And careworn brows forget.

I will sing for the poor and aged,
When shadows dim their sight,
Of the bright and restful mansions,
Where there shall be no right.

Our world, so worn and weary
Needs music, pure and strong
To hush the jangle and discords
Of sorrow, pain and wrong.

Clearly, in this poem and in her other works, Harper assumes the stance of a poet-priestess whose "pure and strong" songs serve to uplift the oppressed in particular and humanity as a whole. The corpus of her poetry indicates that she, like the new black poets, however, is primarily concerned with uplifting the masses of black people. According to William Still the question as to how Harper could best serve her race lay at the very core of her literary and professional career. She answers this question early in her career when she writes to Still in 1853 that she has decided to devote her life to the liberation of her people. As she expresses to him, "It may be that God Himself has written upon both my heart and brain a commissary to use time, talent, and energy in the cause of freedom." This intrinsic concern for black liberation led her to envision herself as a race-builder, the black shepherd who will provide leadership for her flock of sheep (the black masses). In her February 1870 letter to Still, Harper states, "I am standing with my race on the threshhold ⟨sic⟩ of a new era . . . and yet today, with my limited and fragmented knowledge, I may help my race forward a little. Some of our people remind me of sheep without a shepherd."

Patrica Liggins Hill, " 'Let Me Make the Songs for the People': A Study of Frances Watkins Harper's Poetry," *Black American Literature Forum* 15, No. 1 (Spring 1981): 60

FARAH JASMINE GRIFFIN   Much in ⟨Harper's⟩ discourse fore-shadows that of Booker T. Washington, yet there is a sense that Harper, because she lives and identifies with the people, begins to be more concerned

with their day-to-day survival. If as ⟨August⟩ Meier points out, the concerns
of the masses were the acquisition of land, education, and political rights,
Harper's concerns are closely aligned with theirs. She identifies the freed-
man's landlessness as his biggest problem, then his ignorance and finally
his economic powerlessness. She mentions nothing of political rights.

If Harper differed from other educated, middle-class leaders in her identification of goals for the freedmen, her concerns differed in another very
important aspect also: Hers is the voice that emerges regarding the condition
of Black freedmen. She not only speaks to them, but goes on to represent
their concerns to whites and northern Blacks through articles and poems.

In a letter to Still she writes:

> Part of my lectures are given privately to women and for them
> I never make any charge or take up any collection. I am now
> going to have a private meeting with the women of this place. I
> am going to talk to them about their daughters and about things
> connected with the welfare of the race. Now is the time for our
> women to begin to plant the roots of progress under the
> hearthstone.

Harper's notion that reform begins at home emerges from two different but
significant themes. She is certainly influenced by the 19th century cult of
domesticity that stressed the role of women as mothers and wives. However,
Harper is also calling on what historian Jacqueline Jones (1986) has identified as the subversive nature of Black women's roles within their families.

Harper sees Black women, though denied political enfranchisement, as
the bearers of values, stability and strength in their home lives. By doing
this they subvert the intentions of white patriarchal society to keep Blacks
in subordinate positions and strip them of all sense of power. Nowhere is
this theme more evident than in Harper's poem "Deliverance."

Though the poem is full of stereotypes suggesting matriarchal women
and ignorant, easily led Black men, it depicts Black women as politically
enlightened and though disenfranchised, politically powerful in their roles
as wives and mothers:

> But when John Thomas Reder brought
> His wife some flour and meat,
> And told her he had sold his vote
> For something good to eat,

You ought to see Aunt Kitty raise
And head her blaze away;
She gave the meat and flour a toss
And said they should not stay . . .

You'd laugh to see Lucinda Grange
Upon her husband's track
When he sold his vote for rations
She made him take 'em back

Day after day did Milly Green
Just follow after Joe,
And told him if he voted wrong
To take his rags and go.

I think Curnel Johnson said
His side had won the day
Had not we women radicals
Just got right in the way.

Despite the offensive stereotypes of the poem, many of Harper's concepts
are steeped in the reality of the South. The women are strong, politically
enlightened and in control of their homes, through which they influence
society.

In an article entitled "Colored Women of the South" and published in
the January 1878 issue of the *Englishwoman's Review*, Harper provides factual
accounts of individual Black women who make education possible, and
who have gained significant business experience, been successful at farming
ventures as well as organizing themselves for the good of their communities:

> They do a double duty, a man's share in the field and a woman's
> part at home, when the men lose their work through political
> affiliations, the women stand by them and say "stand by your
> principles," by organized effort, colored women have been able to
> help each other in sickness and provide respectable funerals for
> the dead.

The women emerge from the articles not as the henpecking matriarchs of
the poems, but instead as very human wives and mothers who are supportive
of their husbands and who maintain a sense of community through their
mutual aid activities. In this sense they are "women radicals."

Farah Jasmine Griffin, "Frances Ellen Watkins Harper in the Reconstruction South,"
SAGE: A Scholarly Journal on Black Women, Student Supplement 1988, p. 46

DEBORAH E. McDOWELL   Although ⟨the Victorian⟩ ideology
of domesticity was the veritable antithesis of the black woman's reality,
Harper, like the majority of black writers of her era—both men and women—
ironically accommodated her "new" model image of black womanhood to
its contours. ⟨. . .⟩ The image of the Lady combined and conflated physical
appearance with character traits. Immortalized particularly in the southern
antebellum novel, the image required "physical beauty [i.e. fair skin] . . .
fragility, refinement and helplessness." "The closest black women could
come to such an ideal, at least physically," ⟨Barbara⟩ Christian continues,
"would . . . have to be the mulatta, quadroon, or octoroon." Iola ⟨in *Iola
Leroy*⟩ fulfills this physical requirement. "My! but she's putty," says the slave
through whose eyes we first see her. "Beautiful long hair comes way down
her back; putty blue eyes, an' jis' ez white ez anybody's in dis place." ⟨. . .⟩

By giving Iola a role to play in the larger struggle for racial uplift, Harper
modified the image of the southern lady, but it is important to note that
Iola's role in the struggle is enacted within the boundaries of the traditional
expectations of women as mothers and nurturers, expectations that form
the cornerstone of the cult of true womanhood. According to Iola, "a great
amount of sin and misery springs from the weakness and inefficiency of
women." In "The Education of Mothers," one of the two public speeches
she gives in the novel (public speaking being largely reserved for men in
the text), she appeals for "a union of women with the warmest hearts and
clearest brains to help in the moral education of the race." ⟨. . .⟩

In the course of *Iola Leroy*, as Iola fulfills her role as exemplary black
woman she comes to resemble a human being less and less and a saint more
and more. We learn very little about her thoughts, her inner life. Nothing
about her is individualized, nor does this seem to be Harper's chief concern,
for she is creating an exemplary type who is always part of some larger
framework. ⟨. . .⟩ Every detail of Iola's life, down to the most personal
experiences of family life, is stripped of its intimate implications and invested
with social and mythical implications. It is significant that of all the Old
Testament types, she identifies with Moses and Nehemiah, for "they were
willing to put aside their own advantages for their race and country."

Iola's role as social and moral exemplar is paralleled by the novel's role
as exemplum. Like its title character, *Iola Leroy* is on trial before the world.
It aims for a favorable verdict by choosing its models carefully. Harper's
most visible model is Harriet Beecher Stowe's *Uncle Tom's Cabin*, the most
popular novel of the mid-nineteenth century in America. ⟨. . .⟩

Harper's choice of *Uncle Tom's Cabin* as a model is a logical and appropriate one, given the polemical and public role that she expected her novel
to play, a role that Stowe's novel had played to unrivaled success with an
audience comprised mainly of northern white Christians. Harper addresses
and appeals to this audience directly in the afternote of the novel: "From
threads of fact and fiction I have woven a story whose mission will not be
in vain if it awaken in the hearts of our countrymen a stronger sense of
justice and a more Christlike humanity in behalf of those whom the fortunes
of war threw, homeless, ignorant and poor, upon the threshold of a new
era." Those northern whites might be more inclined to lend their assistance
to this homeless and displaced lot if the images of black life that Harper and
her black contemporaries valued and affirmed accorded with that audience's
horizon of social and literary expectations. In this respect, *Iola Leroy* is in
company with a number of novels by black writers of its era, all dedicated
to a public mission, all foundering on the shoals of two contradictory
attempts: "to conform to the accepted social [and] literary . . . standards of
their day and their almost antithetical need to portray their own people
with honesty and imagination" ⟨Arlene Elder⟩.

Deborah E. McDowell, " 'The Changing Same': Generation Connections and Black
Women Novelists," *New Literary History* 18, No. 2 (Winter 1987): 284–85

ELIZABETH YOUNG   ⟨. . .⟩ Frances Harper's 1892 novel, *Iola
Leroy; or, Shadows Uplifted*, offers a powerful vision of the Civil War years
as seen by this prominent activist for black rights, feminism, and temperance.
At sixty-seven, Frances Ellen Watkins Harper was an experienced lecturer,
essayist, short-story writer, and poet when her only novel was published.
Iola Leroy is the story of a woman, the novel's eponymous heroine, raised
as a privileged white daughter of the antebellum South who discovers on
the eve of the Civil War that she is of mixed-race ancestry, and who is
then sold into slavery. Rescued by the Union army, she eventually reunites
with her family when the war is over. Black feminist criticism has recently
brought new attention to *Iola Leroy*. Hazel Carby, for example, argues in a
persuasive reading of the novel that Iola's journey from orphaned youth to
family-filled adulthood both recalls the mid-nineteenth-century domestic
"woman's novel" and recasts its plot in the context of the black family.
Iola's triumphant claim of family at novel's end applies "not only to the

individual heroine but also to the entire race," for it serves, Carby argues, as the vehicle for Harper's observations on the black diaspora and the emerging postwar role of black intellectuals.

We may take the politics of domesticity in another direction, however, by viewing *Iola Leroy* as a domestic novel about a domestic political crisis: the Civil War. Far beyond simply supplying a prelude to the novel's Reconstruction plot, the war profoundly affects the novel's formal and thematic concerns. As a reading of history, *Iola Leroy* rewrites the conventions of war narrative, foregrounding black heroism in combat. Black women are central to this effort, not only as wartime actors but also as mothers whose presence in the narrative frames its war sections. Indeed, Harper embeds the war in a narrative trajectory of maternal quest and reunion, simultaneously feminizing war narrative and using this literary form to represent the importance of maternal and familial structures in the black community.

This use of the Civil War, intercutting the axes of race and gender, is also specific to its meaning as an *internal* conflict. Harper uses "civil war" as a metaphor to describe a variety of conflicts outside the formal battlefield, among them Iola's resistance to the dynamics of interracial rape and her decision, as a light-skinned mulatta, not to pass for white. Engaging and interweaving a variety of antinomies—black/white, male/female, North/South—Harper shows individual identity to be decisively marked by both gender and race. The formations of war, in other words, serve in *Iola Leroy* as a model for the construction of subjectivity.

What complicates this portrayal further is that by the time Harper wrote the novel, the Civil War had already been structured by literary conventions as a series of novelistic plots about sexuality and marriage. Reading Harper's novel against D. W. Griffith's overtly racist 1915 film *The Birth of a Nation*—which elaborates and epitomizes these conventions—suggests the extent to which metaphor determined the politic of Civil War discourse and, consequently, the extent to which Harper's use of metaphor acts as a strategic political intervention. That is, the novel's use of metaphor is reciprocal: *Iola Leroy* simultaneously employs the war as a metaphor for identity and offers a novelistic plot of individual identity that metaphorically restages the Civil War itself. *Iola Leroy*, in short, sets race and gender at battle with war, history at war with metaphor, and representation—political and literary—in conflict with itself.

> Elizabeth Young, "Warring Fictions: *Iola Leroy* and the Color of Gender," *American Literature* 64, No. 2 (June 1992): 273–75

◈ *Bibliography*

Forest Leaves. c. 1845. Lost.

Poems on Miscellaneous Subjects. 1854, 1855.

Poems on Miscellaneous Subjects: Second Series. 1855.

Moses: A Story of the Nile. 1869, 1889.

Poems. 1871.

Sketches of Southern Life. 1872, 1887.

Achan's Sin. c. 1875.

The Sparrow's Fall and Other Poems. c. 1890.

Enlightened Motherhood. 1892.

Iola Leroy; or, Shadows Uplifted. 1892.

The Martyr of Alabama and Other Poems. c. 1894.

Atlanta Offering: Poems. 1895.

Light Beyond the Darkness. c. 1895.

Poems. 1895, 1900.

Idylls of the Bible. 1901.

Complete Poems. Ed. Maryemma Graham. 1988.

A Brighter Coming Day: A Frances Ellen Watkins Harper Reader. Ed. Frances
        Smith Foster. 1990.

⬧ ⬧ ⬧

Georgia Douglas Johnson
1886–1966

GEORGIA DOUGLAS CAMP JOHNSON was born on September 10, 1886, to George and Laura Jackson Camp in Atlanta, Georgia. Johnson attended public schools in Atlanta and went on to Atlanta University. She later attended Howard University in Washington, D.C., and the Oberlin Conservatory of Music in Ohio. She married Henry Lincoln Johnson in 1903. They had two sons, Henry Lincoln, Jr., and Peter Douglas.

Johnson was capable of great periods of creativity, and her interests were as varied as her efforts were concentrated. As early as 1905 her poetry appeared in the *Voice of the Negro* and later in the *Crisis* and other periodicals. Her first book, *The Heart of a Woman*, did not appear until 1918. She was characterized by critics as a black feminist poet, although her early poems do not focus on themes of race or politics. She was essentially of the genteel school and much overshadowed by Sara Teasdale. Her poems, like Teasdale's, are generally conventional in form, romantic in tone, and short in length.

Johnson's second volume of poetry, *Bronze*, was published in 1922. These poems are marked by a clear development of racial consciousness and a focus on black history. By the time *Bronze* was published, Johnson had fallen in with a circle of black notables, such as W. E. B. Du Bois, Countee Cullen, Sterling Brown, Benjamin Brawley, James Weldon Johnson, and others. This volume was more widely read and more favorably reviewed than her first. When Johnson's husband died in 1925, she took on greater financial responsibilities, but her literary career was not dramatically affected. Both of her sons were attending Dartmouth and her literary gatherings were still growing in number. In 1927 Johnson won the *Opportunity* prize for her one-act play *Plumes* and in the same year produced her drama *Blue Blood* in New York.

Johnson's third collection of poetry, *An Autumn Love Cycle*, was published in 1928. It represents something of a departure from *Bronze*. The author returns to her earlier themes of love and loss. During the depression, however, Johnson focused primarily on the writing of drama that addressed racial and

gender concerns. Her play *Sunday Morning in the South* was written to show
support for the antilynching campaign. *Blue-Eyed Black Boy* and *Safe* have
similar themes of social protest and were submitted for production to the
Federal Theatre Projected but rejected along with three of her other plays.
Sunday Morning in the South was published posthumously in *Black Theatre*,
U.S.A., edited by James V. Hatch and Ted Shine (1974). Johnson also
wrote two plays that tell of the struggles of escaping to freedom in the
North, *Frederick Douglass* and *William and Ellen Craft*, both published in
Negro History in Thirteen Plays, edited by Willis Richardson and May Miller
(1935).

Although Johnson focused her efforts on drama at this time, her poetry
continued to appear in various periodicals. She was also much involved
with the social and political life of Washington. She held various government
positions, including Commissioner of Conciliation for the Department of
Labor from 1925 to 1934. Her final volume of poetry, *Share My World*,
appeared in 1962. Atlanta University presented her with an honorary doctor-
ate in literature in 1965. Georgia Douglas Johnson died on May 14, 1966.

Critical Extracts

WILLIAM STANLEY BRAITHWAITE   The poems in this
book are intensely feminine and for me this means more than anything else
that they are deeply human. We are yet scarcely aware, in spite of our
boasted twentieth-century progress, of what lies deeply hidden, of mystery
and passion, of domestic love and joy and sorrow, of romantic visions and
practical ambitions, in the heart of a woman. The emancipation of woman
is yet to be wholly accomplished; though woman has stamped her image
on every age of the world's history, and in the heart of almost every man
since time began, it is only a little over half of a century since she has
either spoken or acted with a sense of freedom. During this time she has
made little more than a start to catch up with man in the wonderful things
he has to his credit; and yet all that man has to his credit would scarcely have
been achieved except for the devotion and love and inspiring comradeship of
woman.

Here, then, is lifted the veil, in these poignant songs and lyrics. To look upon what is revealed is to give one a sense of infinite sympathy; to make one kneel in spirit to the marvelous patience, the wonderful endurance, the persistent faith, which are hidden in this nature.

> The heart of a woman falls back with the night,
> And enters some alien cage in its plight,
> And tries to forget it has dreamed of the stars
> While it breaks, breaks, breaks on the sheltering bars.

sings the poet. And

> The songs of the singer
> Are tones that repeat
> The cry of the heart
> Till it ceases to beat.

This verse just quoted is from "The Dreams of the Dreamer," and with the previous quotation tells us that this woman's heart is keyed in the plaintive, knows the sorrowful agents of life and experience which knock and enter at the door of dreams. But women have made the saddest songs of the world, Sappho no less than Elizabeth Barrett Browning, Ruth the Moabite no less than Amy Levy, the Jewess who broke her heart against the London pavements; and no less does sadness echo its tender and appealing sigh in these songs and lyrics of Georgia Douglas Johnson. But sadness is a kind of felicity with woman, paradoxical as it may seem; and it is so because through this inexplicable felicity *they* touched, intuitively caress, reality.

So here engaging life at its most reserved sources, whether the form or substance through which it articulates be nature, or the seasons, touch of hands or lips, love, desire, or any of the emotional abstractions which sweep like fire or wind or cooling water through the blood, Mrs. Johnson creates just the reality of woman's heart and experience with astonishing raptures. It is a kind of privilege to know so much about the secrets of woman's nature, a privilege all the more to be cherished when given, as in these poems, with such exquisite utterance, with such a lyric sensibility.

William Stanley Braithwaite, "Introduction," *The Heart of a Woman and Other Poems* by Georgia Douglas Johnson (Boston: Cornhill Co., 1918), pp. vii–ix

---

J. R. FAUSET   In these days of *vers libre* and the deliberate straining for poetic effect these lyrics of Mrs. Johnson bring with them a certain sense of relief and freshness. Also the utter absence of the material theme makes appeal. We are all very wary of the war note and are glad to return to the softer pipings of old time themes—love, friendship, longing, despair—all of which are set forth in *The Heart of a Woman*.

The book has artistry, but it is its sincerity which gives it its value. Here are the little sharp experiences of life mirrored poignantly, sometimes feverishly, always truly. Each lyric is an instantaneous photograph of one of the many moments in existence which affect one briefly perhaps, but indelibly. Mr. Braithwaite says in his introduction that this author engages "life at its most reserved sources whether the form or substance through which it articulates be nature, or the seasons, touch of hands or lips, love, desire or any of the emotional abstractions which sweep like fire or wind or cooling water through the blood." The ability to give a faithful and recognizable portrayal of these sources, is Mrs. Johnson's distinction.

In this work, Mrs. Johnson, although a woman of color, is dealing with life as it is regardless of the part that she may play in the great drama. Here she is a woman of that imagination that characterizes any literary person choosing this field as a means of directing the thought of the world. Several of her poems bearing on the Negro race have appeared in the *Crisis*. In these efforts she manifests the radical tendencies characteristic of every thinking Negro of a developed mind and sings beautifully not in the tone of the lamentations of the prophets of old but, while portraying the trials and tribulations besetting a despised and rejected people, she sings the song of hope. In reading her works the inevitable impression is that it does not yet appear what she will be. Adhering to her task with the devotion hitherto manifested, there is no reason why she should not in the near future take rank among the best writers of the world.

J. R. Fauset, [Review of *The Heart of a Woman and Other Poems*], *Journal of Negro History* 4, No. 4 (October 1919): 467–68

W. E. B. DU BOIS   Those who know what it means to be a colored woman in 1922—and know it not so much in fact as in feeling, apprehension, unrest and delicate yet stern thought—must read Georgia Douglas Johnson's *Bronze*. Much of it will not touch this reader and that, and some of it will mystify and puzzle them as a sort of reiteration and over-emphasis. But none can fail to be caught here and there by a word—a phrase—a period that tells a life history or even paints the history of a generation. Can you not see that marching of the mantled with

> Voices strange to ecstasy?

Have you ever looked on the "twilight faces" of their throngs, or seen the black mother with her son when

> Her heart is sandaling his feet?

Or can you not conceive that infinite sorrow of a dark child wandering the world:

> Seeking the breast of an unknown face!

I hope Mrs. Johnson will have wide reading. Her word is simple, sometimes trite, but it is singularly sincere and true, and as a revelation of the soul struggle of the women of a race it is invaluable.

W. E. B. Du Bois, "Foreword," *Bronze: A Book of Verse* by Georgia Douglas Johnson (Boston: B. J. Brimmer Co., 1922), p. 7

ALAIN LEROY LOCKE   In *Bronze*, Mrs. Johnson has at last come to her own—if not also in a peculiar way, *into* her own. A certain maturity that is to be expected of a third volume of verse, is here, but it is the homecoming of the mind and heart to intimately racial thought and experience which is to be especially noted and commended. We can say of this that it is timely both for the author and her readers: for her, it represents the fruition of a premeditated plan not to speak racially until she has learned to speak and attract attention in the universal key; for her readers, of many classes and sections of opinion, it represents more perhaps an occasion of seeing the "color problem" at the heart, as it affects the inner life. Even if it were not very readable poetry, it would, from this latter point of view, be important as human documentation of a much needed sort. "Not wholly this or that"—"Frail children of sorrow, determined by a hue"—"Shall I say, 'My son, you're branded in this country's pageantry' "—the phrase Du Bois has singled out, "With voices strange to ecstasy"—"This spirit-choking atmosphere"—"My every fibre fierce rebels, against this servile rôle"—or

> Don't knock at my door, little child
> I cannot let you in;
> You know not what a world this is—

there are volumes in these phrases. After this, the race question becomes, as it must to all intelligent observers, a human problem, a common problem. One of Mrs. Johnson's literary virtues is condensation. She often distills the trite and commonplace into an elixir. Following the old-fashioned lyric strain and the sentimentalist cult of the common emotions, she succeeds because by sincerity and condensation, her poetry escapes to a large extent its own limitations. Here in the subject of these verses, there is however a double pitfall; avoiding sentimentality is to come dangerously close to propaganda. This is also deftly avoided—more by instinct than by calculation. Mrs. Johnson's silences and periods are eloquent, she stops short of the preachy and prosaic and is always lyrical and human. Almost before one has shaped his life to "Oh! the pity of it", a certain fresh breeze of faith and courage blows over the heart, and the mind revives to a healthy, humanistic optimist. Mrs. Johnson seems to me to hear a message, a message that gains through being softly but intensely insinuated between the lines of her poems—"Let the traditional instincts of women heal the world that travails under the accumulated woes of the uncompensated instincts of men", or to speak more in her way, "May the saving grace of the mother-heart save humanity."

Alain Leroy Locke, [Review of *Bronze: A Book of Verse*], *Crisis* 25, No. 4 (February 1923): 161

EFFIE LEE NEWSOME   It is well-nigh impossible to think of this vital product from the pen of Georgia Douglas Johnson without having communicated to one some of the intense conviction that WROUGHT it into being. It has been stated that authors can convince only to the extent of their persuasion: Georgia Douglas Johnson has molded with the very pulsations of her heart.

Her heart—for this is the potent factor in her creative force—has molded a "Bronze" that challenges not altogether with the sharp angles of accusation, but as well with the graceliness of heart's call to heart for sympathy in the problems of race; as in "The Octoroon;" as also in the ever-recurring light and shadow theme of colored woman's motherhood:

The infant eyes look out amazed upon the frowning earth,
A stranger, in a land now strange, child of the mantled
   birth;
Waxing, he wonders more and more; the scowling grows
   apace,
A world, behind its barring doors, reviles his ebon face!

And we must quote, further, the two lines that conclude if not solve the problem of the poem:

Yet from this maelstrom issues forth a God-like entity,
That loves a world all loveless, and smiles on Calvary!

In ending this finesse of workmanship Mrs. Johnson—or still shall we say, "her heart?"—polishes the bronze with the glory and rich lustre that bronze alone can know. There are inspiring paeans at the end of the work:

Into the very star-shine, lo! they come
Wearing the bays of victory complete!

—to quote in connection with closing tributes to black achievers, the last two verses from the sonnet that opens this book, burnished, in spite of all, now here, now there, with a brave "Optimism" that can glow thus:

We man our parts within life's tragic play.

Effie Lee Newsome, [Review of Bronze: A Book of Verse], Opportunity 1, No. 12 (December 1923): 337

ALAIN LOCKE   Voicing ⟨the⟩ yearning of woman for candid self-expression, Mrs. Johnson invades the province where convention has been most tyrannous and inveterate,—the experiences of love. And here she succeeds where others have failed; for they in over-sophistication, in terror of platitudes and the commonplace, have stressed the bizarre, the exceptional, in one way or another have over-intellectualized their message and overleapt the common elemental experience they would nevertheless express. Mrs. Johnson, on the contrary, in a simple declarative style, engages with ingenuous directness the moods and emotions of her themes.

Through you I entered Heaven and Hell
Knew rapture and despair.

Here is the requisite touch, certainly for the experiences of the heart. Greater sophistication would spoil the message. Fortunately, to the gift of a lyric style, delicate touch, rhapsodic in tone, authentic in timbre, there has been added a temperamental endowment of ardent sincerity of emotion, ingenuous candor of expression, and, happiest of all for the particular task, a naïve and unsophisticated spirit.

By way of a substantive message, Mrs. Johnson's philosophy of life is simple, unpretentious, but wholesome and spiritually invigorating. On the one hand, she belongs with those who, under the leadership of Sara Teasdale, have been rediscovering the Sapphic cult of love as the ecstasy of life, that cult of enthusiasm which leaps over the dilemma of optimism and pessimism, and accepting the paradoxes, pulses in the immediacies of life and rejoices openly in the glory of experience. In a deeper and somewhat more individual message, upon which she only verges, and which we believe will later be her most mature and original contribution, Mrs. Johnson probes under the experiences of love to the underlying forces of natural instinct which so fatalistically control our lives. [Especially is this evident in her suggestion of the tragic poignancy of Motherhood, where the consummation of love seems also the expiation of passion, and where, between the antagonisms of the dual role of Mother and Lover, we may suspect the real dilemma of womanhood to lie.]

Whatever the philosophical yield, however, we are grateful for the pros-pect of such lyricism. Seeking a pure lyric gold, Mrs. Johnson has gone straight to the mine of the heart. She has dug patiently in the veins of her own subjective experience. What she has gleaned has been treasured for the joy of the search and for its own intrinsic worth, and not exploited for the values of show and applause. Above all, her material has been expressed with a candor that shows that she brings to the poetic field what it lacks most,—the gift of the elemental touch. Few will deny that, with all its other excellences, the poetry of the generation needs just this touch to make it more vitally human and more spontaneously effective.

Alain Locke, "Foreword," *An Autumn Love Cycle* by Georgia Douglas Johnson (New York: Harold Vinal, 1928), pp. xvii–xix

---

ANNE SPENCER   Within the last ten years, Georgia Douglas John-son has, through her publishers, brought out three volumes of lyrics, most of which employ—next to food—the oldest theme in the world, and would exquisitely complement a musical setting, here, too, in this united estate of America, where it is decidedly against the law,—Dred Scott, Monroe Doctrine, or, maybe, some unwritten cartel of Marque and Reprisal,—for any person of color to write of love without hypothecating atavistic jungle tones: the rumble of tom-tom, voodoo ebo, fetish of sagebrush and high spliced palm tree—all the primal universal passions often solely associated with Africa,—

Pardon, I did intend writing about Mrs. Johnson's latest book, *An Autumn Love Cycle*, but any digression is logical in an atmosphere where even an offering on the shrine of Parnassus must meet the agony of challenge: Aha! It is white. . . . How important! Lo, it is black! Alas! But Life, the book of poetry, cannot relate itself to unrelated persons. Silk purses are no more made of sows' ears than of rayon. The artificial has nothing to offer but surfaces. In these poems the author has come to terms with life, signed the valiant compromise, the Medean alternative, delivering her awareness over to pain. Her sentience speeds to its martyrdom crying,

> Fire—tears—
> And the torture-chamber,
> With the last maddening turn of the screw—

As one who believes the admixture of what we call human nature to be changeless, I can recall no better for any seasonal lovers than this newest idealization of the emotions:

> Oh night of love, your groves of strange content
> Project a thralldom over coming days;
> Exalted, derelict, and blind I went
> Unmindfully along Life's misty ways.

If with us the practice of a book of verses underneath the bough, or, better still, before the fire, has grown into sneering disrepute, it threatens the obsequies of the finest art, the gentle art of love-making. Lovers are the only persons left to us of any elegance at all. The last of the aristocrats, the Great Lover moves among his menials with a soul all prinked out in plumes, knee-buckles, and *diamant* shoon. Whatever his age, his past experiences, or physical characteristics, the true lover becomes an abstract creature, as shriven and innocent as at the day of his birth—or death . . .

> Consider me a melody
> That serves its simple turn,
> Or but the residue of fire
> That settles in the urn . . .

You will know that such snatches of song are unfair to the singer, but this, and more, Mrs. Johnson has poignantly lineated and set down for whatever God blessed folk remain in this hard-boiled day.

Anne Spencer, [Review of *An Autumn Love Cycle*], *Crisis* 36, No. 3 (March 1929): 87

MARITA ODETTE BONNER   It will have to be the old figure, I guess. It will have to be the figure of fire.—Love is fire.—But surely it is a fire.—Love must be a fire, lit in the beginning to warm us, to light us, to circle us in completely from the iciness of the Struggle—during our Night-of-Passage. In Youth, love is a flame mad and consuming, licking out to eat up Ideas and Ideals, true and false alike.

In Autumn, love is a smoldering fire. A yellow flame burning thinly here, a blue flame pouring steadily there, a red glow everywhere underneath the coals. A red glow smoldering under the coals, that must soon be covered with ashes from the Night.

In Autumn—a smoldering fire. A fire smoldering with yellow and blue jets. Yellow jets. Reflections of other flames. Yellow jets:

> Oh night of love,
> Your rapt ecstatic hours were mine.

Blue, steady, and a red glow all through:—

> Would I might mend
> the fabric of my youth
> For I would go a further while with you
> And drain the cup of Joy.

It is all there. The ashes of experiences burnt through, scorched through and become New "Welt," "Illusion," "Parody," "Delusion,"—Steadily—

And all through the *Autumn Love Cycle* you feel there glows before you, a life that has leapt eagerly to embrace all living, all loving. There is no forced pretences at flights of emotion here—no sycophant, sexual, blue wailings. ⟨. . .⟩

Truly it is a fire that has burned steadily, bravely, unflinchingly. Surely here is a life lived steadily, a life lived whole.

Sticklers with their noses lowered to root out flaws might fail to see the steadiness, the wholeness sometimes when everything seems to sink suddenly laden with the heavy ornateness of the good old language of the nineteenth century. But there will always be rooters for flaws and sticklers for words and seekers for form—divorced—from content. And there will always be content—Life and Love whether it marches proudly and aristocratically in flawless form—whether it labors and heaves under a tangle of rocks and weeds.

And the *Autumn Love Cycle* swings completely—swings fully—glows with a reality that burns off any slight dross, any shade of imperfection and makes you draw deep scorching breath and say,

> Is this what it is to be—
> if you are young.

—If you are old—and if you are old—I guess you know that the fire of love even burns ashes.

Marita Odette Bonner, [Review of *An Autumn Love Cycle*], *Opportunity* 7, No. 4 (April 1929): 130

BENJAMIN BRAWLEY   Georgia Douglas was a teacher in Atlanta before becoming, in 1903, the wife of Henry Lincoln Johnson, later recorder of deeds in the District of Columbia. She is the author of three small volumes, *The Heart of a Woman* (1918), *Bronze* (1922), and *An Autumn Love Cycle* (1928). While much of her work transcends the bounds of race, her second booklet was dominated by the striving of the Negro; and her sympathy may also be seen in such a later poem as "Old Black Men."

> They have dreamed as young men dream
>   Of glory, love and power;
> They have hoped as youth will hope
>   Of life's sun-minted hour.
> They have seen as others saw
>   Their bubbles burst in air,
> And they have learned to live it down
>   As though they did not care.

In her earlier work Mrs. Johnson cultivated especially the poignant, sharply chiselled lyric that became so popular with Sara Teasdale and some other writers a decade or two ago. Later, however, there came into her verse a deeper, a more mellow note, as in "I Closed My Shutters Fast Last Night."

> I closed my shutters fast last night,
>   Reluctantly and slow,

So pleading was the purple sky
With all the lights hung low;
I left my lagging heart outside
Within the dark alone,
I heard it singing through the gloom
A wordless, anguished tone.

Upon my sleepless couch I lay
Until the tranquil morn
Came through the silver silences
To bring my heart forlorn,
Restoring it with calm caress
Unto its sheltered bower,
While whispering, "Await, await
Your golden, perfect hour."

Benjamin Brawley, *The Negro Genius* (New York: Dodd, Mead, 1937), pp. 219–20

CEDRIC DOVER   Georgia Douglass ⟨*sic*⟩ Johnson's poems were published in the anthologies of the Renaissance, her books appeared in the decade that marked its beginning and end, and her home has always been a center for the writers and artists who gave it color and shape. She is definitely of it; but equally definitely not in it. Her first volume, *The Heart of a Woman* (1918), echoes Sara Teasdale and shows real sensibility, but contains no hint of the ferment which, a little later, inspired Claude McKay's moving sonnets of protest, his evocative explorations of the Harlem scene, and his exquisite lyrics of nostalgia. ⟨. . .⟩

Mrs. Johnson's second book, *Bronze* (1922), reflects these departures from the poesy of the comfortable villa in the manner indicated by its title. The subject is still the heart of a woman, but now it is the heart of a colored woman aware of her social problem and the potentiality of the so-called hybrid. Therefore, it is unfortunate that *An Autumn Love Cycle* (1928) failed to concentrate her awareness. Instead of enlarging the new vitality, it reverts to the personal notes of her first poems, though it adds the aching maturity of a sensitive woman in her forties. The poet is again overwhelmed by herself.

Soon after the *Cycle*, the Depression swept away the Golden Brown and everything else that was supposedly golden in the days of mad prosperity. It should, by all analogies, have swept Mrs. Johnson away too, but she survived by turning her attention to other forms of writing. They did not get published, but they kept the flame alive.

The War might easily have extinguished it, but Mrs. Johnson responded with revived vigor to the changing scene. She added her voice to the Negro struggle for a full share in the democracy that demanded Negro lives and labor. She gave herself unstintingly and, at the same time, poured out a stream of effective poems and fighting songs. Today she is a poet born again of suffering and the social Holy Ghost.

It is an exceptional record. All the more exceptional when we view the sad procession of middle-class poets silenced by inability to find some dynamic in a transitional society. Mrs. Johnson has been saved from this fate, I think, by the circumstance of being a Negro. It has prevented class limitations from enclosing, and finally stifling, her. It has roused her passionate belief in ultimate justice and the coming brotherhood of man. It has given her that extra something apparent in her great sincerity and appealing simplicity.

These are qualities that assure admiration, even from those who have gone beyond idealization to the real means, the critical disciplines and endeavors, by which ideals are realized. They would be quite striking in an adequate and long overdue sifting of her collected poems. Such a bouquet would certainly have the fragrance of a rich and mellow personality, near enough to less generously endowed folk to be typical of cultivated thought in a large part of the colored world.

Indeed, her affinities are as integral to the interest of her poems as the quietly sharp differences. We expect chords of conventional familiarity amongst the offerings of her womanly heart—and we find them in abundance, as in these lines:

> I want to die while you love me,
> While yet you hold me fair;
> While laughter lies upon my lips
> And lights are in my hair.

Cedric Dover, "The Importance of Georgia Douglass Johnson," *Crisis* 59, No. 10 (December 1952): 633–44

WINONA L. FLETCHER   Encouraged by expectations that the Federal Theatre would be a haven for fledgling playwrights, that experimental productions not likely to get produced elsewhere would be mounted, that plays of social protest would be judged on their merits, Georgia Douglas Johnson submitted at least five plays to the Federal Theatre Project between 1935 and 1939, the year the project closed. *None* were accepted for publication in any of the producing units of FTP. Three of the plays submitted are specifically on the theme of lynching and rape; two are historical sketches based on the desperation of slaves to escape from servitude to freedom. The lynch mob lurks ubiquitously in the minds of the author and the characters of both of these dramas. A brief analysis of the dramas and of the FTP playreaders' evaluations of them can lead to an understanding of why Mrs. Johnson, and black playwrights in general, failed in the American theatre of the thirties—and any time when their serious dramas expose the evils of a racist society.

In the one-act drama, *Blue-Eyed Black Boy*, Jack Walter, a 21-year-old black man on his way home from work, innocently brushes against a white woman, is charged with an attempted attack, arrested and jailed. He becomes the intended victim of a lynch mob. Jack's mother, hearing the mob moving toward the jail to get her son, in desperation, retrieves a small ring from a secret hiding place. She then sends the black doctor, who is soon to marry her daughter, in haste to the governor with a message from "Pauline who gave birth to a son 21 years ago." She adds with emphasis:

> Just give him the ring and say, Pauline sent this, she says they goin' to lynch her son born 21 years ago, mind you say twenty-one years ago—then say—listen close—look into his eyes and you'll save him.

The ring and the message are delivered, the governor remembers, the militia is called out, the lynching is stopped, and Jack is sent home safely to his mother.

Like many of the revolutionary dramas of the sixties that are reminiscent of the social protest plays of the thirties, *Blue-Eyed Black Boy* is a tightly structured drama with compressed action. The entire playing time of the script is less than twenty minutes. Johnson, having already exhibited technical aptitude of high quality in her writing, handles exposition well through inference and understatement, plants a note of suspense, and concentrates on protesting the social realism of black women and their mulatto sons. The dialogue distinguishes between the simple dialect of the uneducated, older characters and the more polished speech of the young, educated characters. The audience never sees the blue-eyed boy and, while this contributes to the suspense, the omission might have contributed to the play being attacked as an "incomplete drama." ⟨. . .⟩

The action of A Sunday Morning in the South takes place in 1924 in a humble cottage occupied by a grandmother, Sue Jones, and her two young grandsons, Tom (19) and Bossie (7). Church music is heard from nearby as a neighbor, on her way to morning services, reports that a white woman has claimed "rape by a young black man." They all suspect that the rape charge is untrue but know it will fan more racial hatred and shudder at the thought of what will happen if the young man is found. Almost immediately, two white officers come with the girl who vaguely identifies Tom as the man who raped her. Despite the grandmother's pleas and assurance that Tom was at home asleep all night, the 19-year-old boy is arrested and supposedly taken to jail. Sue (in the second version) sends for help from "Miss Vilet, the good white woman," but learns that Tom is lynched before anybody can save him. The shock of the news kills Sue as the curtain falls.

Of the three plays specifically on lynching, this was the only one that met with the approval of all the FTP readers. ⟨. . .⟩ The clue to approval of Sunday Morning may be found in the reader's phrase "it is not offensive to either group." The persistent dilemma of which audience to address rears its head again, but sympathy for the characters seems to overcome the need to take sides and makes the play more acceptable. Subtextual statements on the hypocrisy of the Christian religion may also have touched sensitive chords in the readers' consciences. Nevertheless, the play was not given a production by The Federal Theatre Project.

Winona L. Fletcher, "From Genteel Poet to Revolutionary Playwright: Georgia Douglas Johnson," *Theatre Annual* 40 (1985): 52–53, 57–58

▣ Bibliography

The Heart of a Woman and Other Poems. 1918.
Bronze: A Book of Verse. 1922.
Blue Blood. 1927.
Plumes. 1927.
An Autumn Love Cycle. 1928.
Share My World: A Book of Poems. 1962.

◈ ◈ ◈

June Jordan

b. 1936

JUNE JORDAN was born in New York on July 9, 1936. Her parents, who were immigrants from Jamaica, wanted their daughter to be a doctor and sent her to the Northfield School, an exclusive girls' school in Massachusetts. One of the few black students in her class, Jordan graduated in 1953 and entered Barnard College in New York City that fall. Two years later she married a Columbia graduate student, Michael Meyer, and abandoned her own studies to take care of their son.

After moving with her husband to Chicago, Jordan returned to Harlem around 1960 and began working on Frederick Wiseman's film about life in the ghetto, *The Cool World*. Around this time she became interested in city planning and met R. Buckminster Fuller, with whom she devised plans for the revitalization of Harlem. In 1969 Fuller nominated Jordan for the Prix de Rome in Environmental Design, which she won. She spent the next year studying at the American University in Rome. Her marriage ended in 1965, and she continued to work as a freelance journalist, writing poetry in her spare time. A long poem titled *Who Look at Me* was published in 1969. It reflects the racial and political concerns that mark much of her poetry.

Since *Who Look at Me* appeared in 1969, Jordan has published seven more volumes of poetry, including *Some Changes* (1971), *New Days* (1974), and *Things That I Do in the Dark: Selected Poetry* (1977). *Passion* (1980) and *Living Room* (1985) gather the poems she wrote between 1977 and 1984, while *Lyrical Campaigns* (1989), *Naming Our Destiny* (1989), and *Haruko/Love Poetry* (1993) present selections of her best poetic work. Jordan has also written several plays, including *The Issue* (1981) and *Bang Bang Uber Alles* (1986), which have been performed but not published.

In 1971 her first novel, *His Own Where*, was nominated for a National Book Award. This young adult book is written in dialect, referred to as Black English, which aroused much protest from parents who felt that their children should not be guided toward nonstandard English models of writing and dialogue. The case was decided in the Michigan courts, where a judge ruled that Black English was a viable alternative to standard English and could not be banned in public schools. Jordan continued writing fiction for children: the novels *Dry Victories* (1972), *New Life: New Room* (1975), and *Kimako's Story* (1981), and the biography *Fannie Lou Hamer* (1972). She has also published several collections of essays: *Civil Wars* (1981), *On Call* (1985), *Moving towards Home* (1989), and *Technical Difficulties* (1992). These essays, like much of her poetry, express Jordan's challenging and uncompromising views on political, literary, and social issues.

Jordan has held teaching positions at various colleges, including City College of the City University of New York, Connecticut College, Sarah Lawrence, and the State University of New York at Stony Brook. Since 1989 she has been a professor of Afro-American studies and women's studies at the University of California at Berkeley.

✣ Critical Extracts

JAMES A. EMANUEL   Opposite the title page of *Who Look at Me* is a painting simply entitled "Portrait of a Gentleman." The gentleman is black. June Jordan's book suggests all black Americans are as unknown as the anonymous early 19th-centuury artist and his subject.

"We do not see those we do not know," she writes. "Love and all varieties of happy concern depend on the discovery of one's self in another. The question of every desiring heart is, thus, 'Who Look at Me?' In a nation suffering fierce hatred, the question—race to race, man to man, and child to child—remains: 'Who Look at Me?' We answer with our lives. Let the human eye begin unlimited embrace of human life."

By intermixing 27 paintings of black Americans from colonial times to the present with an original, understated but intense poem that comments indirectly on the paintings and enhances their meaning, she has given children a splendid opportunity to "begin unlimited embrace of human life."

James A. Emanuel, [Review of *Who Look at Me*], *New York Times Book Review*, 16 November 1969, p. 52

LOUIS L. MARTZ   June Jordan's book, *Some Changes*, inaugurates the new "Black Poets Series" edited by Julius Lester, who provides a brief introduction to the volume, where he says: "For some, her poetry may not qualify as 'black poetry' because she doesn't rage or scream. No, she's quiet, but the intensity is frightening. Her poetry is highly disciplined, highly controlled." It is indeed the skill of her control that is at a first reading most impressive about this volume ⟨. . .⟩ At the same time, the temper of the volume is tough-minded. There is a harsh poem in memory of Martin Luther King; there is a bitter rejoinder to L.B.J.:

> He lost the peace so
> he can keep the peril he
> knows war is nothing like please.

Louis L. Martz, "New Books in Review," *Yale Review* 59, No. 4 (June 1970): 561–62

SARAH WEBSTER FABIO   This book ⟨*His Own Where*⟩ begins: *"You be different from the dead. All them tombstones tearing up the ground, look like a little city, like a small Manhattan . . . Cemetery let them lie there belly close. . . ."*

Whose where? Why cemetery? How sex? At what early age? Between the first and last pages, for Buddy Rivers, 16-year-old protagonist, and his first love, Angela, the only progression is the short sleep in the cemetery, time for her young dream. The story of their trials, the immediacy of their physical attraction is told in flashback and dream flashes, filling the pages of the chapters from one to 17.

June Jordan, author and poet (*Who Look At Me* and *Some Changes*) knows the abandonment of this age. It is a limbo between childhood and young adult, where the void is so great as to be unbearable. It is true here that the mind often stammers for language and the heart only responds to song— to the radio, which you use like a compass on a music map. Angela, at 14, trying to understand Buddy, tells him, "Tune the dial to what you want." There must be bridges if we are to reach our young. *His Own Where* promises to be one. ⟨. . .⟩

Buddy's immediate problem is his father's hospitalization. This, when coupled with his mother's earlier desertion, creates alienation. Although his father has taught him how to fend for himself; how to clean, build, plant, draw plans, he still needs adult contact. At school, he agitates for free and healthy sex, contraceptives, a turned-on lunchroom, coeducational classes in anatomy; his principal suspends him from school and he is told not to return without a parent. Complications arise when he becomes involved with Angela, recognizing her imprisonment and seeing himself as the force of her liberation. Her cab-driving father, who drinks heavily, and her overworked mother, who is a nurse at the hospital, are united in their suspicion of her evilness. She is humiliated and beaten daily to keep her straight. This ends when she is beaten unmercifully; the parents are investigated for child abuse; the home is shattered. ⟨. . .⟩

Buddy sees himself as a man of action. In dream flashes, we see him attending to emergency room patients, liberating Angela from St. Margaret's, a Catholic Home for Girls, filling empty skyscrapers with children who need space to breathe. Finally, he moves with runaway Angela to the cemetery to create, even for a moment, "His own where, own place for loving made for making love."

Sarah Webster Fabio, [Review of *His Own Where*], *New York Times Book Review*, 7 November 1971, pp. 6, 28

JASCHA KESSLER   June Jordan assembles *Some Changes* out of the black experience, and she does so coherently. Her expression is developed out of, or through, a fine irony that manages to control her bitterness, even to dominate her rage against the intolerable, so that she can laugh and cry, be melancholic and scornful and so on, presenting always the familiar faces of human personality, integral personality. She adapts her poems to the occasions that they are properly, using different voices, and levels of thought and direction that are humanly germane and not disembodied rages or vengeful shadows; thus she can create her world, that is, people it for us, for she has the singer's sense of the dramatic and projects herself into a poem to express its special subject, its individuality. Of course it's always her voice, because she has the skill to use it so variously: but the imagination it needs to run through all her changes is her talent. Moreover she seems not to have rejected on principle what has been available to poets in the way of models; in other words, you can see all the white poets she has read, too. She has been assimilating their usages of phrase and stanza; she sees with her own eyes through them, speaks them with her own voice, which is another way of remarking that she is interested in poetry itself. No matter how she will use her poems, and most of them are political in thrust, she has the great good sense, or taste, not to politicize her poetry. There is a difference, even in love poetry, nature poetry, and she has some of that sort, between speaking as yourself and editorializing for others. She is both simple and strong; she is clear in the head, besides. Her compassion and suffering for others is put into lyrical statement, and not into poems which are weapons. I can't shield myself against her, and have no wish to do so, let alone feel myself forced to deliver counter-blows, forced to feel gratuitous pain, gratuitous outrage. It may be because Jordan is a woman, that even her anger and despair are kept within the bounds of the humane, where poetry is too. That is the circle I draw round myself, though it is often broken into, or broken out of, as the case may be. ⟨. . .⟩

When June Jordan goes through her changes, she does it; she doesn't talk about doing it. For us there is pleasure in that, because we can go through them with her. And that means she has poetry near her.

Jascha Kessler, "Trial and Error," *Poetry* 121, No. 5 (February 1973): 301–3

JUNE JORDAN   *The Black Poem . . . Distinctively Speaking.* What is it? Quite apart from individual volumes of Black poetry, I have learned that I hold decidedly different expectations of a Black Anthology, as compared to any other kind. If the single poem, or if the anthology qualifies as distinctively Black, then, as compared to a "white anthology" or a "white poem," I expect the following:

> *A striving for collective voice, or else its actual, happy accomplishment. Even if the person proceeds in the 1st person singular, I expect a distinctively Black poem to speak *for* me-as-part-of-an-*us*, a bounded group that the poem self-consciously assumes as an integral, guiding factor in her/his/their individual art.
> *From a reaching for collective voice, as a self-conscious value, it follows that a distinctively Black poem will be accessible to random readers, rather than "hard," or arrantly inaccessible. (This does not mean that prolonged/repeated study will not yield new compulsion. But it does mean that the first time around, which may be an only time, the poem has to "hit" and "stick," clearly, and openly, in a welcoming way.)
> *Collective voice necessarily refers to spoken language: Distinctively Black poems characteristically deal memories and possibilities of spoken language, as against literary, or written,

language. This partially accounts for the comparative *directness*
and force of Black poetry; it is an intentionally collective, or
inclusive, people's art meant to be shared, heard and, therefore,
spoken—meant to be as real as bread.
  *Sound patterns, rhythmic movement and change-ups often
figure as importantly as specific words, or images, in distinctively
Black poetry. (Even if the poet says nothing especially new, I can
expect to take pleasure in the musical, textural aspects of the
poem; they will be as intrinsic to the work, as the words.)

  To conclude this second point: Distinctively Black poetry adheres to
certain, identifiable values—political and aesthetic—that are open to adoption, enjoyment by anyone. Overriding everything else is the striving and
respect for collective voice. These distinctive values also constitute the
main sum of what I look for, and prize, in The Black Poem.

  June Jordan, "The Black Poet Speaks of Poetry," *American Poetry Review* 3, No. 3
  (May–June 1974): 50

DORIS GRUMBACH   In the *American Poetry Review* issue for May/
June 1974 there are a number of interesting contributions, not the least of
which, to my biased mind, is June Jordan's "The Black Poet Speaks of
Poetry." Her thesis is that "white people/white editors, of major/nationwide
magazines and publishing houses simply do not read and do not value and
do not publish what I would call The Black Poem." There follow citations
of who those major/nationwide magazines are and lo, *The New Republic*
leads all the rest: "Although *TNR* regards itself as a political journal, when
have you seen a political poem published there?"
  You will note that the black poem, in the course of a few sentences, has
transmuted itself to something called the *political* black poem. When I wrote
to her to point out the notice *TNR* has taken of black poets and writers,
she made this distinction: "The kind of poetry I am referring to is Distinctly
Black/Political poetry." Disclaiming my citations of Alice Walker, Sterling
Brown, Barbara Smith, Michael Harper, Ishmael Reed, Ivan Webster as
examples of writers whom *TNR* either has published, is about to publish,
or has dealt with critically, she said none of them qualified under her
stringent definition, which by now had acquired a new word, "Distinctly."
She accused *TNR* of "having been offered, and has steadily refused to publish
Distinctly Black/Political Poetry many times in the last several years" (capital

letters are all hers). My response was that I had no way of knowing for
certain from the ms. that the DBP poetry *was* black, or was by a black. So
it was entirely possible that, for reasons other than racist, I or my predecessor
had returned the poetry offered to us by DBP poets. Our correspondence
went on in this fashion, she accusing me of "patronizing response" that is
"so apparently the nature of your immediate reaction to criticism by Black
People."

This drove me not so much to anger as to June Jordan's own poetry, the
only DBP poet she cited in her letter as having been rejected by us. (I am
constrained to add that when I wrote telling her the names of other noted
poets—*white*—whose poems I had rejected she suggested we discontinue
our correspondence because she could not read my handwriting.) Her newest
book is called *New Days*, published in September of this year by Emerson
Hall publishers. It contains some very admirable poems, some very angry
ones (clearly what she would call Political), but an even greater number
that I would call love poems, or poems of exile and return in her words in
which neither the color of the poet nor her politics are apparent. ⟨. . .⟩
There are other very good ones, some I like somewhat less, though they
are not necessarily the Distinctly Black Political ones, and a few I liked not
at all, convincing me that *TNR* or the other media she accuses—*NY Times*,
New Yorker, *NY Review of Books*, *American Review*, *Harper's*, *Atlantic*, and
a number of publishing houses—may have rejected poets for a number of
reasons besides racism, among them, the private esthetic of the literary
editor, the poetic value of the submitted poem, the state of things at the
publishing house at the moment (some publications, like ours, are stocked
for a year or more with accepted poetry) and, God help us, space limitations.

Doris Grumbach, "Fine Print," *New Republic*, 9 November 1974, p. 44

NTOZAKE SHANGE   To be in exile & be a poet is to be turned
in on oneself / more than to be free of the trauma / there is a case that the
whole nation of us who are African are in exile / here in this english-
speakin place / but the collections of poems by june jordan ⟨*New Days*⟩ / &
joseph jarman ⟨*Black Case*⟩ steer us away from a sense of dislocation / these
are exiles returned / & more ourselves than many of us who stayed durin
the holocausts & frenzy of sixties / illusions grow in newark & paris /
whatever we have stepped outta cycle / outside ourselves / ⟨. . .⟩ aside from

confrontin the vast disarray that is the contemporary world / circlin on itself / maybe swallowin us / loosin us in the momentum / less we do as jarman chants:

> can you look at your black skin
> your black self if you got one
> and then do itit is
> time
> say do it yes
> go sing
> the sound the music it is *fire*.

& jordan incants:

> YOUR BODY IS A LONG BLACK WING
> YOUR BODY IS A LONG BLACK WING

we shall twist in despair & distortion / in conceits & wrong information same as those jarman's ODAWALLA moved through 'the people of the Sun' teachin through 'the practice of the drum and silent gong' / or jordan's "Gettin Down to Get Over":

> momma momma
> teach me how to kiss
> the king within the kingdom
> teach how to t.c.b. / to make do
> an be
> like you
> teach me to survive my
> momma
> teach me how to hold a new life
> momma
> help me
> turn the face of history
> *to your face*

movin back in on ourselves / to discover all that is there / is not lovely worth holdin / but necessary to know / what is real / who we are / jordan & jarman examine mercilessly their own dilemmas / which become / all of ours

Ntozake Shange, [Review of *New Days: Poems of Exile and Return*], *Black Scholar* 8, No. 5 (March 1977): 53–55

DARRYL PINCKNEY   "Passion" is an appropriate title for this gathering of 51 new poems. Miss Jordan, in the preface, calls for a "people's poetry," hailing Walt Whitman and Pablo Neruda as notable examples. It is impossible to accept her charge that there is a "vendetta" against Whitman in America. Even before recent scholarly work that sympathetically discusses the homoerotic in Whitman's sensibility, there was Randall Jarrell's important essay. It is also difficult to understand why the quest for a "New World" poetry must entail the rejection of T. S. Eliot, Robert Lowell, Wallace Stevens or Elizabeth Bishop, four of the finest poets in the language. There is no contradiction in admiring *The Waste Land* as well as lyrics from the streets. One can learn from any tradition.

The poems in *Passion*, mostly in free verse, share many of the themes of the essays. These poems are confidently within an oral tradition, and although the oral can often mean the merely rhetorical, Miss Jordan serves the tradition well, with a sensitive ear for the vernacular, for the ironic tone. ⟨. . .⟩

The energy and seriousness of these poems are impressive and, like the essays, they are the work of a writer of integrity and will.

Darryl Pinckney, [Review of *Civil Wars* and *Passion*], New York Times Book Review, 9 August 1981, p. 26

PETER ERICKSON   Those who come to June Jordan's poetry because of her reputation as a strictly political poet will be surprised at the large number of love poems and of her constant recourse to this genre. Setting aside political concerns, the poet indulges her erotic longing: "I can use no historic no national no family bliss / I need an absolutely one to one a seven-day kiss" ("Alla Tha's All right, but," *Passion*). What is here a raucous assertion and celebration of sexual need has earlier—more often than not—been an expression of intense vulnerability in love. Jordan's first collection of poetry, *Some Changes* (1971), is divided into four untitled sections, the implicit rationale for section two being love. This second section, arguably the richest in the volume, has an important long-term effect on Jordan's overall poetic development, thus providing a key to that development.

An atmosphere of deep malaise—interrupted by occasional, though still muted, bursts of erotic release of self-affirmation—dominate section two of

Some Changes. The last poem of section one, "I Live in Subtraction," makes the transition to the next section by firmly setting a dejected tone. Though "I" is the first word and subject of every line, the action of the poems is to reduce rather than enlarge this self, the continual subtracting effect culminating in the contemplation of suicidal gesture: "I can end a dream with death." We are not told how this psychological state came about, though we might guess the poet has been hurt by love when she says that she has forgotten or directs herself to "forget you name." Her demoralization is presented as a given, its origin and cause left a mystery.

Nor are we told the reason for the sadness in "My Sadness Sits Around Me." This title is reiterated in the poem's first and last lines, creating a literal enclosure which represents the emotional isolation that envelops the poet. We are forced simply to note and to accept this sadness which the poems gingerly explore without explaining more precisely. The same image of being cut and sealed off is reproduced in "Nobody Riding the Roads Today," where the last stanza can only repeat the first: "Nobody riding the roads today / But I hear the living rush / far away from my heart." The formal circularity mimics and heightens the poet's desolation.

The troubled mood of these poems can be usefully associated with the general background of Jordan's life during this period, so long as we do not insist on a one-to-one correspondence by which the life is supposed to explain the poetry. The two crucial events of which the reader needs to be aware are, in successive years, Jordan's divorce from her husband (1965) and her mother's suicide: first with a brief mention in *Civil Wars* (p. xvii), then at length in her second address at Barnard College. In the latter, Jordan presents her recollection of the suicide with such vivid immediacy that it is almost as if it were occurring in the present rather than fifteen years ago, as if Jordan must relive her confused feelings in order finally to attain expiation.

Peter Erickson, "The Love Poetry of June Jordan," *Callaloo* 9, No. 1 (Winter 1986): 223–24

SARAH BENTON   The threat of annihilation by white America is the pulse of June Jordan's writings. This makes hers a rare voice in the refined world of the political essay. From her account of a riot in Harlem in 1964 to her oration for the death of ⟨Jesse⟩ Jackson's Presidential bid in

1988 she measures all political movement against this irreducible standard: does it combat the likelihood of death by violence, by suffering or by suicide? With her fingers on this fear, she keeps herself in the bloodstream of the peoples to whom she feels herself thrice kin: blacks, women and the third world. For unlike them, June Jordan has earned an audience through her work as poet, public speaker and academic. ⟨. . .⟩

When she sees the world in simple black and white she jeopardises the fragile alliance for which she speaks, as in her attack on a group of Hassidic Jews. But she is again rare in her efforts to describe the conflicts between black, and women's and third world movements. Rarer still in seeing the solution in love, as in: "It is against such suicide, and is against such deliberate strangulation of the possible lives of . . . powerless peoples . . . everywhere that I work and live, now, as a feminist, trusting that I will learn to love myself well enough to love you . . ." The vulnerability of a form of writing that does not investigate, or write directly from, the lives of the oppressed, is that it can fall into a sententious moralism. Most of the time, the power of her words carries her argument through.

Sarah Benton, "A Rare Voice" [Review of *Moving towards Home* and *Lyrical Campaigns*], *New Statesman and Nation*, 7 April 1989, p. 46

MARILYN HACKER   June Jordan's new book ⟨*Naming Our Destiny*⟩ is an anthology of causes won, lost, moot, private and public, forgotten and remembered. Anyone who doubts the relevance and timeliness of poetry ought to read Jordan, who has been among the front-line correspondents for almost thirty years and is still a young and vital writer. So should anyone who wants his or her curiosity and indignation aroused, or wants to read a voice that makes itself heard on the page. ⟨. . .⟩

What makes politically engaged poetry unique, and primarily poetry before it is politics? Jordan's political poetry is, at its best, the opposite of polemic. It is not written with a preconceived, predigested agenda of ideas and images. Rather, the process of composition is, or reproduces, the process of discovering how events are connected, how oppressions are analogous, how lives interpenetrate. Jordan's poems are strongest when they deal with interior issues, when she begins with a politics of the personal, with the articulate and colloquial voice of, if you will, "a woman speaking to women" (and to men) and ranges outward to illustrate how issues, lives and themes are inextricably interconnected. ⟨. . .⟩

How can a white critic say that a black poet has a spectacular sense of rhythm? Modestly, or courageously. Jordan writes (mostly) free verse. Many writers of free verse produce a kind of syntactically disjointed prose, expecting line breaks to provide a concentration and a syncopation not achieved by means of language. In Jordan's best poems there is a strong, audible, rhythmic counterpart to the line breaks, a rhythm as apparent to the reader as it is to the auditor who hears the poet deliver them. This is true of her poems that have been set to music by Bernice Reagon of the a cappella group Sweet Honey in the Rock ("Alla Tha's All Right, but" and "A Song of Sojourner Truth"), but it's equally true of dramatic monologues like "The Talking Back of Miss Valentine Jones" and "Unemployment Monologue," and of the interior monologues evolving into public declaration, like "Poem About My Rights."

The fluid speech-become-aria quality of Jordan's free verse poems also makes them difficult to quote, though never difficult to remember. They are not made of lapidary lines and epigrammatic stanzas. They gather momentum verbally, aurally. Most often, the effects of the voice and the statement are cumulative.

Why is this important? Because it fixes the poems in the reader's memory; because it makes these poems, even those on the most serious subjects, paradoxically fun to read. It is a reason for these texts to be written in verse, to be poetry. They are not fiction, journalism, essays or any other form of prose, even when they share qualities with these other genres. When Jordan's poems are unambiguous and straightforward, as well as when they are figurative, ironic or complex, her words create a music, create voices, which readers must hear the way they were written. Her poems read themselves to us.

Marilyn Hacker, "Provoking Engagement," *Nation*, 29 January 1990, pp. 135–36

DAVID BAKER   The issues of race and self-reliance (artistic and otherwise) are not the only political topics to which Jordan returns persistently. She speaks searingly in behalf of the hitherto silenced or subjugated: women, the poor and hungry, the imprisoned, the politically tyrannized in Nicaragua, the enslaved in Manhattan. I can think of very few contemporary

American poets who have been so willing to take on other people's troubles; decidedly, this is not the poetry of a sheltered, introspective confessional, not the work of a tidy scholar or a timid dormouse. Jordan's variety of poetic stances enacts her drive to connect and represent, for in addition to her principal mode of delivery—the poet talking directly to an audience—she also speaks through a number of other characters in persona poems, giving sympathetic articulation to lives, idioms, and concerns beyond her own. Like Carl Sandburg, she makes public art out of public occasion and the available word, and she does so with confidence and conviction.

> David Baker, "Probable Reason, Possible Joy," *Kenyon Review* 14, No. 1 (Winter 1992): 154–55

ADELE LOGAN ALEXANDER   *Technical Difficulties* is a book about America—subtitled, as it is, "The State of the Union." This is America observed and found both noble and nurturing, brutal and malformed—often at the same time—by a brilliant and mature African American scholar who has looked at our country with her own unique clarity of vision and focus. Her subjects include affectionate tributes to her own Jamaican heritage ("For My American Family") and that of those other immigrants, not the Poles, Russians, Irish, or Germans but the too-often invisible and darker-skinned newcomers whose journeys through New York harbor, past the Statue of Literty and Ellis Island, have been largely overlooked in our romantic imaging of the American melting-pot. ⟨. . .⟩

Jordan tackles and dissects familiar themes: family, race, neighborhood ("two-and-a-half years ago," she writes, "I . . . returned to my beloved Brooklyn where, I knew, my eyes and ears would never be lonely for diversified, loud craziness and surprise"), the love of men, women and children, the mutable American Constitution, education, creativity and politics (of nations and of sexuality, the "correct" and the "incorrect"). For many years she has been a teacher and writer, with several books of essays, including *Civil Wars, Moving towards Home* and *On Call,* to her credit, as well as collections of poetry, including the less well-known *Who Look at Me—* poems for children about African American artists and their work. These new essays, though they cover a variety of topics, come together into a unified and consistent whole. Adapting the Cubists' technique of viewing a subject from many different perspectives at once, Jordan sees all sides and then reassembles the fragments into a consistent, if multifaceted, whole. One should not say *Technical Difficulties* is "better" than what preceded it, but it is surely "more," and though a little of Jordan's well-muscled prose goes a long way, in this case it is also true that "more is better." ⟨. . .⟩

Jordan vigorously rants at our familiar "emperors," from George Washington to Ronald Reagan. She reminds us of the meaty, but non-mainstream, substance that has been deliberately omitted and obscured from our educational, cultural and political lives. I look to her not only to rail at the way things have been ("if you're not an American white man and you travel through the traditional twistings and distortions of the white Western canon, you stand an excellent chance of ending up *nuts*," she says) but to knock our white, male-centered world cockeyed from its moorings and provide more of the revised visions that we need.

Adele Logan Alexander, "Stirring the Melting-Pot," *Women's Review of Books* 10, No. 7 (April 1993): 6–7

Bibliography

Who Look at Me. 1969.

The Voice of the Children (editor; with Terri Bush). 1970.

Soulscript: Afro-American Poetry (editor). 1970.

Some Changes. 1971.

His Own Where. 1971.

Dry Victories. 1972.

Fannie Lou Hamer. 1972.

Poem: On Moral Leadership as a Political Dilemma (Watergate, 1973). 1973.

New Days: Poems of Exile and Return 1970–1972. 1974.

New Life, New Room. 1975.

Niagara Falls. 1977.

Things That I Do in the Dark: Selected Poetry. 1977.

Unemployment: Monologue. 1978.

Passion: New Poems 1977–1980. 1980.

Kimako's Story. 1981.

Civil Wars. 1981.

Living Room: New Poems. 1985.

On Call: Political Essays. 1985.

Bobo Goetz a Gun. 1985.
Naming Our Destiny: New and Selected Poems. 1989.
Moving towards Home: Political Essays. 1989.
Lyrical Campaigns: Selected Poems. 1989.
Technical Difficulties: African-American Notes on the State of the Union. 1992.
Haruko/Love Poetry: New and Selected Poems. 1993.

❖ ❖ ❖

Audre Lorde
1934–1992

AUDRE GERALDINE LORDE was born on February 18, 1934, in New York City, to Frederic Byron and Linda Belmar Lorde. She attended public schools in Manhattan and, at an early age, began to write poetry. In 1951 she enrolled at Hunter College, working at a number of odd jobs to support herself and graduating in 1959. In 1954 she spent a year studying at the National University of Mexico.

Shortly after graduation Lorde entered a library science program at Columbia University, receiving the M.L.S. degree in 1961. During the next seven years Lorde worked at Mount Vernon Public Library and the Town School Library in New York City. In her spare time she wrote poetry and in 1968 her first collection, *The First Cities*, appeared. This volume received little attention but was praised for its originality of language. In that same year Lorde received a National Endowment for the Arts grant, resigned her position as librarian, and became poet-in-residence at Tougaloo College in Mississippi. Tougaloo presented Lorde with her first reprieve from urban life. The city, however, is a significant influence in Lorde's poems, being generally a place of confinement and deterioration.

Lorde's second book of poetry, *Cables to Rage* (1970), was published in England but distributed in America by the Broadside Press. The poems, like those in *The First Cities*, largely focus around human relationships. With *From a Land Where Other People Live* (1973; nominated for a National Book Award), the evolution of Lorde's concerns became evident. Unlike many of her contemporaries, Lorde's themes progressed from personal awareness toward a larger societal vision. Her vision of the world somewhat resembled her description of the city: it is a place of oppression, large and uncaring, walled in by racism and injustice. In *The New York Head Shop and Museum* (1974), Lorde's politics became more explicit. She also adopted much of the militant black rhetoric of the radical black poets of the 1960s.

Lorde, however, came to be known primarily as a lesbian feminist poet. She had become involved in the Greenwich Village "gay-girl" milieu as early as 1955, and although she married an attorney, Edwon Ashley Rollins, in 1962 and had two children with him, she was divorced in 1970. From that time onward, Lorde's efforts to win respect for lesbians were unremitting. Many of the poems in such collections as *Coal* (1976), *The Black Unicorn* (1978), *Chosen Poems, Old and New* (1982), *Our Dead Behind Us* (1986), and *The Marvelous Arithmetics of Distance* (1993), as well as the autobiographical novel *Zami: A New Spelling of My Name* (1982), examine such issues.

Lorde also published two collections of essays, *Sister Outsider* (1984) and *A Burst of Light* (1988), as well as *The Cancer Journals* (1980), an account of her fight against breast cancer. She helped found the Kitchen Table: Women of Color Press, a black feminist publisher, and Sisters in Support of Sisters in South Africa.

Audre Lorde taught at several universities, including the City University of New York, John Jay College of Criminal Justice, and, from 1978, at Hunter College, where she was Thomas Hunter Professor of English. She died of liver cancer on November 17, 1992, in St. Croix in the U.S. Virgin Islands.

◈ *Critical Extracts*

ANTAR SUDAN KATARA MBERI   There are many poems ⟨in *Coal*⟩ such as "Coal," "Summer Oracle," "Generation," "Poem for a Poet," "Hard Love Rock," "Bridge through My Window," and "Conversations in Crisis" which are good to excellent poems. At the same time, there is a marked, uneven and sometimes ambiguous character to the book. The long poem "Martha" is extremely reflective of this. It seems an unwieldy attempt to convey poetically an accident, the victim, in relationship to life and the crucifixion. The idea is not a bad one in itself, but despite the occasional insights, the narrative fails badly; is dead. The poem itself in its persona almost borders on the neurotic and is not always clear; this may be its justification and intent but I am not convinced.

Coal is not as strong and well-knit a collection as the aforementioned collection ⟨*From a Land where Other People Live*⟩ which won a National Book Award nomination. Yet there is this argument to be made in its behalf. What comes through is the "stretchingness" of Audre Lorde's poetry into new poetic vistas of the Afro-American and general human experience. This book almost seems a transition, a harbinger of an entire new world and way of defining it.

Antar Sudan Katara Mberi, "Poetic Vistas of Afro-American Experience," *Freedomways* 16, No. 3 (Third Quarter 1976): 195

R. B. STEPTO   In contrast to ⟨Maya Angelou's⟩ *And Still I Rise,* Audre Lorde's seventh volume of poems, *The Black Unicorn,* is a big, rich book of some sixty-seven poems. While *The Black Unicorn* is as "packaged" as *And Still I Rise* (the prominent half-column of authenticating commentary from Adrienne Rich constitutes much of the wrapping), it really does not need this promoting and protecting shell. Perhaps a full dozen—an incredibly high percentage—of these poems are searingly strong and unforgettable. Those readers who recall the clear light and promise of early Lorde poems such as "The Woman Thing" and "Bloodbirth," and recall as well the great shape and energy of certain mid-1970s poems including "To My Daughter the Junkie on a Train," "Cables to Rage," and "Blackstudies," will find in *The Black Unicorn* new poems which reconfirm Lorde's talent while reseeding gardens and fields traversed before. There are other poems which do not so much reseed as repeople, and these new persons, names, ghosts, lovers, voices—these new I's, we's, real and imagined kin—give us something fresh, beyond the cycle of Lorde's previously recorded seasons and solstices.

While *The Black Unicorn* is unquestionably a personal triumph for Lorde in terms of the development of her canon, it is also an event in contemporary letters. This is a bold claim but one worth making precisely because, as we see in the first nine poems, Lorde appears to be the only North American poet other than Jay Wright who is sufficiently immersed in West African religion, culture, and art (and blessed with poetic talent!) to reach beyond a kind of middling poem that merely quantifies "blackness" through offhand reference to African gods and traditions. What Lorde and Wright share, beyond their abilities to create a fresh, Now World Art out of ancient Old World lore, is a voice or an *idea* of a voice that is essentially African in that it is communal, historiographical, archival, and prophetic *as well as* personal in ways that we commonly associate with the African *griot, dyeli,* and tellers of *nganos* and other oral tales. However, while Wright's voice may be said to embody what is masculine in various West African cultures and cosmologies, Lorde's voice is decidedly and magnificently feminine. The goal of *The Black Unicorn* is then to present this fresh and powerful voice, and to explore the modulations within that voice between feminine and feminist timbres. As the volume unfolds, this exploration charts history and geography as well as voice, and with confluence of these patterns the volume takes shape and Lorde's particular envisioning of a black transatlantic tradition is accessible.

> R. B. Stepto, "The Phenomenal Woman and the Severed Daughter," *Parnassus: Poetry in Review* 8, No. 1 (Fall–Winter 1979): 315–16

ROSEMARY DANIELL   Throughout ⟨*Zami: A New Spelling of My Name*⟩, ⟨Lorde's⟩ experiences are painted with exquisite imagery. Indeed, her West Indian heritage shows through most clearly in her use of word pictures that are sensual, steamy, at times near-tropical, evoking the colors, smells—repeatedly, the smells—shapes, textures that are her life. Her attention to detail is exacting whether she's describing a supper of hot tamales and cold milk in Mexico City or an evening of bar-hopping in the West Village of two decades ago. Her use of language is often imaginative but uncontrived, as in her description of her first lover, Ginger, as having "hight putchy cheeks" or her reference, in one of the many meals deliciously detailed in the book, to "chopped onions quailed in margarine."

Yet Miss Lorde is at her best when her images become—as they often do—metaphors for states of being: A torn stocking caught in the wind on the side of a tenement building becomes symbolic of her terror when, as a small child, she hangs by one hand from the window of her apartment, only to be saved by her mother's timely return home. Or the day she has begun her first menstrual period: Left alone by her usually ever-present mother in the kitchen, she crushes with mortar and pestle the garlic, onions and celery leaves that will season the meat for dinner; as she pounds—and pounds and pounds—she becomes carried away, the scents from the ground herbs mixing with her own. And her membership at Junter High School in what she calls The Branded, The Lunatic Fringe, is really her wider membership in that part of the population made up of artists, blacks, women, and homosexuals.

Despite her obvious poet's ease with symbol, metaphor, image, her references to herself as poet—a vocation held since childhood—are unemphatic:

". . . sometimes there was food cooked, sometimes there was not. Sometimes there was a poem, and sometimes there was not. And always, on weekends, there were the bars," she writes, describing life with her lover Muriel. And while her downplaying of her commitment to poetry may be partly an attempt to avoid widening the distance between the reader and herself, there is the sense, in *Chosen Poems* as in *Zami*, of a writer who has other, more pressing concerns—such as cooking a meal, making a living, or simply living out the life style that for many homosexuals is an avocation in itself.
Rosemary Daniell, "The Poet Who Found Her Own Way," *New York Times Book Review*, 19 December 1982, pp. 12, 29

CLAUDIA TATE   C.T.: Would you describe your writing process?
LORDE: I keep a journal and write in it fairly regularly. I get a lot of my poems out of it. It's like the raw material for my poems. Sometimes I'm blessed with a poem that comes in the form of a poem, but other times I've worked for two years on a poem.

For me, there are two very basic and different processes for revising my poetry. One is recognizing that a poem has not yet become itself. In other words, I mean that the feeling, the truth that the poem is anchored in is somehow not clearly clarified inside of me, and as a result it lacks something. Then it has to be re-felt. Then there's the other process which is easier. The poem is itself, but it has rough edges that need to be refined. That kind of revision involves picking the image that is more potent or tailoring it so that it carries the feeling. That's an easier kind of rewriting and re-feeling.

My journal entries focus on things I feel: feelings that sometimes have no place, no beginning, no end; phrases I hear in passing; something that looks good to me; sometimes just observations of the world.

I went through a period once when I felt like I was dying. I wasn't writing any poetry, and I felt that if I couldn't write I would split. I was recording in my journal, but no poems came. I know now that this period was a transition in my life.

The next year, I went back to my journal, and here were these incredible poems that I could almost lift out of it. Many of them are in *The Black Unicorn*. "Harriet" is one of them; "Sequelae" and "The Litany for Survival" are others. These poems came right out of the journal. But I didn't see them as poems then.

"Power" was in the journal too. It is a poem written about Clifford Glover, the ten-year-old black boy shot by a cop who was acquitted by a jury on which a black woman sat. In fact, the day I heard on the radio that O'Shea had been acquitted, I was going across town on 88th Street [New York City] and I had to pull over. A kind of fury rose up in me—the sky turned red. I felt so sick. I felt as if I would drive the car into a wall, into the next person I saw. So I pulled over. I took out my journal just to air some of my fury, to get it out of my fingertips. Those expressed feelings are that poem. That was just how "Power" was written.

C.T.: A transition has to occur before you can make poetry out of your journal entries.

LORDE: There is a gap between the journal and my poetry. I write this stuff in my journal, and sometimes I cannot even read my journals because there is so much pain and rage in them. I'll put it away in a drawer, and six months later, I'll pick up the journal, and there will be the seeds of poems. The journal entries somehow have to be assimilated into my living; only then can I deal with what I have written down.

Art is not living. It is the use of living. The artist has the ability to take the living and use it in a certain way and produce art.

Claudia Tate, "Audre Lorde," *Black Women Writers at Work* (New York: Continuum, 1983), pp. 111–12

BARBARA CHRISTIAN   As a black, lesbian, feminist, poet, mother, Lorde has, in her own life, had to search long and hard for *her* people. In responding to each of these audiences, in which a part of her identity lies, she refuses to give up her differences. In fact she uses them, as woman to man, black to white, lesbian to heterosexual, as a means of conducting creative dialogue. Thus, she asserts that "the results of woman-hating in the Black communities are tragedies which diminish all Black People" and that the black man's use of the label "lesbian" as a threat is an attempt to rule by fear. She reminds white women who fear the anger of black women that "anger between peers births courage, not destruction, and the discomfort and sense of loss it often causes is not fatal but a sign of growth." In "Eye to Eye," she acknowledges the anger that black women direct toward each other, as well as our history of bonding, in a society that tells us we are wrong at every turn. In discussing our condition she reminds black women who attack lesbianism as anti-black of "the sisterhood of work and play and power" that is a part of our African tradition, that we have been taught to see each other as "heartless competitors for the scarce male, the all important prize that could legitimize our existence." This dehumanization of the denial of self, she asserts, "is no less lethal than the dehumanization of racism to which it is so closely allied." And underlying all of Lorde's attempts to have creative dialogue with the many parts of her self is her recognition that the good in this society is tragically defined in terms of profit rather than in terms of the human being.

Lorde's essays are always directed toward the deepening of self, even as she analyzes the ways in which society attempts to dehumanize it. In showing the connections between sexism, racism, ageism, homophobia, classism, even as she insists on the creative differences among those persons they affect, she stresses the need to share the joy and pain of living, through language. In speaking, in breaking the silences about what each of us actually experiences, what we think, in voicing even our disagreements, we bridge the differences between us. Like ⟨June⟩ Jordan and ⟨Alice⟩ Walker's essays, Lorde's collection "broadens the joining," even as it exemplifies another way in which a black woman interprets her experiences.

Barbara Christian, "The Dynamics of Difference: Book Review of Audre Lorde's *Sister Outsider*" (1984), *Black Feminist Criticism: Perspectives on Black Women Writers* (New York: Pergamon Press, 1985), pp. 209–10

JOAN MARTIN   *The Cancer Journals* is an autobiographical work dealing with Audre Lorde's battle with cancer, her horror at discovering that she was being forced to face her own mortality head on, and the lessons she learned as a result of this most painful experience. She talks constantly of fear, anxiety, and strength. And strength is the substance of which she seems made. The opening statement of the Introduction addresses the problem immediately. "Each woman responds to the crisis that breast cancer brings to her life out of a whole pattern, which is the design of who she is and how her life has been lived. The weave of her everyday existence is the training ground for how she handles crisis." She further states, "I am a post-mastectomy woman who believes our feelings need voice in order to be recognized, respected, and of use." And we hear her feelings voiced in a manner both eloquent and disturbingly prophetic. As in her poetry, Lorde states her truths with no holds barred in this short but powerful prose work. Her biggest fear beyond the loss of her breast and the possibility of imminent death is that she should die without having said the things she as a woman and an artist needed to say in order that her pain and subsequent loss might not have occurred in vain. In her own words, she says, "I had known the pain, and survived it. It only remained for me to give it voice, to share it for use, that the pain not be wasted." And like the love she lost as a child and learned to survive without, Lorde has taken the loss imposed on her by death-dealing breast cancer and survived with dignity and new strength. Her adamant refusal to wear a prosthesis after the removal of her breast is an example of that self-esteem we saw developing in the young child. It has emerged complete in Audre Lorde the woman.

Joan Martin, "The Unicorn Is Black: Audre Lorde in Retrospect," *Black Women Writers (1950–1980): A Critical Evaluation*, ed. Mari Evans (New York: Anchor Press/ Doubleday, 1984), pp. 287–88

AMITAI F. AVI-RAM   One of the most powerful of Lorde's later poems, both emotionally and politically, is "Afterimages" (1981). Thematically, the poem is concerned with two painful historical events in Jackson, Mississippi: a flood of the Pearl River, which the speaker must witness through a television interview of a woman victim, and the notorious lynching of Emmett Till in 1955, which the speaker had witnessed through the proliferation of print-media images of his dead and mutilated body. The second and third of four sections are respectively devoted to each of these events. The first section provides a controlling metaphor for the speaker's relation to the violence she must witness and somehow learn and grow from: her eyes are

> rockstrewn caves where dragonfish evolve
> wild for life, relentless and acquisitive
> learning to survive
> where there is no food. . . .

The dragonfish must "learn / to live upon whatever they must eat / fused images beneath my pain." The final section brings all three thematic strands together, and it is this section in particular, along with the close of section

III (on Emmett Till), that avails itself of some interesting uses of *apo koinou* ⟨"in common"⟩.

> A black boy from Chicago
> whistled on the streets of Jackson, Mississippi
> testing what he'd been taught was a manly thing to do
> his teachers
> ripped his eyes out his sex his tongue
> and flung him to the Pearl weighted with stone
> in the name of white womanhood
> they took their aroused honor
> back to Jackson
> and celebrated in a whorehouse
> the double ritual of white manhood
> confirmed.

Here, the phrase "in the name of white womanhood" stands in common as an adverbial modifier both of the lynch mob's horrible acts against Emmett Till (*ripped, flung*) and of the lynchers' exultant trip to the brothel. The sentence thus represents mimetically the position of the White women beneath the Black victim and the White male oppressors, between the agents and the object of violence. At the same time, it associates the men's "protection" of the women (or rather of their *name*) with their sexual exploitation of those same women. This in turn makes possible the comparison between Till and the White women who suffer from a common oppressor, while the women additionally must bear the *name* of the violence against Black men as one of the aspects of their own victimization: "the double ritual."

The irony of the pivotal line, "in the name of white womanhood"—its use of the men's own language to reveal their deceptions and delusions—is signalled by the *name* that is obviously—for us—not the name of the women themselves, their own proper names, but a name placed upon their "womanhood." Thus, to the White men, the women are not so much living beings as a conglomerate abstract symbol; the very sublimation of their bodies into such a symbol is then revealed to be simultaneously also a subordination and an effacement in the White men's trip to the brothel "in [their] name." Indeed, it is that same simultaneous sublimation and effacement that initially encodes the mob's inscription of their power into the body of their victim, as they remove from him specifically all the outward signs of the Black man's ability to receive and to create meaning: "his eyes . . . his sex his tongue." Upon such a deprivation of the Other's body and its meaning, and *only* upon such violence, can the mob rest its own power to create a name, which it then places upon the sex whom they perceive as initially and naturally powerless to speak their own name for themselves.

Amitai F. Avi-ram, "*Apo koinou* in Audre Lorde and the Moderns: Defining the Differences," *Callaloo* 9, No. 1 (Winter 1986): 203–4

GLORIA T. HULL   Lorde's first language was, literally, poetry. When someone asked her "How do you feel?" "What do you think?" or any other direct question, she "would recite a poem, and somewhere in that poem would be the feeling, the vital piece of information. It might be a line. It might be an image. The poem was my response." Since she was hit if she stuttered, "writing was the next best thing." At this point, Audre was well on her way to becoming schizophrenic, living in "a totally separate world of words." She got "stoned on," retreated into poetry when life became too difficult. As miscellaneous poems no longer served to answer questions from herself and others, she began to write her own. These she did not commit to paper, but memorized and kept as a "long fund" in her head. Poems were "a secret way" of expressing feelings she was "still too afraid to deal with." She would know that she "finally had it" when she spoke her work aloud and it struck alive, became real.

Audre's bizarre mode of communication must surely have meant frequently tangential conversations, and certainly placed on her listeners the burden of having to "read" her words in order to connect her second-level discourse with the direct matter at hand. At any rate, her answer to "How do you feel?" or "Do you want to go to the store with me?" could rarely be a simple "fine" or a univocal yes or no.

In high school, she tried not to "think in poems." She saw in amazement how other people thought, "step by step," and "not in bubbles up from chaos that you had to anchor with words"—a kind of "nonverbal communication, beneath language" the value of which she learned intuitively from her mother. After an early, pseudonymously published story, Lorde did not write another piece of prose until her 1977 essay "Poetry Is Not a Luxury." Even though she had begun to speak in full sentences when she was nineteen and had also acquired compositional skills, "communicating deep feeling in linear, solid blocks of print felt arcane, a method beyond me." She "could not focus on a thought long enough to have it from start to finish," but she could "ponder a poem for days." Lorde possessed an admirable, innate resistance to the phallogocentric "white pencil," to being, as she put it, "locked into the mouth of the dragon." She had seen the many errors committed in the name of "thought/thinking," and, furthermore, had formed some precious convictions about her own life that "defied thought." She seems always to have been seeking what she calls, in *Our Dead Behind Us*, "an emotional language / in which to abbreviate time."

Gloria T. Hull, "Living on the Line: Audre Lorde and *Our Dead Behind Us*," *Changing Our Own Words: Essays on Criticism, Theory, and Writing by Black Women*, ed. Cheryl A. Wall (New Brunswick, NJ: Rutgers University Press, 1989), pp. 170–71

ANN LOUISE KEATING   According to both Chinosole and ⟨Claudine⟩ Raynaud, Lorde's poetic voice has its roots in her mother's "special and secret relationship with words." But by focusing solely on the specialness of the mother's relationship with words—on her euphemisms for unmentionable body parts and the puzzling phrases reminiscent of her island home—it is easy to overlook the effects of her secrecy. Although Lorde does "use the written word to translate the oral poetry of her mother's language," it is the mother's secretiveness, her selective silence, which shapes the daughter's lifelong belief in language's power. In an early section of the novel ⟨*Zami: A New Spelling of My Name*⟩ entitled "How I Became a Poet," Lorde sharply distinguishes her own voice from her mother's by declaring that when her *"strongest words"* remind her of those she heard as a child, she must reevaluate everything she wishes to say. Again, in an interview with Adrienne Rich, Lorde contrasts her own words with those of her mother and explains that while she was growing up she wanted nothing to do with her mother's use of language.

From her mother's silence, Lorde learns the importance of words. As she asserts in "The Transformation of Silence into Language and Action," speech is essential and silence does not really protect. In both this essay and *Zami*, she equates "the tyrannies of silence" with white patriarchal oppression and insists that without language, without the ability to express themselves, women of all colors are powerless to control their own lives. They must "swallow" the words of the father until they "sicken and die . . . still in silence." Forced to accept the language of others, they lack self-definition and are invisible—even to themselves. This inability to reject patriarchal language and speak freely leads to further oppression. As Lorde explains in a 1978 interview, when the dominant ideology is so interiorized that it becomes a part of women's consciousness, they repress both their own speech and that of others, they become the oppressor and the oppressed. Lorde associates her mother's use of language with this internalized oppression. During childhood, her father and mother spoke as "one unfragmentable unappealable voice." Together, they chose to withhold "vital pieces of information," the realities of racism in everyday life, from their daughter. Perhaps most importantly, Lorde writes that it was "from the white man's tongue" that her mother learned to use language defensively, to ignore or misname those aspects of reality she was unable to change.

    Ann Louise Keating, " 'Making Our Shattered Faces Whole': The Black Goddess and Audre Lorde's Revision of Patriarchal Myth," *Frontiers* 13, No. 1 (1992): 22–23

KATIE KING   Gay girls selectively reveal and conceal the paradoxes of race and sex. Lorde wants to remember the connections among women; doing so requires putting together the sexual and psychic attractions to white women with the realities of racism and survival. A little desperately, since the assurance is only partial, but also generously, Lorde offers: 'Lesbians were probably the only Black and white women in New York City in the fifties who were making any real attempt to communicate with each other.' Writing it over at another point, Lorde adds qualifications and alters emphasis—'*So far as I could see*, gay-girls were the only Black and white women who were even talking to each other'—and generalises beyond New York City ('*in this country* in the 1950s') while dismissing the possibilities of other political solidarities: 'outside of the empty rhetoric of patriotism and political movements' (emphasis added). The sacred bond of gayness, always insufficient, is still motivating and hungry. Inside the lesbian bar the meanings of the intersections of race and sex implicitly shift from circumstance to circumstance, and these shifts are reflected in subtle rewritings, partial repetitions, revealing editing, reordered valuations and reordered connections. These shifts destabilise the oppositions black/white, butch/femme, Ky-Ky/role-playing, celebration of women's community/internalisation of homophobia.

    One could easily read *Zami*'s depiction of the bar as an indictment of role-playing, even as a 1982 historical reinscription, a response against lesbian s/m with an assimilation of 1950s role-playing into a paradigm of dominance/submission that must be politically rejected. This is surely one lacquered written layer of history in *Zami*. Some of Lorde's judgements and interpretations of the meanings of role-playing are straightforwardly rejecting and certainly spoken from the early 1980s in retrospective analysis:

> For some of us, role-playing reflected all the depreciating attitudes toward women which we loathed in straight society. It was a rejection of these roles that had drawn us to 'the life' in the first place. Instinctively, without particular theory or political position or dialectic, we recognized oppression as oppression, no matter where it came from.

As Lorde writes on here, she offers two simultaneous connections, connections both retrospective and historically separated out. First, she puts role-playing in association with 'the pretend world of dominance/submission'. At the same time, she also depicts its former hegemony in lesbian culture, a hegemony effectively routed now as reflected in the current weight of judgement against it. Lorde continues: 'But those lesbians who had carved some niche in the pretend world of dominance/subordination, rejected what they called our "confused" life style, and they were in the majority.' ⟨. . .⟩

Audre Lorde's biomythography *Zami*, with its focus on the intersection of race and sexuality in the lesbian bar, does not at all reflect the same story as D'Emilio's *Sexual Politics, Sexual Communities*, which is told at the intersection of class and political affiliation. None the less, *Zami*, with its lacquered histories—restricted, salvaged, dreaming of choice and its absence, even at times also 'whitelisting' the gay past—constructs lesbian personal and political identity out of many of the same resources and materials. These resources, materials, and also political investments mark our current productions of gay identities. *Zami* manages too to exemplify what Chicana theorist Chela Sandoval calls 'oppositional consciousness'—in the *rewritings themselves* of the meanings of the bar scene and in the transparent *processes* of rewriting which reveal the locations of the intersections of race, sexuality, language, culture, class, education, age and politics.

The value of this kind of process-bound political specificity I have learned about most clearly from Sandoval and Cherríe Moraga. I believe these two theorists describe especially convincingly the complexities of political identity, as they use creative and intellectual tools made within those overlapping feminist territories, 'the politics of identity' and 'the politics of sexuality'. Lorde belongs with these and other political workers, often women of colour, who are now powerfully reconstructing feminism.

Katie King, "Audre Lorde's Lacquered Layerings: The Lesbian Bar as a Site of Literary Production," *New Lesbian Criticism: Literary and Cultural Readings*, ed. Sally Munt (New York: Harvester Wheatsheaf, 1992), pp. 56–57, 69–70

ANNA WILSON   In the absense of a Black tradition, then, Lorde's biomythography *Zami* initially constructs a lesbian existence that has needs and features in common with the lesbian myth produced by white Anglo-American novelists. Her sexual coming out is described within a series of metaphors for recognition familiar from that tradition: making love is 'like coming home to a joy I was meant for'; the act of lesbian sex is naturalised through being presented as a return to an original knowledge that the protagonist has temporarily forgotten: 'wherever I touched, felt right and completing, as if I had been born to make love to this woman, and was remembering her body rather than learning it deeply for the first time.' This is a country of the body rather than of a people. Audre's community as a young lesbian in New York is defined as sexuality, and it is a community that attempts the utopian separation and newness of lesbian nation: 'We were reinventing the word together'; 'we had no patterns to follow, except our own needs and our own unthought-out dreams'. Yet membership in such a community is purchased at the price of non-recognition of Blackness; Lorde repeatedly describes Audre's 'invisibility' to the white lesbian community as Black; she is admitted only under the assumption of sameness. The lesbian community believes in itself as obliterating difference, 'that as lesbians, we were all outsiders and all equal in our outsiderhood. "We're all niggers," [Muriel, Audre's white lover] used to say.' Yet in Lorde's analysis the lesbian community is not elsewhere but is rather a microcosm of the world outside ⟨. . .⟩ In the white model, the real world recedes before the lesbian community's power to redefine: one reclothed oneself in a new identity and a new way of relating. It is one of Orlando's freedoms in Virginia Woolf's imaginary biography that s/he is able effortlessly to switch between costumes; her sexual fluidity is signalled by this flexibility, and in the same moment it indicates a crucial aspiration: the capacity both to switch between costumes and to cross-dress stands for freedom from gender imprisonment. George Sand said of her experience of cross-dressing, 'My clothes knew no fear.' But for Audre a rigidly stratified dress-code, each item signifying a particular class or role position, expresses not freedom of play but her imprisonment within a system of hierarchised differences. The 'uncharted territory' that she finds in trying to discover new ways of relating in 'a new world of women' is not just uncharted but inaccessible: there is no pathway for the Black lesbian nation. It is from this experience that Lorde constructs the 'house of difference' that she finally articulates as 'our place'; it is a refusal of the aspiration to unity that lesbian nation encodes. The 'house of difference', then, is a movement away from otherworldliness. It accepts the inevitability of a material world where class, race, gender all continue to exist. It is, therefore, a step back towards acknowledging the necessity of reasserting ties of identity with the Black community.

> Anna Wilson, "Lorde and the African-American Tradition: When the Family Is Not Enough," *New Lesbian Criticism: Literary and Cultural Readings*, ed. Sally Munt (New York: Harvester Wheatsheaf, 1992), 81–82

◈ Bibliography

The First Cities. 1968.

Cables to Rage. 1970.

From a Land Where Other People Live. 1973.

New York Head Shop and Museum. 1974.

Between Our Selves. 1976.

Coal. 1976.

The Black Unicorn. 1978.

Use of the Erotic: The Erotic as Power. 1978.

The Cancer Journals. 1980.

A Litany of Survival. 1981.

Chosen Poems, Old and New. 1982, 1992 (as *Undersong: Chosen Poems, Old and New*).

Zami: A New Spelling of My Name. 1982.

Sister Outsider: Essays and Speeches. 1984.

I Am Your Sister: Black Women Organizing across Sexualities. 1985.

Our Dead Behind Us. 1986.

A Burst of Light. 1988.

Apartheid U.S.A. ⟨with *Our Common Enemies, Our Common Cause* by Merle
    Woo⟩. 1990.
Hell under God's Orders: Hurricane Hugo in St. Croix—Disaster and Survival
    (with Gloria I. Joseph and Hortense M. Rowe). 1990.
Need: A Chorale for Black Women Voices. 1990.
The Marvelous Arithmetics of Distance: Poems 1987–1992. 1993.

Thylias Moss
b. 1954

THYLIAS MOSS was born Thylias Rebecca Brasier on February 27, 1954, in Cleveland, Ohio, the only child of Calvin Theodore and Florida Missouri Gaiter Brasier. Both of Thylias's parents came from the South: her father originated from Cowan, Tennessee, and worked for the Cardinal Tire Company, while her mother was the daughter of a farmer from Valhermosa Springs, Alabama. Thylias grew up in a loving and stable environment, with her parents encouraging her youthful attempts at literature: she wrote a short story at the age of six and a poem at seven.

After graduating from Alexander Hamilton Junior High School and John Adams High School, Thylias entered Syracuse University. She remained there for two years (1971–73) but found the racial tensions at the college difficult to endure and withdrew. Shortly afterward, in July 1973, she married John Lewis Moss, a man she had met at the New Bethlehem Baptist Church in Cleveland when she was sixteen.

Moss eventually returned to college, this time attending Oberlin and receiving a B.A. in creative writing in 1981. Two years later she earned an M.A. from the University of New Hampshire. In that same year, 1983, she published her first book of poetry, *Hosiery Seams on a Bowlegged Woman*. Moss had won the Academy of American Poets College Prize in 1982 for the poem "Coming of Age in Sanduski" and was encouraged by the Cleveland State University Poetry Center to compile a volume of her poetry. *Hosiery Seams* attracted relatively little attention but was representative of many of the themes found in Moss's work: deep concern about the role of both minorities and women in society, a religious sensibility that is nonetheless highly critical of the social and intellectual repressiveness of conventional religion, and a probing of her own mental and emotional states as she encounters the varied phenomena of life.

Moss has received many awards and grants to continue her work, including grants from the Kenan Charitable Trust and the National Endowment for the Arts and a fellowship from the Artists' Foundation of Massachusetts.

Since the mid-1980s she has been teaching at Phillips Andover Academy in Massachusetts.

Moss subsequently published three books of poetry in three years: *Pyramid of Bone* (1989), *At Redbones* (1990), and *Rainbow Remnants in Rock Bottom Ghetto Sky* (1991). The first, solicited by Charles Rowell of the University Press of Virginia, was first runner-up for the National Book Critics Circle Award. Moss attained celebrity with *Rainbow Remnants*, which won the Wytter Bynner Award. She has won other awards as well, including the Pushcart Prize and the Whiting Writer Award.

In 1993 Moss published a children's book, *I Want to Be*, and *Small Congregations*, a volume containing selections from her earlier work along with new poems. She is at work on a collection of short stories and another volume of poetry.

Critical Extracts

UNSIGNED   This ⟨*Hosiery Seams on a Bowlegged Woman*⟩ is a fitting title for Thylias Moss's first book of poems because in it she reveals how women-related subjects such as marriage, motherhood, rape, abortion, and the complicated emotions between fathers and daughters all contribute to the slight bending of a sensitive individual's poetic vision. She builds many of her images and metaphors on passages from the Bible and rituals in the Baptist church. ⟨. . .⟩ In several poems, she explores her own ethnic roots as an American with Cherokee, Choctaw, and African ancestry; however, Moss is not calling for bold, public, political action as do some of the black women poets in Erlene Stetson's *Black Sister* or Amiri and Amina Baraka's anthology *Confirmation*. Instead, Moss is at her best as an artist when she is engaged in the autobiographical mode—the act of self-discovery through writing one's personal history.

Unsigned, [Review of *Hosiery Seams on a Bowlegged Woman*], *Choice* 21, No. 6 (February 1984): 823

UNSIGNED   If Thylias Moss's résumé is sedate (attended Oberlin, teaches at Phillips Academy, has earned an artist's fellowship), her poetry is anything but. These poems ⟨*Pyramid of Bone*⟩ are raw, violent, full of anger, self-loathing, and defiance. And there is humor, albeit perverse, as in "The Undertaker's Daughter Feels Neglect"; like her father, whose wife "played dead" at the conception, she is "attracted / to things that can't run away from me." Moss's imagination is fantastical and mythical—she reads the minds both of a seamstress and of God.

> Unsigned, [Review of *Pyramid of Bone*], *Virginia Quarterly Review* 65, No. 3 (Summer 1989): 100

SUE STANDING   If *At Redbones* were a lightbulb, it would be 300 watt; if it were whiskey, it would be 200 proof; if it were a mule, it would have an awfully big kick. The poems in Thylias Moss's third collection ⟨. . .⟩ crackle with wit and wild surmise. In Moss's poems, wild women might get the blues, but the meek don't inherit the earth. Apothegms follow one another like a series of karate blows: "Absence of prejudice is a white lie"; "Birds of prey aren't holy"; "Monastic silences govern many marriages." ⟨. . .⟩

Sometimes Moss takes a one-shot idea and rides it a little too hard, as in "Faith in a Glass" (the speaker keeps faith instead of dentures in a glass by the bed) or "Provolone Baby" (variations on the cliché of throwing the baby out with the bathwater). But while a few of the poems are slight, they are never predictable. And when she's on target, as she is most of the time, Moss's verbal energy and righteous anger fuse into a cocktail as potent as one you might get at Redbones, the bar to which the book title refers and in which several poems in the book are set: "You go to Redbones after / you've been everywhere else"; "Free love had / been Redbones since black unemployment / and credit saturation."

In *At Redbones*, the neo-surrealism of Moss's earlier work has been transformed into a powerful blend of riveting imagery and dead-on social commentary. The communion wafers, grits, and sugar of these poems are "put on the table for surgery, not feast."

> Sue Standing, [Review of *At Redbones*], *Boston Review* 16, No. 1 (February 1991): 28

GLORIA T. HULL   ⟨Moss⟩ possesses absolutely stunning poetic skill and wields a kind of deceptively prose-like line and narrative sensibility that are still loaded with brilliant images, word play, and pregnant ellipses. This skill she unites with one of the bleakest, most sardonic visions I have ever encountered in an African American woman writer (for a comparison, think of Adrienne Kennedy, although Moss is the more assured and palatable of the two). With Moss, we have to give up cultural shibboleths about family, religion, nurturing, strength, and survival and be confronted with a lack of hope/hopefulness, which I admit was somehow disturbing to me. Here is the imprint of a casualty who not only walks among us, but speaks with eloquent savagery about the lost battles and doomed, ongoing war. As careful as I am about autobiographical criticism, I would nevertheless like to know more about the person who set this world in motion. ⟨. . .⟩

⟨. . .⟩ The entire book ⟨At Redbones⟩ is filled with ⟨. . .⟩ bloody Eucharistic imagery, Biblical lore, sacrilegious bitterness, and existential reliance on the ravaged self within a malevolently regimented universe—all juxtaposed with quotidian matter from our daily (white and black) lives. The only redemption here is the seeing, not the vision.

Gloria T. Hull, "Covering Ground," *Belles Lettres* 6, No. 3 (Spring 1991): 3–4

MARILYN NELSON WANIEK   Last week when two of my gradu-ate students looked up for breath from a discussion about who owns the signifiers in *Invisible Man*, I thought, "Say what?" But I said, "That's very interesting" and wondered silently whether we could take our break a few minutes earlier than usual. So I feel I must define my use of the word "interesting" when I write here that Thylias Moss's third collection, *At Redbones*, is a very interesting book. What I mean is that although there are individual passages which seem private or weak to me, I recognize that a fine rage is at play in these pages. Moss's rage is distinctly Black, but more than that; it is the rage of faith. From an apparently Catholic upbringing and equipped with a sound theological background, Moss asks wide ranging questions about contemporary society and world history, confessing her doubt while offering an authentically Christian response. ⟨. . .⟩

Moss's quarrel is not with Christ, but with the distant silence of God, who, in "The Adversary," is

> . . . a man, subject to
> the quirks of maleness, among them that need
> for adversary, for worthy opponent, for just short
> of equal. And that's Satan, the runner up . . .

In "Spilled Sugar" she tells us that "we have to redefine God; he is not love at all. He is longing." God's silence allows the reading of Christianity which turns it into an instrument of oppression, not of liberation. For the ghetto-bound people who crowd the pages of her book, Christianity teaches utter submission. ⟨. . .⟩

Yet Moss rejects neither God nor Christ. She understands the ironic liberation of Christian love. In "A Catcher for an Atomic Bouquet," a poem which begins with a reference to the PBS series about the Civil Rights Movement, "Eyes on the Prize," she describes a life filled with the family responsibilities we recognize as characteristic of many Black women's lives: "a / baby from a teen-ager's body, a daughter from / a sister-in-law declared unfit." Where is the vaunted prize, she asks;

> When the baby tugs at me he is no prize; a prize
> just doesn't force its acceptance. You could
> easily look at him thinking how you didn't bring
> him into the world, he isn't really your
> responsibility. You just signed your name on
> a sheaf of paper that could have been one of the
> usual bad checks. You know, however, who's doing
> all the insisting that the baby stay in the world.
> Who's loving the insistence. Insistence is the prize.

In the suffering love of the people—most of them Black women—who crowd the pages of this collection, Moss finds an image of sainthood. Love becomes a powerful liberating force, a Eucharist of human community ⟨. . .⟩

At *Redbones* is a powerful and a painful book, a book which takes many risks. It's very interesting. I admire it greatly.

Marilyn Nelson Waniek, "A Multitude of Dreams," *Kenyon Review* 13, No. 4 (Fall 1991): 220–23

SUZANNE GARDINIER   Thylias Moss's poetic re-vision of history ⟨in *Rainbow Remnants in Rock Bottom Ghetto Sky*⟩ comes through a polished magnifying glass, in an intensely focused beam with the power to expose and to burn. ⟨. . .⟩

This poet has published three books in three years ⟨. . .⟩ and the work is similar enough to be taken as a whole, divided by chance into three parts. ⟨. . .⟩

Pyramid of Bone is dedicated to "my mother who made it to the dean's list of preferred housekeepers; she is a maid of honor." In the three books there are several poems that center on her; but the most revealing glimpses come in the middle of discussions of other things ⟨. . .⟩

In *Rainbow Remnants*, the poet's mother appears most fully in "Poem for My Mothers and Other Makes of Asafetida"; asafetida is a folk medicine, one the poet calls "my church in a bottle": "nasty asafetida, tastes like the bootleg, jackleg / medicine it is / curing me as only generations can . . ." In this poem Moss's sharp humor is evident, but doesn't require understatement; the praise words roll on and on, incantatory, invoking the unlikely character of what heals, searching it out of its hiding places:

> . . . there are
> no eyes except the ones I look into and fall in love, right
> into Mama's pupils, the past dark with dense ancestry, all
> who came before having to fit into the available space of
> history which is existence's memory and year after year
> the overcrowding worsens . . .
> . . . asafetida still on the shelf, oil in the puddle
> still ghetto stained glass, still rainbow remnants in rock
> bottom ghetto sky like a promise of no more tears, asafetida
> bottle floating there, some kind of Moses, some kind of
> deliverer . . .

You don't have to walk far from here to find the deep, nourishing current that is this poet's preoccupation with God. These books chart the stages of her private re-creation; in a note to "The Warmth of Hot Chocolate" in *The Best American Poetry 1989*, she writes that she will have none of "that voyeur God I met in Sunday school before old enough to start kindergarten, not the one who created weak flesh then condemned, *damned* for that very weakness; not him." The path to reconciliation is not simple for this poet of sass and backtalk, who describes a buffalo stampede as "footsteps whose sound / is my heart souped up / doctored, ninety pounds / running off a semi's invisible engine." ("The Rapture of Dry Ice Burning Off Skin as the Moment of the Soul's Apotheosis"—what a maker of titles she is!) Her nearest saint is Thomas, "jugging his hands into / wounds" ("Eucharistic Options"); her verse theology pivots on the argumentative distinctions and qualifications of a Talmudic scholar, laced with "Not even," "Yet also," "But" and "Besides," and with credos of unbelief. "Now the cyclone spirals above my house," she writes in the last poem of *Pyramid of Bone*; "I vow not to go to heaven / if that's the only ladder."

Suzanne Gardinier, "Bootleg, Jackleg Medicine: Curing as Only Generations Can," *Parnassus: Poetry in Review* 17, No. 1 (1992): 66–69, 71–72

ALVIN AUBERT   There is a bountiful tension in Thylias Moss's poetry between her Afro- and Euro-American cultural and literary lineages. Her inventive amalgamation of material from these two sources generates a strikingly witty and allusive style. The result is surrealistic, binary poems in which the *real* is never overwhelmed, as it might easily be, by its dream opposite. The poems are shielded from that hazard, principally, by the concreteness and humor with which they emphasize important issues.

⟨. . .⟩ From her first publications, *Hosiery Seams on a Bowlegged Woman* (1983) and *Pyramid of Bone* (1989), Moss establishes a "province" in which imaginatively conceived speculation lays claim to bona fide cognition. Through a unique, extraordinarily complex, surrealistic combination of the real and the fantastic, Moss claims magic realism as a place for sociopolitical discourse—even a singularly appropriate territory for that purpose, in its radical unsettling of the senses and concurrent limbering of the imagination for heightened perceptions and keener perspectives on things. ⟨. . .⟩

Moss's poems reflect not only a deep emotional capacity on the part of their personae but a profound intellectual commitment as well, in that balancing of emotion and thought many still acknowledge as essential to the creation of fine poetry. Her eyes seek everywhere for apt juxtapositions, and they are marvelously comprehending. Her ear is finely tuned to the right intonation and pitch, and her precise, at times metaphysical wit never fails to spark life into the experiences she renders with unfailing fidelity throughout her work.

Moss's poetry sensitively and unapologetically melds materials from the poet's African- and European-American cultural and literary traditions, while it affirms universal human values. The poems are richly complex and not always immediately accessible, but that is part of their aesthetic value; they impel re-reading as—to borrow an expression from ex-slave Frederick Douglass's *Narrative of the Life*—the light breaks upon us by degrees.

Alvin Aubert, "Bountiful Tension," *American Book Review* 13, No. 6 (February—March 1992): 29

ALDON L. NIELSEN   If the poems of Thylias Moss have always employed an imagery more insistently surreal than ⟨Lucille⟩ Clifton's, they worry some of the same blue notes. Often that imagery adds just the needed grace note, as in the closing of the poem "Lunchcounter Freedom": "When knocked from the stool / my body takes its shape from what / it falls into. The white man cradles / his tar baby. Each magus in turn. / He fathered it, it looks just like him / the spitting image. He can't let go of / his future. The menu offers tuna fish, / grits, beef in a sauce like desire. / He is free to choose from available / choices. An asterisk marks the special." Few among us can bring such particulars of new comprehension to such well-known events.

Aldon L. Nielsen, [Review of *At Redbones*], *MultiCultural Review* 1, No. 2 (April 1992): 73–74

MARK JARMAN   There is a handful of successful poems in Thylias Moss's fourth book ⟨*Rainbow Remnants in Rock Bottom Ghetto Sky*⟩. One of them, "Poem for My Mothers and Other Makers of Asafetida," which contains the phrase that is the book's title, is first rate. These poems succeed for many of the same reasons that the others fail. Moss constructs an elaborate syntax, often discursive, yet seeking always to make distant connections and to illuminate them by the flame of her insight and imagination. When she succeeds, the results are breathtaking ⟨. . .⟩ But often Moss does not find her way. Though every poem contains something brought to radiance, many poems begin nebulously and grope their way to an almost crystallized argument-in-an-image; or, after a clear start, the poem ends in murk. Sometimes the murk is opaque syntax; sometimes it is changing subject in mid-stream. ⟨. . .⟩

Moss's large and expansive poems many times seem like exercises in association. She gives us everything she has thought of without pruning. I am ambivalent about the necessity of all the verbiage in her poems, but recognize that she is trying to manipulate a narrative syntax that poets like Norman Dubie and Roger Weingarten have often worked with. The difference between these poets and Moss is that she is not narrative at all. Charles Simic, who chose her book for the National Poetry Series, calls her a "visionary storyteller," but she tells no stories. She pirouettes in place, flinging sparks and cinders. The book is quite a performance. Curiously one of the best poems is "Interpretation of a Poem by Frost." It deserves a place in future anthologies and ends movingly with an echo of Frost's most famous poem:

> She has promises to keep . . .
> And miles to go, more than the distance from Africa to
>   Andover
> more than the distance from black to white . . .

I wish I liked all the poems better than I do, but while I admire her ambition, I find that Moss shows a kind of complacence in assuming that putting one thing on one side of an equals sign and one on another is imagination. Consider her image of a bible in "Congregations."

> His bible warms his hands, never
> leaves them, a dialysis, transfusion that keeps him alive . . .

A dialysis is not a transfusion. In "Time for Praise," extending a metaphor of a car as a whale that has swallowed Jonah and his family, she is led to call a Toyota "a whale with a door." Finally, this is the first poet I have encountered who, in the poem "News," actually has used the word *hopefully* as it is currently employed, which is to say incorrectly. Moss's errors appear to be the result of hurried composition. Often they are part of her poetry's dazzling improvisatory effects, but just as often they are not.

Mark Jarman, "The Curse of Discursiveness," *Hudson Review* 45, No. 1 (Spring 1992): 163–65

RITA SIGNORELLI-PAPPAS   I wish that I could ⟨. . .⟩ recommend the work of Thylias Moss for its graceful staying power, but I cannot. ⟨. . .⟩ While the poems in her fourth collection, *Rainbow Remnants in Rock Bottom Ghetto Sky*, are attractive in their verbal energy, most fail to cohere.

No less a poet than Charles Simic praises Moss's "wildness," but what he sees as a virtue strikes me as a central deficit of her work. That is, she keeps the surfaces of her poems so active that meaning seldom has a chance to clear. In poem after poem, images are introduced but not expanded to allow reader involvement, and questions raised go unresolved.

Moss's problem with writing accessible work becomes apparent in the book's very first poem, "Renewal at the Pediatric Hospice." The title suggests that the speaker has gained something from seeing children under the duress of imminent death, but the tone of the poem that follows is oddly breezy and disaffected. The focus on the children's brave suffering never successfully condenses; exactly how and why they provided inspiration is not apparent as the maker watches them:

> fill the whites of their eyes with snow, sculpt
> the iris into the pupil's plow that clears
> the field of vision for spring in which the white
> becomes shells and the irises, emerging chicks.

In this passage the random movement from snow-playing, to sculpting, to plowing, and, finally, to the first stirrings of spring in the short space of four lines distracts and confuses; there is no recovery time for the reader to make the transition from one disparate action to the next. ⟨. . .⟩

Still, Moss's work is rich in inventiveness. If in time she achieves a greater artistic discipline, we can look forward to a poet of considerable power.

Rita Signorelli-Pappas, "Poets Practiced and Premiering," *Belles Lettres* 7, No. 4 (Summer 1992): 63

UNSIGNED   A much-lauded poet brings her gifts for stretching language and patterning images to the perennial, pedestrian query, "What do you want to be?" An African American girl ⟨in *I Want to Be*⟩ ponders this question as she meanders home, and her thoughts seem to take as many detours as she does on her journey. She begins playfully—"I made a grass mustache, a dandelion beard, and bird nest toupee"—and grows ever more abstract: "I double-dutched with strands of rainbow. Then I fastened the strands to my hair and my toes and became a fiddle that sunbeams played. Then I sang with the oxygen choir." When she reaches home, the girl voices a string of aspirations: "I want to be quiet but not so quiet that nobody can hear me. I also want to be sound, a whole orchestra with two bassoons and an army of cellos. Sometimes I want to be just the triangle, a tinkle that sounds like an itch." Some readers may need to be guided through the kaleidoscope of metaphors that tumble across the pages; considering each image individually may elicit the greatest response.

Unsigned, [Review of *I Want to Be*], *Publishers Weekly*, 5 July 1993, p. 71

▦ *Bibliography*

Hosiery Seams on a Bowlegged Woman. 1983.
Pyramid of Bone. 1989.
At Redbones. 1990.
Rainbow Remnants in Rock Bottom Ghetto Sky. 1991.
I Want to Be. 1993.
Small Congregations: New and Selected Poems. 1993.

⊞ ⊞ ⊞

Carolyn M. Rodgers
b. 1945

CAROLYN MARIE RODGERS was born on December 14, 1945, in Chicago, the daughter of Clarence and Bazella (Colding) Rodgers. After attending public schools in Chicago, she entered the University of Illinois in 1960 but left the next year; she then enrolled at Roosevelt University in Chicago, where she received a B.A. in 1965.

During college and after graduation, Rodgers held various jobs to support herself, mostly in community service. She also became a political activist in the 1960s, fighting for the rights of blacks in a white society and the rights of women in a male society. Rodgers met various black writers in Chicago and joined the Organization of Black American Culture Writers Workshop and Gwendolyn Brooks's Writers Workshop, where she worked on her poetry.

Rodgers's first collection, *Paper Soul*, was published in 1968; it won the Conrad Kent Rivers Memorial Fund Award. The poems in this volume reveal Rodgers's revolutionary ideology and are written in dialect, often with experimental grammar and syntax. *Songs of a Black Bird* and *2 Love Raps* appeared the next year. In 1975 Rodgers published *how i got ovah: New and Selected Poems*, which brought her much celebrity and critical acclaim (it was nominated for a National Book Award). Revolutionary politics still appear in the collection, but overall it is highly autobiographical, with the focus shifting from the communal to the personal. In the process of fashioning her own rhythms and examining more personal topics, Rodgers has perhaps written more original and distinctive poems in *how i got ovah* than in her previous collections. Her next volume, *The Heart as Ever Green* (1978), also reveals a noticeable maturity of theme and refinement of technique.

After spending five years as a social worker, Rodgers began a teaching career in 1968 at Columbia College in Chicago. She has subsequently taught at the University of Washington, Albany State College, Malcolm X College, and Indiana University. In 1983 she received an M.A. from the University of Chicago. Her poetic output has been slim in the last decade or so, although she has published two more collections, *Translation* (1980) and *Finite Forms* (1985), and a novel, *A Little Lower Than Angels* (1984). She has also written short stories and has served as a book reviewer for the *Chicago Daily News* and a columnist for the *Milwaukee Courier*.

◈ *Critical Extracts*

SARAH WEBSTER FABIO   "Great!" was my first reaction to *Paper Soul*. "Why great?" was "something else." Carolyn Rodgers seems to know what she is about in each poem, and she does whatever it is she sets out to do with utmost precision. I think that this mastery of material is very important.

Hoyt Fuller's description of this writer in the introduction is very appropriate, and his comments on her poetry intimate the integration of artist and artistry so evident in her work. She is "boldly eloquent, brandishing words like steel knuckles . . . sometimes cold . . . young and vulnerable and open to life . . . But she is real . . ." And of her work:

> Her poems are bridges on which the heart and will may pass from the world her disgust would level, to the world her love would build. Her prose is spare and angular, geared to essence, but hard only when she wills it; and always it is stamped with an elegance so effortless and deep that it seems inborn: it is like her own frame, slim and straight, and as subtly feminine as a virgin's blush.

"Eulogy" and "Now Ain't That Love" are fine poems: the first is filled with pathos and rhetoric of concern and the latter with the stutter of fluttering pulse, knocking knees, drooled words marking a bad case of puppy love. Sometimes, in a poem such as "Soliloquy," the aim is to project a human voice and the special quality of that voice—the rhythm, force, persuasion in the direction, in this case 13 words. The title and the description of the setting, ironically, use twice as much language as does the actual capsule drama; this economy of words is a very black thing, I think, almost as black as the young fellow's cool stance toward an affair and the excess of feeling involved by it which threatens to "sweat up! / mah / do . . ."

Sarah Webster Fabio, [Review of *Paper Soul*], *Negro Digest* 17, No. 11 (September 1968): 51

DUDLEY RANDALL   She has satiric and witty poems also. "The Last M. F.," where she renounces the word *muthafucka* but uses it no less than 11 times, is clever. "Year, i is uh shootin off at the mouth" uses surprises effectively. "Greek Crazeology," I think, fails. The poet doesn't keep her cool enough to generate wit or humor. The victim should be impaled on a jest, but there is no jest here. It's interesting to note how in amorphous free verse there is a striving toward shape, toward form, like water shaping itself into raindrops as it falls from clouds. Often it takes the form of repetition or parallelism. In this poem the words *ducks, weeds, dogs, tics* and *worms* are repeated like the studied repetitions of some satiric poem. It cuts like a knife. It has brevity, surprise, and point.

There are other poems of delicate lyricism, intense feelings: "What Color Is Lonely," "6:30," "Breakthrough," "Me, In Kulu Se & Karma," with fine lines like "the sweet changes we are as Blacks;" "hours that / trickle befo me like unfreezin water;" "spread my fingers / in hair coarse thickets;" "and wish us me to sleep."

In her second book, Carolyn Rodgers shows herself as a sensitive and gifted poet, with variety and richness. The flaws and fripperies are minor, and could have been eliminated by careful revision, scrupulous editing (but again the poet has to heed the editor), or frank comment from a friend (but again the poet has to heed the friend; some poets jump bad at criticism).

Dudley Randall, [Review of *Songs of a Black Bird*], *Black World* 19, No. 10 (August 1970): 52

DON L. LEE   Carolyn Rodgers reveals obvious elements of her personality in her poetry. In her first book, *Paper Soul*, there are glimpses of greatness. ⟨. . .⟩ The poems are controlled and heavy. For a first book, she definitely cuts the smell of newness. In her latest book, *Songs of a Black Bird*, she continues to break rules and suggest the real, but doesn't carry the power or the creativeness of *Paper Soul*. There is feeling in the new book, but nothing to match "Now Ain't That Love" or "For Some Black Men" from her first volume.

The first "pome" in the new book is not a poem. It is not even a prose poem and belongs more in the category of a short story or prose sketch. "Jesus was crucified or It Must Be Deep" is a good piece of work but does not stand up as poetry. The only part that approaches poetry in style, line arrangement and images is the first page, but beyond that we have pure and good prose. In the poem "Greek Crazeology," she fails by using too many words. ⟨. . .⟩

Yet to sense the weaknesses of Sister Rodgers in a few poems only makes us more aware of her strengths in others. She works well in poems like "Breakthrough," "Me, in Kula Se & Karma" and "for h. w. fuller." It is difficult to believe that the care, time and effort that produced these poems went into the book as a whole. If she had been as careful with many of the poems in this second volume as she is in "for h. w. fuller," the book would have been a success.

Don L. Lee, *Dynamite Voices I: Black Poets of the 1960's* (Detroit: Broadside Press, 1971), pp. 54, 57, 59

JOSEPH McLELLAN   These short lyrics ⟨*how i got ovah*⟩ were written over a period of years and deal with a variety of subjects: revolution, generation conflict, people known and loved and lost, growing up in Chicago where "just living was guerrilla warfare," and a slow discovery of the enduring values in a black religious heritage that was once scorned. Read together, they blend finally into one eloquent poem which is the story of a life.

Joseph McLellan, [Review of *how i got ovah*], *Washington Post Book World*, 18 May 1975, p. 4

UNSIGNED   This collection of new and selected poems ⟨*how i got ovah*⟩ gives a representative view of the sensitivity and integrity Miss Rodgers brings to the act of writing black poetry. Her forte is the personal narrative poem, the impact of which is strongest in oral performance. Thus a number of the poems here, unfortunately, suggest the poet is more interested in pure experience than in rendering experience as poetry. Nevertheless, the poet treats spiritual aspects of black life, the getting over, with a tenderness that is rare in the new black poetry.

Unsigned, [Review of *how i got ovah*], *Virginia Quarterly Review* 52, No. 1 (Winter 1976): 21, 24

HILDA NJOKI McELROY   It is interesting to note that most of
the poems in *How I Got Ovah* are written in the lyric mode from a first-
person perspective. The *persona* in each poem is so well established and
developed that one feels well acquainted and involved with this speaker in
a very personal manner. Though some poems are deeply personal at times,
the reader/audience is never excluded from these experiences. Probably
because Carolyn Rodgers' works cover such a wide range of human experiences her sermons/songs/tales seem to often be addressed to us though we
know the poet is female and the poems reveal a female *persona*. I have noticed
that male students in my Interpretation of Black Poetry class frequently find
Rodgers' works to be equally valid for male or female.

Skillfully utilizing rhythmic devices from our Afrikan oral tradition in
the title poem, "how i got ovah," the *persona* seems to be speaking directly
to those of us in the Black diaspora who share the sufferings of a displaced
people:

> i can tell you
> about them
> i have shaken rivers
> out of my eyes
> i have waded eyelash deep
> have crossed rivers
> have shaken the water weed out
> of my lungs
> have swam for strength
> pulled by strength
> through waterfalls with electric beats
> i have bore the shocks
> of water deep deep
> waterlogs are my bones
> i have shaken the water free of my hair
> have kneeled on the banks
> and kissed my ancestors of the dirt
> whose rich dark root fingers rose up reached out
> grabbed and pulled me rocked me cupped me
> gentle strong and firm
> carried me
> made me swim for strength
> cross rivers
> though i shivered
> was wet was cold
> and wanted to sink down

and float as water, yea—
i can tell you.
i have shaken rivers
out of my eyes. ⟨. . .⟩

In "The Children of Their Sin," Rodgers is like the old Afrikan folk-teller—entertaining and instructing us about our weakness, contradictions and inner conflicts. Combining many devices from the African folk tale, Rodgers deals basically with self-hatred. In order to re-inforce this theme, Rodgers, in a fantastic display of craftpersonship, utilizes present/mythic time, cosmic sounds/rhythms, and vivid imagery. In the present time in part one, the *persona* establishes the irony and contradictions by explaining how she left her job one evening of poet-teaching Black people how to love one another and on the way home she refused to sit next to a Black brother because he looked "mean and hungry, poor and damply cold." Rather, she chose to sit next to a white man because he "was neatly new yorkish antiseptically executive."

Hilda Njoki McElroy, [Review of *how I got ovah*], *Black World* 25, No. 4 (February 1976): 51–52

GEORGE E. KENT   Carolyn M. Rodgers' *how i got ovah* contains new and selected poems from the body of her work. Such older favorites as "Jesus Was Crucified, or It Must Be Deep," "It Is Deep," "Somebody Call," "c. c. rider," "U Name This One," "to Gwen," and "For H. W. Fuller," are included.

Newer poems often involve a revaluation of older values. The simplicities about the black church and religion are re-studied ⟨. . .⟩ The church gets praise for its communal work and for steady building, in contrast to the unproductiveness of the militant rhetoric which criticized it and tried to give instruction. Other successful religious poems include "how i got ovah," "how i got ovah II," and "Living Water." ⟨. . .⟩

The religious poems are occasionally threatened by the attempt to mix religious and hip diction, as the term "shimmy" would illustrate. The poem "Jesus must of been some kind of dude" seems also to suffer from this mixture of diction. In addition to new poems devoted to religion, there are also simply new poems which reveal sharp craftsmanship, and an interesting poem of introduction by Angela Jackson.

George E. Kent, "The 1975 Black Literary Scene: Significant Developments," *Phylon* 37, No. 1 (March 1976): 112–13

WALTER SUBLETTE   Carolyn Rodgers' poetry has received more than mild critical interest for some time. It was considered special well before 1976, when her collection, *How I Got Ovah*, was a National Book Award nominee. Yet since that time, Rodgers' reputation has spread considerably. Her poetry is tightly crafted free verse that unpretentiously combines the black American vernacular and the straightforward American style. It is absent of fashionably extreme attitudes, and achieves a distinct presence by cementing private poetic vision with grim but poignant understanding. In *The Heart as Ever Green*, this fusion of poetic vision and spiritual compassion is extremely pronounced, producing a kind of contemporary black American poetry that is warmly honest, immediately direct, and clearly accessible.

Rodgers makes strong use of the word "heart" in the title. As supported in the poems, the heart is meant to be a reservoir of containment. In it the patiently waiting expectations of all black people are protectively housed. It is a place of necessity from which the black race observes life, the observation itself made tolerable through the realization of inevitable social change. That change will one day bring freedom as well as personal and collective growth. It seems important to realize that the image of the heart is not used to express pessimistic hope, but realized certainty. It is a place of warm solidity, of relative security, whose sustaining power is the awareness of past and present suffering. It is a place of pride and dignity, of indestructible strength and enormous love. And since the heart is suspended in time as an impregnable constant, it is appropriately affixed with the color green in anticipation of the time it may realize its full fruition.

The Heart as Ever Green is a poetic statement on the condition, attitude, and determination of black people. Carolyn Rodgers has given us a strong, dignified, and beautiful book of poems. At the core of this work is a sensibility that is framed in the notion that black suffering will be alleviated in time.

That may be an accurate, perceptive, and honorable belief, but is nonetheless one that not all black contemporary poets would agree with.

Walter Sublette, "Poetic Voices of Hope and Rage," *Chicago Tribune Book World*, 19 November 1978, p. 10

ESTELLA M. SALES   The expression "how I got ovah" slips fluently from black colloquialism into a black gospel song and on into the black slang vernacular with unobstructed ease. Presently it is the title of Carolyn Rodgers' latest volume of poetry, *How I Got Ovah*.

The meaning of the recurring expression is generally defined by its contextual usage and can be appropriately connotative of how one has triumphed spiritually; how one has overcome worldly hardships; how one has outwitted his adversary; or merely how one has swindled his loved ones. In Carolyn Rodgers' book, many of these connotations emerge; however, another unique connotation is given shape by the thematic structuring of the book. The poet writes on the seemingly disjointed and ostensibly contradictory aspects of black life. She is not afraid of the contradictions; she consciously seeks them out, then reconciles their differences by poetically presenting their interrelatedness. The poet 'gets ovah' the waters of confusion that flow between the contradictions by crossing certain metaphorically symbolic bridges. These bridges she comes to recognize are her own inner voice, her ancestral rootedness, her Christian faith, and her parental support. Other supportive structures in the bridges are her church community and her extended black community. So the unique connotation of 'getting ovah' in Carolyn Rodgers' book would be bridging the separating waters, reconciling the contradictions or piecing together the seemingly dichotomous entities of black life.

The major dichotomies that are patterned throughout the book are (1) black revolutionary tactics as opposed to Christian ethics, (2) the black past as opposed to the present, (3) the black younger generation as opposed to the older generation, (4) idealistic dreams as opposed to dead-end awakenings, and (5) the individual poetic voice as opposed to the conscious, collective poetic voice. Often, more than one dichotomous pattern is being dealt with simultaneously in the same poem. ⟨. . .⟩

In her untitled poem (p. 6), the poetic statement is consummated. The persona realizes, after being caught up in a whirlwind of voices, that she is confused and "cannot remember / where to listen." Once away from the screaming voices, silence reflows and the poet returns "cradling creation in the silences." The poet has listened to the (ideological) voices till deafened by them and only after that point does she realize that through creative silence, or listening to her own inner voice, she is able to create. Listening to her own inner voice is her poetic bridge of "getting ovah."

Estella M. Sales, "Contradictions in Black Life: Recognized and Reconciled in *How I Got Ovah*," *CLA Journal* 25, No. 1 (September 1981): 74–75, 81

ANGELENE JAMISON   Rodgers treats a wide range of topics in her poetry, including revolution, love, Black male-female relationships, religion, and the complexities of Black womanhood. Not only does she bring a Black perspective to these subjects, but through keen insight, intuition, and expert craftsmanship she brings the unique vision and perception of the Black woman. Through a skillfully uncluttered use of several literary devices, she convincingly reinterprets the love, pain, longings, struggles, victories, the day-to-day routines of Black people from the point of view of the Black woman. Gracefully courageous enough to explore long-hidden truths, about Black women particularly, her poetry shows honesty, warmth, and love for Black people. Rodgers is a "straight-up" poet, a "singer of sass and blues" with a "sanctified soul." Forcing one to recognize the complexities of being, she "make u testify to truth." Her language "remind u of the people on the corner / her words be leaning on the building there." Eloquently employing various Black linguistic forms, she speaks in the idiom of those whose sentiments she reflects. ". . . country and street and proper too," as Angela Jackson points out, Carolyn Rodgers is "a choir in herself."

Most striking about her poetry was her ability to describe so realistically the emotional dilemmas of the Black female artist in a poem entitled "Breakthrough." Originally published in *Songs of a Black Bird*, "Breakthrough" describes the poet's "tangled feelings . . . about ev'rything. . . ." What is perhaps the most outstanding quality of the poem is the poet's use of rhythmic Black speech and imagery to describe the inner turmoil of the Black woman as artist, and her coming to grips with the confusion.

"Breakthrough" sent me searching for other works by and about this woman who had put in poetic form such feelings and emotions, those with which so many Black women struggle. I discovered there is very little criticism, but there is poetry, poetry which particularly reflects not only an incredible honesty and perception about Black women but an ability to articulate "what Black women mean." With depth and insight, she reveals the fears, insecurities, needs, yearnings, etc., with a poetic "I know, I've been there, I *am* there" realness.

> Angelene Jamison, "Imagery in the Women Poems: The Art of Carolyn Rodgers," *Black Women Writers (1950–1980): A Critical Evaluation*, ed. Mari Evans (New York: Anchor Press/Doubleday, 1984), p. 378

BETTYE J. PARKER-SMITH   It can be fairly accurately claimed that Carolyn Rodgers' artistic achievements have undergone two distinct and clear baptisms. The first can be viewed as being rough-hewn, folk-spirited, and held 'down at the river' amid water moccasins in the face of a glaring midday sun; the climax of a 'swing-lo-sweet-chariot' revival. These were her OBAC (Organization of Black African Culture) years. This organization, a Petri dish for young Black writers of the sixties, was guided principally by the late Hoyt W. Fuller, Jr., then editor of *Black World*, and served, if only temporarily, to arrest the psychological frailty of Carolyn Rodgers, who was "slim and straight, and as subtly feminine as a virgin's blush." Fuller recalled that when he first met her at an OBAC social function, she was "skinny and scared," verbalized an interest in writing, and telegraphed a need to be stroked. Being the unhealthy flower she was, Carolyn Rodgers responded naturally to his quiet mood and healing voice. ⟨. . .⟩ The format of the OBAC workshops helped cushion Rodgers' insecurities; its members provided a strong support system for each other. It was as a member of this literary coterie, this small in-group of novice writers and intellectuals, that she made her initial impact. In introducing her first volume of poetry, *Paper Soul*, Fuller prepared us for what was to come: "Carolyn Rodgers will be heard. She has the artist's gift and the artist's beautiful country." This first period of her writing includes her first three volumes, *Paper Soul*, *2 Love Raps*, and *Song of a Black Bird*. It is characterized by a potpourri of themes and demonstrates her impudence, through the use of her wit, obscenities, the argumentation in her love and revolution poems, and the pain and presence of her mother. She questions the relevance of the Vietnam War, declares war on the cities, laments Malcolm X, and criticizes the contradictory life-style of Blacks. And she glances at God. These are the years that she whipped with the lean switch, often bringing down her wrath with stinging, sharp, and sometimes excruciating pain. She is very exact about her focus:

> I will write about things that are universal So that hundreds, maybe even thousands of years from now, White critics and readers will say of me, Here is a good Black writer, who wrote about truth and universal topics. . . . I will write about Black people repossessing this earth, a-men.

To be sure, she was clairvoyant and uncompromising. Her poetry was colored by a young woman's contempt for injustice and a young rebel's sensitivity to the cost of freedom in a corrupt world where race takes precedence over everything else.

On the other hand, the second baptism takes place just before Carolyn Rodgers is able to shake herself dry from the first river. This one can perhaps be classified as a sprinkling and is protected by the blessings of a very fine headcloth. It is more sophisticated. It is cooler; lacks the fire and brimstone of the first period. But it is nonetheless penetrating. The two volumes that characterize this phase are How I Got Ovah and The Heart as Ever Green. At this point, Rodgers moved away from Third World Press, the publisher that accommodated most of the OBAC writers and which published her first three volumes, to a larger commercial publishing house. She also broke, it seems, abrasively with OBAC. She moved back inside her once lone and timid world. With OBAC she had demonstrated signs of strength and assertiveness. These characteristics are not visible in this stage and she returned to her old form of insecurity. In fact, her frailty seemed to have returned doublefold, wrapped itself around her physical and psychological self. This was the moment when she received recognition from a larger and more diverse reading audience. However, her celebrity was short-lived. The poetry that represents this period is rather specific. She cross-examines the revolution, its contradictions, and her relationship to it. She listens to her mother's whispers. And she embraces God.

Bettye J. Parker-Smith, "Running Wild in Her Soul: The Poetry of Carolyn Rodgers," Black Women Writers (1950–1980): A Critical Evaluation, ed. Mari Evans (New York: Anchor Press/Doubleday, 1984), pp. 395–97

◈ Bibliography

Paper Soul. 1968.

Songs of a Black Bird. 1969.

2 Love Raps. 1969.

For Love of Our Brothers (editor). 1970.

Now Ain't That Love? 1970.

For H. W. Fuller. 1971.

A Long Rap: Commonly Known as a Poetic Essay. 1971.

Roots (editor). 1973.

how i got ovah: New and Selected Poems. 1975.

The Heart as Ever Green. 1978.

Translation. 1980.

A Little Lower Than Angels. 1984.

Finite Forms. 1985.

⬛ ⬛ ⬛

Sonia Sanchez
b. 1934

SONIA SANCHEZ was born Wilsonia Driver on September 9, 1934, in Birmingham, Alabama, to Lena and Wilson L. Driver. Sonia's mother died when she was one, and she and her sister Pat spent several years with various relatives before being taken by their father to New York City. There Sanchez attended public schools and then Hunter College, where she received a B.A. in 1955. After graduating, she entered a graduate program at New York University but withdrew after a year.

Sanchez became swept up in the revolutionary social movements of the 1960s. Her first two collections of poetry, *Home Coming* (1969) and *We a BaddDDD People* (1970), reflect her militant, antiwhite stance, inspired in part by the example of Malcolm X. She incorporates dialect and profanity into her pithy, biting poems, and the tone is usually combative. Sanchez unleashed some of her rage at America's Anglocentric educational system. Her criticisms, however, were followed by suggestions, and she has become a powerful advocate of black studies programs.

Sanchez herself began a long teaching career in 1965 at the Downtown Community School in New York. After stints at several universities, including San Francisco State College, the University of Pittsburgh, Rutgers, Amherst, and the University of Pennsylvania, she joined the staff of Temple University in Philadelphia in 1977, where she is currently a professor in the departments of English and women's studies. Her anthology, *Three Hundred and Sixty Degrees of Blackness Comin at You* (1972), collects poetry written by her students in a creative writing class in Harlem.

In 1968 Sanchez married activist Etheridge Knight, with whom she had three children. The marriage, however, was troubled, and Sanchez and Knight later divorced. This experience may perhaps have helped to make her aware of the increasing tensions between black men and black women, which she has addressed both in poems and in the play *Uh Huh: But How Do It Free Us?* (1975). Sanchez has written several other plays, including

189

Sister Son/ji (1969), *The Bronx Is Next* (1970), and *I'm Black When I'm Singing, I'm Blue When I Ain't* (1982).

Sanchez's later poetry volumes—including *A Blues Book for Blue Black Magical Women* (1974), *I've Been a Woman* (1978), and *Generations* (1986)—are more specifically feminist in orientation, treating Sanchez's personal growth while celebrating women in general. One of her most celebrated volumes is *homegirls & handgrenades* (1984), a collection of autobiographical prose poems. The volume received an American Book Award from the Before Columbus Foundation.

Sanchez has also done considerable writing for children. *It's a New Day* (1971) is a poetry collection for "young brothas and sistuhs," while *The Adventures of Fathead, Smallhead, and Squarehead* (1973) is a juvenile short story. Sanchez has also compiled a collection of short stories for young readers, *A Sound Investment* (1980).

Sanchez continues to teach and write in Philadelphia.

▨ *Critical Extracts*

DON L. LEE   Sonia Sanchez has moments of personal loneliness that are not akin to some philosophical abstraction, but come because of the absence of someone, her man, who is real. She is intense, able to do many things simultaneously, as in "Short Poem," from her first book *Homecoming*:

> My old man
> tells me i'm
> so full of sweet
> pussy he can
> smell me coming.
> maybe
>   i
>   shd
>   bottle
>   it   and
>   sell it
>   when he goes.

It screams the fertile sense of being a woman desired. Irony suggests an attitude toward sex life that's natural. It can't be sold. She reveals a self-blues and an obscenity that's funny and easy for Black people to relate to. Sonia Sanchez understands that the mind of the negro works at a very conscious level; his skin tonality maintains this consciousness. Sonia enables us to move under her conscious tonality into blackerfields. Truedarkness. She pushes. Her one word lines are like well worked sentences and her metaphors and images are those we go to sleep/wake up with for days. We identify, double. The poems in the first book are not those of a first book poet. The poet is skilled/confident to the point of oversay. Saying more than it be's. Her poems/poetry will not fail to impress the stagnant mind and will open little holes in the blk/brain with poisonlines as indicated in "Homecoming."

> this is for real.
>   black.
>   niggers.
>   my beauty.
> baby.
> i have learned it
> ain't like they say
> in the newspapers.

For the negro, reality is real (reality: whatever controls yr/thought process, controls yr/pure & unpure actions). Blackpeople's reality is controlled by alien forces. This is why Sonia Sanchez is so beautiful & needed; this is also why she is dangerous. The Black artist is dangerous. Blk/art moves to control the negro's reality, moves to negate the influences of the alien forces. Sonia's word usage is positive. Her direction is aimed/armed to do damage to the nigger's control center. His mind. Poeple will be looking/ hoping/trying to shoot her down. Back shooting, they will not face her. We know that "fuck u muthafuckas" will turn a lot of evil minds around. The true/pure people will read on. they will confess, to themselves. That's important—her poetry helps you face yr/self. Then, actually, u will be able to move thru/out the world an face otherpeople as true Blackperson.

Don L. Lee, *Dynamite Voices 1: Black Poets of the 1960s* (Detroit: Broadside Press, 1971), pp. 48–49

SEBASTIAN CLARKE   The ordering of the role the Black woman can play as designated by Sonia corresponds to the philosophy of the Bantu in relation to the three phases of evolution as Man, as complete Man. First, she accepts that she is a woman, the feminine dimension, which is an acceptance of the first principle—man, Monad, revealed in his masculinity; the second principle in man's evolution to becoming *humanized*, towards becoming a person, is revealed in Woman, Dyad, fecundity; Man is now responsible to each other, but is not freedom, and is incomplete without Triad, child, i.e., without becoming mother. The complete cycle—Man-Woman-Child. These priciples as designated by the Bantu, as unconsciously designated by Sonia, reveal the extent and degree to which the depth of an African sensibility still pervades her consciousness despite the severance from native Africa for over 400 years. This philosophy is essentially the key towards achieving harmony and unity within the Black family.

In terms of the stylistic quality of her writing it is incontestable that she is one of the forerunners of the New Breed. The language and rhythm of her poetry reflect the language and speech-rhythm of Black people—revealing her most pristine desire as that of maximum communication to her audience in a language that they are not foreign to. One white critic said that the "young" Black writers are fakes because they use "word-acrobatics" in their writing. But the vibrations of Black people would have manifested itself adversely if the "fakery" of these poets was a reality, since the Black poets function within and for the Black community. Black people are a vibratory, emotional and all-feeling people, they are moved very much by their feeling-being. So that the rhetoric of that white critic has no foundation or relevance to the feelings of the Black poets' audience. In fact, the style, the writing style, of these Black poets is not unique or original—it is a very old form that has its tradition in white writers like William Carlos Williams and Lawrence Ferlinghetti. The *innovative difference* is that the style is transformed, is given creative life, by the uniqueness of the content of these poets' creations.

In terms of the negativism or positivism of Sonia's work, there is one thing that is certain—that nowhere in her poetry is there a question of "identity" posed in any form. Sonia Sanchez has transcended that, and so have most of the other writers and poets of this generation; it has never been a question or a theme in her poetry. Hers is more significant and profound—like the releasing of the *id*, the demon of the new Black Magic. It is a poetry of destiny, a declaration of self-determination, Black people as intrinsically being separated, in their philosophy and essentially in their sensibility as a nation, from the murderous, masochistic and decadent society that is called white America.

Sebastian Clarke, "Sonia Sanchez and Her Work," Black World 20, No. 8 (June 1971): 98

BARBARA WALKER   In a time when society breeds groups like the Women's Liberation Movement, blacks have begun to reflect on their roles as women. The theatre continuously utilizes the stage as an exclusive device to portray the innermost feelings of the people in their society. One of the controversial figures of the theatre today, who has made a unique attempt in her writing to present us with a realistic look at the "woman thing," is Sonia Sanchez.

There is more than just being witty and 'heavy on the cap,' because Sonia's writing is not the result of a meticulously developed writing style colored with "it's hip to be black" now syndrome. Her writing is her lifestyle colored with a natural warmth and honest outlook on people and herself.

Most of us identify best with her poetry. Only recently, people have become aware of her ability as a playwright.

"It's sort of a different kind of writing," she said. "I've always written poetry since I was a little girl. In terms of plays, sometimes you can't always say things in poems. You can't always say what you want to say. People don't always listen.

"I moved into plays in the 60's specifically because of my dialogue and poems," she explained. "Imamu was doing *Black Fire*. He asked me to do a play and I did *The Bronx Is Next*. It got there too late, so only my poems were in it. The next time, Ed Bullins was doing the Tulane Drama Review. So I did *The Bronx Is Next* for that. I constructed a play where Black revolutionaries decide to burn out Harlem. My vision at the time was that the buildings in Harlem were full of rats and roaches. The only way to get them out was by burning them. In the play is a character called the 'black bitch.' A woman who is all of us. I took women who I had seen, heard, talked about in the community. What's interesting is that she has this white lover, a policeman, this kind of gets her into difficulties with the band of black revolutionists.

"Not long after Ed Bullins called me long distance when I was in California organizing a Black studies program. He was doing *Plays from the Black Theatre*.

'I want you to do a play for me.' Then I had twins and was feeling sorry for myself, tired and beat up because twins will do that to you. He called. I knew I hadn't got the plays out. So I said 'I just had twins.' He said, 'Don't tell me your problems. I don't tell you to have twins.' I needed that kind of thing because it just made me pop up and I wrote *Sister Sonji*. I worked from 10:30 p.m. to 5 a.m. in the morning."

> Barbara Walker, "Sonia Sanchez Creates Poetry for the Stage," *Black Creation* 5, No. 1 (Fall 1973): 12

GEORGE E. KENT   Sonia Sanchez's latest book, *A Blues Book for Blue Black Magical Women*, possesses an extraordinary culmination of spiritual and poetic powers. It is in part an exhortation to move the rhythms of black life to a high peak through deep and deeper self-possession; in part an address to all, with specific emphasis upon women; in part, a spiritual autobiography. Actually, one gets trapped in rhetoric; the separate strands entwine themselves together and are pervasive, for the most part. The book consists of five parts: Part I, urging women to move out of false paths created by racism into the queenly existence of self-possession, purpose, direction; Part II, describing autobiographically Sonia's own psychological and spiritual evolution in the past; Part III, focusing on the present and giving her transition and rebirth into the Muslim vision; Part IV, a brief celebration of rebirth; and Part V, ringing with visions and celebrations. Although the spiritual journey finds its vitalizing point in a movement toward the Muslims, the spiritual and poetic power has nourishment even for the unready. In the book's conception of woman and her role, there seems to be both the influence of the Baraka group and that of the Muslims.

A *Blues Book* is a mountain-top type poem. That is, it is the poetic rhythms of one who has climbed from the valleys and is now calling others up from the low, the misted flats. A number of radical writers have attempted to create the mountain-top type, without sufficient awareness of the traps to be evaded. At the very least, it seems to require that one dislodge the ego from the center of one's concerns. If one has not dealt with the ego, if one is not really at the top or at one of the peaks, the ego whips out patronizing gestures and tones to the multitude.

It seems to me that the author has escaped such traps. I feel in the poems a genuine humbleness, love, and thankfulness, brightly leavening the exhortations. The voice is that of a struggler mindful of the journey and further humanized by it, an achievement emphasized by the confessional and testifying parts of the book.

George E. Kent, "Notes on the 1974 Black Literary Scene," *Phylon* 36, No. 2 (June 1975): 197–98

CLAUDIA TATE   C.T.: How does being black, female, and a one-time member of the Nation of Islam constitute a particular perspective in your work?

SANCHEZ: I wrote as a child. When I first started to write, I stuttered. Always at the core of my being was the realization that I was black, not that I knew I was oppressed, but that I knew I was black. I might have said "Negro" years ago. I knew something was wrong, but I didn't know the terminology to explain it or what to do about it. I was in Alabama then. There were simple things, like going to a house where my grandmother worked, and we were in the kitchen and heard the way she was talked to. But I could not verbalize my feelings. When we went into elevators in stores, white people always wanted to touch us and say, "Aren't they some nice little children." I would always draw back because I knew something was wrong, but my stepmother allowed this to happen, and I was always very angry about that. Because I knew they had no business touching me. I somehow knew that because she was black, she let that happen. I remember asking my stepmother four times why she couldn't try on a hat she wanted to buy, and each time I didn't get an answer. That I remember. ⟨. . .⟩

Although I was a very shy child, a very introspective child, one who stuttered, one who was not very self-confident, there were some things that I was sure of. One of the things which has propelled me all my life is when a principle is violated. America has violated many principles as far as black people are concerned and that's why I do battle with her. I do battle not because I think it's cute or militant but because America has violated a race of people. This means that my whole life has been dedicated toward the eradication of those violations.

I went into the Nation of Islam in 1972. I had been in New York for a couple of years, and had watched a lot of people who were "in the Nation." When I joined I didn't change my basic lifestyle, my writing. I had children, and I thought it was important for them to be around people who had a sense of nationhood, a sense of righteousness and morality. I wanted them to be exposed to this behavior. You cannot talk about progress for people unless you also talk about morality. The Nation was the one organization that was trying to deal with the concepts of nationhood, morality, small business, schools. . . . And these things were very important to me.

Claudia Tate, "Sonia Sanchez," *Black Women Writers at Work* (New York: Continuum, 1983), pp. 138–39

D. H. MELHEM   In both poetry and drama, Sanchez maintains she is trying to reach all kinds of audiences. She sees no real change in Black life since the sixties, and says, "I couldn't write *Homecoming* and *We a BaddDDD People* now." While the point of Black Pride has been made, it is time to progress from there toward concrete gains, by organizing well and powerfully through—and here she differs radically from Madhubuti—interracial coalitions. "Organize in terms of particular issues?" I ask her. "Always, always, always," she replied.

Sanchez offers this advice to beginning writers:

> Read and read and read and read everything you can get your hands on. One of the things Louise Bogan told me was, "Whatever you write, read aloud. Your ear will be the best friend you will ever have." And join a workshop at some point when you really feel you want to work more and/or apprentice yourself to a poet or writer and study with her or him. ⟨. . .⟩

In a recent telephone conversation, I discussed with the poet her latest book, *homegirls & handgrenades* ⟨. . .⟩ Lyricism, the gift of her love poetry, moves the first two sections, "The Power of Love" and "Blues Is Bullets"; animates the humanitarian poems of "Beyond the Fallout"; and splashes the public poems of "Grenades Are Not Free."

In stories like "Just Don't Never Give Up on Love," relating an encounter with an old woman on a park bench, and "Bluebirdbluebirdthrumywindow," about a chance encounter with a homeless Black woman ("This beached black whale.") in a Pennsylvania Station restroom; "Bubba" and "Norma," bright friends from her childhood and school, who stayed behind in Harlem among the rubble of their thwarted dreams, Sanchez reveals the compassionate immediacy with which she relates to the lost ones of earth, and her felt responsibility as an artist to voice their inarticulate despair.

Richness of that voice culminates in public poems of the last section. As she writes to Ezekiel Mphahlele, the exile returning to South Africa after twenty years; addresses Dr. Martin Luther King, Margaret Walker, Jesse Jackson; reflects on the June 12, 1983 March for Disarmament; and exhorts Third World working-class people in "MIA's (missing in action and other atlantas)"; visionary hopefulness transforms her anger and pain into a call for action. "MIA's," the concluding poem, interspersed with Spanish and Zulu, explodes its real and surreal images to light a landscape of suffering from Atlanta to Johannesburg, South Africa.

D. H. Melhem, "Sonia Sanchez: Will and Spirit," *MELUS* 12, No. 3 (Fall 1985): 95–97

JAMES ROBERT SAUNDERS   It is appropriate when analyzing a work such as *Homegirls and Handgrenades* (1984) to wonder about what might have been the motivation for its subject matter and form. It might be declared by some that this is just another long line of Sonia Sanchez's books of poems. Her very first volume, *Homecoming* (1969), was an impressive display of staggered-lined poems with word-splitting diagonals. *We a BaddDDD People* (1970) and *It's a New Day* (1971) contained even more of the same stylistic devices. Part of Sanchez's early effort was to experiment with words in verse to create a new perspective on how blacks should perceive themselves within the context of a nation struggling to admit them into the fold of social equality. Although the task remains incomplete, one can nevertheless sense a development on the part of the poet as she advances her work to include the mystical *A Blues Book for Blue Black Magical Women* (1973) as well as *Love Poems* (1973) where there can be seen an attempt to reconcile all the various aspects of black culture for the benefit of progress. *I've Been a Woman* (1978) and *Under a Soprano Sky* (1987) are further examples of how the author has examined, in particular, the plight of black women as they strive toward freedom in a world not always conducive to that undertaking.

Nonetheless, it is in *Homegirls* where Sanchez delivers what Henry Louis Gates has characterized as "the revising text . . . written in the language of the tradition, employing its tropes, its rhetorical strategies, and its ostensible subject matter, the so-called Black Experience." Gates further explains how many black writers have either consciously or subconsciously "signified" on previous authors' works so as to explore their own impressions while yet remaining faithful to certain literary strategies used by their predecessors. The former slave, Olaudah Equiane, wrote his narrative based to a large extent on what a previous slave narrator, James Gronniosaw, did. Ralph Ellison's *Invisible Man* (1952) is largely a response to the literary work of Richard Wright. And recently, Alice Walker has drawn on the basic themes and dialect style of Zora Neale Hurston to render her prize-winning novel, *The Color Purple* (1982). This tradition of signifying on what other writers have done is a deep-rooted feature of black writing that has as its origin the culture of blacks as a whole. It is, interestingly enough, the mark of black culture in its most creative posture, that of being able to play upon what is available, in terms of form and substance, and convert it into something new and unique.

Such is the achievement of Sanchez who, in *Homegirls*, has rendered a marvelous collage of thirty-two short stories, poems, letters, and sketches that often ring loudly with the truth of an autobiographical fervor.

James Robert Saunders, "Sonia Sanchez's *Homegirls and Handgrenades:* Recalling Toomer's *Cane*," *MELUS* 15, No. 1 (Spring 1988): 73–74

HOUSTON A. BAKER, JR. The riddle for the critic who would deal with the *sound* of Sonia Sanchez—the renaissancism of *her* transmission and passage of the word through a community of sharers—is how did an Alabama black child who turned away from the world surrounding her and found introspective refuge and psychological defense in stuttering move in her maturing years to achieve her own resonant articulation? When asked how she ceased stuttering, Ms. Sanchez tells of an act of will in which she simply decided to cure herself. When asked how she moved from introspection and moderate Americanism to active, nationalist cadences, she points to a moment on a Sunday evening in the sixties when she put aside a resolution to avoid Malcolm X's speeches and refused to be bound by an agreement among fellow workers in New York CORE that Malcolm was a racist to be shunned at all costs.

> Malcolm sent the word out that you could not have any kind of demonstration in Harlem unless he was a part of it. And so I remember saying to some people in the [CORE] office: "God, this man, he's nothing but a racist anyway. What is he gonna do?"

Everytime he'd come to speak at demonstrations we were having, we'd walk back over to the office and go in there until he was finished and then come back for our part. But one day, a rainy day . . . I listened to Malcolm as the rain was drizzling . . . And I stood there with the rain hitting me and I kept looking and I kept listening . . . The danger of Malcolm and probably of Farakann, is that they . . . pull middle class people toward them . . . Our poems were almost direct results of how [Malcolm] presented things . . . always that strong line at the end—the kick at the end that people would repeat, repeat, and repeat, always a finely tuned phrase or line that people could remember.

Malcolm's speech, with its penetrating logic and obvious commitment, converted Sanchez forever. The vision that she seized on a rainy New York afternoon comes powerfully home in a characterization found in elegiac stanzas that she wrote for the brilliant Muslim leader:

> he was the sun that tagged
> the western sky and
> melted tiger-scholars
> while they searched for stripes.
> he said, "fuck you white
> man. we have been
> curled too long. nothing
> is sacred now. not your
> white faces nor any
> land that separates
> until some voices
> squat with spasms."

Houston A. Baker, Jr., "Our Lady: Sonia Sanchez and the Writing of a Black Renaissance," *Reading Black, Reading Feminist: A Critical Anthology*, ed. Henry Louis Gates, Jr. (New York: Meridian, 1990), pp. 327–28

JOANNE VEAL GABBIN   *Homecoming* (1969), Sanchez's first book of poems, is her pledge of allegiance to blackness, to black love, to black heroes, and to her own realization as a woman, an artist, and a revolutionary. The language and the typography are experimental; they are aberrations of standard middle-class Americanese and traditional Western literary forms. As such, they reflect her view of American society, which perceives blacks as aberrations and exploits them through commercialism, drugs, brutality, and institutionalized racism. In this book and the poetry that follows, the vernacular and the forms are clear indications of her fierce determination to redefine her art and rail against Western aesthetics. *Homecoming* also introduces us to a poet who is saturated with the sound and sense of black speech and black music, learned at the knees of Birmingham women discovering themselves full voiced and full spirited. The rhythm and color of black speech—the rapping, reeling, explosive syllables— are her domain, for she is steeped in the tradition of linguistic virtuosity that Stephen Henderson talks about in *Understanding the New Black Poetry*. Black music, especially the jazz sounds of John Coltrane, Ornette Coleman, and Pharoah Sanders, pulse, riff, and slide through her poetry.

In her second volume, *We a BadDDD People* (1970), Sanchez is wielding a survival sword that rips away the enemy's disguise and shears through the facade of black ignorance and reactionism. Arranged in three groups, "Survival Poems," "Love/Songs/Chants," and "TCB/EN Poems," the poems extend the attack begun in *Homecoming* and tell black people how to survive in a country of death traps (drugs, suicide, sexual exploitation, psychological slaughter via the mass media) and televised assassination. Her message, however, is not one of unrelieved gloom, for it is rooted in optimism and faith: "know and love yourself." Like Sterling A. Brown's "Strong Men" and Margaret Walker's "For My People," "We a BadDDD People," the title poem of the volume, is a praise song that celebrates black love, talent, courage, and continuity. The poems appear rooted in a courage learned early from aunts who spit in the face of Southern racism and sisters who refused to be abused by white men or black men. In this volume, Sanchez reveals her unmistakable signature, the singing/chanting voice. Inflections, idiom, intonations—skillfully represented by slashes, capitalization (or the lack of it), and radical and rhythmic spelling—emphasize her link with the community and her role as ritual singer.

Joanne Veal Gabbin, "The Southern Imagination of Sonia Sanchez," *Southern Women Writers: The New Generation*, ed. Tonette Bond Inge (Tuscaloosa: University of Alabama Press, 1990), pp. 181–82

FRENZELLA ELAINE DE LANCEY   One of the few titled haiku written by Sonia Sanchez, "Walking in the rain in Guyana" is an excellent example of both the poet's artistic vision and artistry:

watusi like trees
holding the day like green um/
brella catching rain.

Elements consistent with definitions of classical Japanese haiku as a lyric
verse form in three unrhymed lines, with a 5-7-5 syllable count are evident,
so, too, is the requisite emphasis on external nature. The clarifying title
tells us that this haiku derives from a walk in the rain in Guyana and
announces the poet's intention to "localize" the haiku in a particular manner.
Sanchez uses Afrocentric motifs to textualize the haiku, making it not some
universal statement about rain and tree but a particular experience, filtered
through the poet's consciousness. Though Guyana is located in South
America, African people are among its inhabitants; the watusi trees evoke
images of the Burundi Watusi, again, images associated with Africa. Sanchez
localizes this image by inserting "like" in the first line, forcing it into service
as she forges an adjective-phrase, "watusi-like" to describe the trees. Such
techniques signal the reader: this is haiku with a difference. ⟨. . .⟩

Sanchez's transformation of the form is more radical than mere structural
alteration, although she sometimes changes the structure of the haiku by
using simile, conjunction, and metaphor. Her use of these structural markers
can always be identified as functional; they are used to make the haiku
speak her words, reveal her vision. In fact, Sanchez's use of the form is a
revolutionary textualization of both structure and form. Sometimes working
within the structural strictures of classical Japanese haiku form, other times
altering the form to fit her needs, and always textualizing it, Sanchez forces
the form to accommodate her vision. By imbuing the haiku form with
Afrocentric motifs, Sanchez textualizes the form in a specific manner, and
in the instances where she must abrogate universally observed strictures,
she does so to force the haiku to conform to her needs and her vision. In
her haiku, then, the effect is a movement through the uneven strictures
imposed by dicta reintroduced for the English haiku. Referring specifically
to her book *I'VE BEEN A WOMAN*, Sanchez discusses her use of haiku
and tanka, and her conscious use of African themes. In *I'VE BEEN A
WOMAN*, she points out, "I have haiku, tankas, and again, the movement
towards what I call 'African' ideas and feelings and also the movement
toward a black ethic and a feminine one too."

Frenzella Elaine De Lancey, "Refusing to Be Boxed In: Sonia Sanchez's Transformation of the Haiku Form," *Language and Literature in the African American Imagination*,
ed. Carol Aisha Blackshire-Belay (Westport, CT: Greenwood Press, 1992), pp. 21–23

REGINA B. JENNINGS   It is obvious that revolutionary fervor characterized some of Sanchez's work, but it is essential for understanding her poetics, as well as the neo-aesthetic of the sixties, to recognize that anarchy was not the goal. These poets considered themselves to be word soldiers for black people, defending their right to have equality, honor, and glory. In each of Sanchez's volumes of poetry, for example, one finds the artist handling themes that include love, harmony, race unification, myth, and history. Her poetic personas are diverse, incorporating themes from China, to Nicaragua, to Africa. Yet, there is a pattern in her figurative language that blends an African connection. In this article, I shall examine the Afrocentric tropes that embody Sanchez's poetics. To use Afrocentricity in this regard is to examine aspects of traditional African culture not limited by geography in Sanchez's work. A body of theory that argues such an African commonality is in Kariamu Welsh's *The Concept of Nzuri: Towards Defining an Afrocentric Aesthetic*. Using her model will enable this kind of topological investigation.

Houston A. Baker, Jr. presents a different aesthetic in *Blues, Ideology, and Afro-American Literature*. This book is a point of departure from Africa, concentrating solely on discussions of African American art from a black American perspective. On the back cover of *Under a Soprano Sky*, Baker maintains that blue/black motif appears in selected works by Sanchez. Baker's definition of the blues constitutes a transitory motion found precisely in this motif. The blues manifests itself in Sanchez's prosody in varying degrees and in differing forms. It determines shape and category, directs the vernacular, and informs the work. To demonstrate this specific vitality in Sanchez's poetry, Baker's construct of a blues matrix is an apt qualifier.

One can identify the blues as matrix and Afrocentric tropology in Sanchez's literary vision when one understands the significance of her axiology. Her ethics informs not only her creativity but her essays and articles as well. Her focus is to inscribe the humanity of blacks to challenge the Eurocentric perspective of black inferiority. Her particular axiology emerged during the greatest period of social unrest between white and blacks. In the sixties, African American artists deliberately fused politics and art to direct social change. That Sanchez's axiology influenced her ethics has to be considered in order to understand why her poetry inverts the tropology of "white" and "black." The artists of the black Arts Movement were at war with America. Their tone and perspective encouraged black people to rethink their collective position and to seize control to direct their destiny.

Regina B. Jennings, "The Blue/Black Poetics of Sonia Sanchez," *Language and Literature in the African American Imagination*, ed. Carol Aisha Blackshire-Belay (Westport, CT: Greenwood Press, 1992), pp. 119–20

▨ Bibliography

Home Coming. 1969.

Liberation Poem. 1970.

We a BaddDDD People. 1970.

It's a New Day: Poems for Young Brothas and Sistuhs. 1971.

Ima Talken bout the Nation of Islam. 1972.

Three Hundred and Sixty Degrees of Blackness Comin at You (editor). 1972.

We Be Word Sorcerers: 25 Stories by Black Americans (editor). 1973.

The Adventures of Fathead, Smallhead, and Squarehead. 1973.

Love Poems. 1973.

A Blues Book for Blue Black Magical Women. 1974.

I've Been a Woman: New and Selected Poems. 1978.

A Sound Investment: Short Stories for Young Readers. 1980.

Crisis in Culture: Two Speeches ("The Poet as a Creator of Social Values"; "The Crisis of the Black Community"). 1983.

homegirls & handgrenades. 1984.

Generations: Poetry 1969–1985. 1986.

Under a Soprano Sky. 1987.

Autumn Blues: New Poems. n.d.

Behind the Bamboo Curtain. n.d.

Continuous Fire: A Collection of Poetry. n.d.

Ntozake Shange
b. 1948

NTOZAKE SHANGE was born Paulette Williams on October 18, 1948, in Trenton, New Jersey, the oldest child of a surgeon and a social worker. With her two younger brothers and sister she grew up in Trenton, at an air force base in upstate New York, and in St. Louis, Missouri. Her father painted and played percussion in addition to his duties as a physician, and she met many leading black figures in sports and the arts. She read widely as a child, and in her teens began to rebel against her privileged life. A turning point occurred when she was bussed to an all-white school for the gifted in St. Louis; she was, she says, unprepared for the hostility and harassment of white students.

Paulette Williams went on the Barnard College, where she majored in American studies, specializing in black American music and poetry. At Barnard she became active in the civil rights movement. After graduation in 1970 she went to the University of Southern California, teaching while earning a master's degree in American studies; the following year she changed her name, after consulting friends from the Xhosa tribe, who baptized her in the Pacific Ocean with her new African name. *Ntozake* means "she who comes with her own things"; *Shange* means "who walks like a lion."

Shange went on to teach in the women's studies program at Sonoma State College and began writing poetry intensively. Soon she was reading it at women's bars, accompanied by friends who were musicians and dancers. Out of these performances grew her first theatrical production, or "choreopoem," *For Colored Girls Who Have Considered Suicide/When the Rainbow Is Enuf*, a celebration of the survival and triumph of black women. Shange and her friend, choreographer Paula Moss, moved to New York City in the mid-1970s and first performed *For Colored Girls* in a jazz loft in SoHo in July 1975. The show evolved through a series of highly successful Off-Broadway productions, then opened uptown at the Booth Theatre in the fall of 1976; it was published in book form the next year. Shange, who had been in the show's cast since its first performance, remained in the Broadway production for one month. *For Colored Girls* played on Broadway for two years, then was taken by touring companies to Canada, the Caribbean, and other cities in the United States.

Shange's second major work to be staged in New York was *A Photograph: A Study of Cruelty*, termed a "poemplay" by its author. The production, which explores the relationship between a black woman dancer and her talented but unsuccessful photographer lover, ran at the Public Theatre during the 1977–78 season but received mixed reviews; it was published in a revised version as *A Photograph: Lovers in Motion* (1981). Shange did not appear in this play, having formed a three-woman ensemble called the Satin Sisters, who read their poetry against a background of jazz at the Public Theatre Cabaret.

Shange has written and performed in several theatrical pieces in New York in recent years, including *From Okra to Greens* (1978; published 1985). Her adaptation of Bertolt Brecht's play *Mother Courage and Her Children* was presented at the Public Theatre in 1980. Of her other plays, only *Spell #7* (1981) has been published. Her published books of verse include *Nappy Edges* (1978), *A Daughter's Geography* (1983), *Ridin' the Moon in Texas* (1987), and *The Love Space Demands* (1991). Shange has issued the novels *Sassafrass, Cypress & Indigo* (1982) and *Betsey Brown* (1985) as well as a volume of essays, *See No Evil* (1984).

▨ *Critical Extracts*

HAROLD CLURMAN   In a number of respects this work ⟨*For Colored Girls Who Have Considered Suicide/When the Rainbow Is Enuf*⟩ is unique. Its stress is on the experience of black women—their passionate outcry, as women, within the black community. There is no badmouthing the whites: feelings on that score are summed up in the humorously scornful lines addressed to a black man which begin: "ever since I realized there was someone callt a colored girl, a evil woman, a bitch or a nag, I been tryin' not to be that and leave bitterness in somebody elses cup. . . . I finally bein real no longer symmetrical and inervious to pain . . . so why don't we be white then and make everythin' dry and abstract wid no rhythm and no feelin' for sheer sensual pleasure. . . ." The woman who utters these words, like all the others, speaks not so much in apology or explanation of her black condition but in essential human protest against her black lover whose connection with her is the ordinary (white or black) callousness toward women. Thus she asserts "I've lost it / touch with reality / I know who's doin' it. . . . I should be unsure, if I'm still alive. . . . I survive on intimacy and to-morrow. . . . But bein' alive and bein' a woman and bein' colored is a metaphysical dilemma."

This gives only a pitifully partial notion of the pain and power, as well as the acrid wit—"so redundant in the modern world"—which much of the writing communicates. The thematic emphasis is constantly directed at the stupid crudity and downright brutality of their own men, which, whatever the causes, wound and very nearly destroy their women. These women have been driven to the very limits of their endurance (or "rainbow") and are desperately tired of hearing their men snivel that they're "sorry." Part of the joy in the performance lay in the ecstatic response of the women in the audience!

Harold Clurman, "Theatre," *Nation*, 1 May 1976, p. 542

JANET BROWN   Although *For Colored Girls* has many protagonists rather than one, its pattern of symbolic action is clearly a search for autonomy opposed by an unjust socio-sexual hierarchy. The search for autonomy in *For Colored Girls* succeeds, however, more thoroughly than in any of the other plays studied. Thus, it is the most idealistic of the plays examined as well.

The successful resolution to the search for autonomy is attributable first to the communal nature of the struggle. *For Colored Girls* has many agents who share in the same struggle, but just as significantly, none of these agents is able to transcend the unjust hierarchy alone. Rather the play's pattern of symbolic action shows a progression of sympathetic sharing and support among women culminating in the communal recitation and singing that ends the play.

Secondly, the play's optimistic resolution results from the agents' affirmations of self building through the play. The colored girl who at the beginning of the play "doesn't know the sound of her own voice: her infinite beauty," affirms by the end of the play that she has found God in herself. These two elements in the achievement of autonomy, sisterhood and self-realization, are symbolically united in the final song which affirms the holiness of self and which is sung by the whole community of women on stage.

Finally, the achievement of autonomy in *For Colored Girls* is not only socio-sexual or psychological but spiritual as well. The spirituality of the play's resolution, reflected in images of blessing hands, the spirits of women of the past haunting present-day women and the female god women find in themselves suggests the spiritual transcendence of sexism described by Mary Daly in *Beyond God the Father*. Such a transcendence, Daly says, will be "an ontological, spiritual revolution, pointing beyond the idolatries of sexist society and sparking creative action in and toward transcendence."

Just as Daly describes, the agents in *For Colored Girls* confront their own "non-being" in the fact of their "non-existence" as persons in the unjust hierarchy. Sechita has learned to disbelieve the grotesque distortion which is society's reflected image of her. The lady in sequins and feathers understands that without her costume she is nothing to the men who court her. The woman who lives in Harlem knows that she has no right to live and move freely in the world. ⟨. . .⟩

Thus, *For Colored Girls* is among the most idealistic of the plays studied, reflecting the feminist philosophy outlined by Daly more fully than any of the other plays studied. As Daly does, the play goes beyond denunciation of the unjust *status quo* to evoke an alternative, non-hierarchical order based on sororal community and a recognition of the worth of each individual. In *For Colored Girls* the agents' affirmation of individuality and community transcends the socio-sexual hierarchy, making the play an idealistic statement of the feminist impulse.

Janet Brown, *Feminist Drama: Definition and Critical Analysis* (Metuchen, NJ: Scarecrow Press, 1979), pp. 129–31

SANDRA HOLLIN FLOWERS   ⟨. . .⟩ there is definitely a crisis.
Individually we have known this for some time, and lately black women as well as black men are showing growing concern about the steady deterioration of their relationships. Black literature, however, has lagged somewhat behind. The works which usually comprise Afro-American literature curricula and become part of general reading materials, for instance, show the position of the black man in America; but generally we see the black woman only peripherally as the protagonist's lover, wife, mother, or in some other

supporting (or detracting) role. Certainly black women can identify with the predicament of black men. Black women can identify, for example, with the problems articulated in Ellison's Invisible Man because they share the same predicaments. But for black women the predicament of the black male protagonist is compounded by concerns which affect them on yet another level. This, then, is what makes Colored Girls an important work which ranks with Ellison's Invisible Man, Wright's Native Son, and the handful of other black classics—it is an artistically successful female perspective on a long-standing issue among black people. If, however, black men fail to acknowledge the significance of Colored Girls, if they resent it or insist that it does not speak to their concerns or is not important because it deals with "women's issues," then the crisis is more severe than any thought it to be.

Colored Girls is certainly woman's art but is also black art, or Third World art, as Shange probably would prefer to have it designated. Its language and dialect, its geography, its music, and the numerous allusions to Third World personalities make it an intensely cultural work. Many of these characteristics, however, are peculiar to Shange's upbringing, education, and experiences, with the result that the piece loses universality at points, as in the poem "Now I Love Somebody More Than." But even here, black audiences are sure to know which lady loved gardenias; they will know the Flamingoes and Archie Shepp and Imamu. Then there is the poem "Sechita" in which the dancer is linked to Nefertiti, hence to Africa and Olduvai Gorge, the "cradle of civilization"—all of which puts into perspective the cheapening of Sechita by the carnival audience. While "Sechita" speaks to the degradation of black womanhood, "Toussaint" speaks, with subtle irony, of the black woman's awakening to the black man.

Sandra Hollin Flowers, "Colored Girls: Textbook for the Eighties," Black American Literature Forum 15, No. 2 (Summer 1981): 51–52

SANDRA L. RICHARDS   Although the epistemology of experience within an African world view is inseparably cognitive *and* intuitive, Shange's protagonists, who are African people raised within the Western perspective, tend to feel that they must opt for one mode of knowledge over the other. Their Western heritage teaches them to see experience as fragmented rather than holistic and to value rational over emotional systems—hence, the dialectic of combat breath vs. will to divinity.

In *Spell #7*, subtitled a "quick magic trance manual for technologically stressed third world people," Shange tackles the iconography of "the nigger." Underneath a huge blackface minstrel mask, a master of ceremonies promises to perform a different kind of magic designed to reveal aspects of Black life authentically. The minstrel performers move through the pain of dance steps and memories associated with Black entertainment for white America on to the release of more private, improvisational party styles. In doing so, they banish the hideous mask along with their stage personae, thereby creating a safe space in which to expose secret hopes, fears, or dreams. ⟨. . .⟩

Shange draws upon two distinct traditions in contemporary Western theatre. In her commitment to combat breath, she achieves some of the effects described in Bertolt Brecht's dramatic theories. Chief among the German dramatist's tenets is the view that theatre must be an analytical forum which exposes bourgeois illusions and stimulates audiences to think objectively about the causes of social and personal ills. By constructing most of her plays as a series of poetic monologues, occasionally interrupted by conventional dialogue, she takes advantage of the telegraphic, elusive quality of poetry to encourage audiences to listen with close, critical attention; the resultant episodic structure diminishes the audiences' empathetic tendencies by denying them the opportunity to gain a more rounded sense of character. Additionally, the women's contrariness can function like Brecht's *Verfrem-dung* effect as an alienation device which keeps observers at a more objective, thinking distance from the characters. But because this contrariness also emotionally engages spectators, after a performance they are apt to demand answers to questions like, "Why are these women so strange; what does it mean? Is Shange describing reality accurately? How do I feel about what she describes?" Most importantly, in debating their responses to Shange's views, they can initiate a process of change in the world outside the theatre.

Sandra L. Richards, "Conflicting Impulses in the Plays of Ntozake Shange," *Black American Literature Forum* 17, No. 2 (Summer 1983): 74–75

CLAUDIA TATE   C.T.: When did you first know you were a writer? SHANGE: I wrote when I was a child. I wrote stories. Then it became very difficult for me to get through school because somebody told me that "Negroes"—we weren't "black" then—didn't write. Some racial incident blocked my writing, and I just stopped. I can't remember exactly when it was. I started writing again in high school. I wrote some poetry, and it was published in a high-school magazine. That same year I'd been writing a lot of essays in English class, and I would always write about black people. Then I was told that I was beating a dead horse, so I stopped writing again. I started back at it when I was nineteen.

C.T.: Do you intend to include white people in your work?

SHANGE: I would never have a white person in a story I wrote with the possibile exception of "the white girl" [*Spell #7*] piece. I have no reason to do it. I was writing this real funny thing last night in my head. It was about my putting a story in a time capsule so that people in the year 20,000 could find it. It was a conversation with a white director: "Yes, I think it's wonderful that you think it's so good that you think it should be all white. Yes, I think it's fine that you think, even though the character is black, a white actress could do it so much better because you know black people really can't talk, although I remember that when my mother was speaking to me in my house, I never heard her talk like the white girl you're going to hire is going to talk like a black person. Then again, I'm only black, so how would I know how best to do it? Yes, I think it's wonderful that you think that because it's a black character you absolutely have to have this white actress play her because she's so good. And where in the world could you find a black person who could play her? I mean, after all it is a black character, and you know a black actress isn't perfectly trained to do this. So, yes, I think you should take my name off it and give me my money. Yes, it's perfectly all right if you use the story as is, but remember nobody in the world will believe that these people were really white. I mean, after all, they sweat."

This business is very sick. The theater is very sick. I feel really badly about it, though I'm compelled to keep working in this medium. What keeps me in the theater has nothing to do with an audience. It has to do with the adventure that's available in that little, three-dimensional stage. I can see a character who exists for me in one way become a real human body. That's a great adventure for me. I don't care. Theater gives my stuff what I cannot give it. Actors spend as many years learning how to act as I've spent learning how to write. Actors spend many years trying to give me something that I don't have. They make the piece come alive in a new way. For example, writers think they know how their characters sit. But if you give a piece to Avery Brooks or Laurie Carlos or Judy Brown or Mary Alice, how they sit can change everything. The timbre of their voices, how they walk, what they do, become available as a communal experience. You cannot read a book with somebody. Whereas, when you have a character there in front of you, that's somebody you know and anybody else sitting there with you would know also. Theater helps me, as a writer, known where I didn't give a character enough stuff, or where I told a lie. It's just a glorious thing to see actors make my characters come alive. But I don't like it when my artist-self has to be confined so that other people can understand. In the theater you have to do this; otherwise, they call your work "performance pieces," which means that you should be a white person and live downtown. Obviously, I can't do that.

Claudia Tate, "Ntozake Shange," *Black Women Writers at Work* (New York: Continuum, 1983), pp. 171–73

MAUREEN HONEY   Ntozake Shange dedicates her latest book of poems ⟨A *Daughter's Geography*⟩ to her family, most especially to her daughter; and it opens with an epigraph consisting of a poem written by a woman in revolutionary Cuba. Both the dedication and the epigraph anticipate the major theme of the book, which is that Third-World peoples are united by a long history and current oppression: that all of them are members of the same family with a common enemy. This theme is rendered by a voice more fierce than angry, more determined than defiant. It is a revolutionary volume, informed by a sensibility of struggle and hope. ⟨. . .⟩

This volume delights, inspires, and enlightens. Shange's political astuteness, ear for the street, and earthiness are a rare combination and one to be savored.

Maureen Honey, "A Sensibility of Struggle and Hope," *Prairie Schooner* 58, No. 4 (Winter 1984): 111–12

ELIZABETH BROWN-GUILLORY   Shange's theater pieces, beyond the commercially successful *For Colored Girls Who Have Considered Suicide/When the Rainbow Is Enuf*, have gone virtually unnoticed in critical studies. One case in point is Shange's *A Photograph: Lovers in Motion*, a drama that "comes closest to play form in that there is a logical progression of action and dialogue, with some detectable growth in at least one of the five characters." Though the stages of growth are not as readily detected as in plays by ⟨Alice⟩ Childress and ⟨Lorraine⟩ Hansberry, Michael in *A Photograph: Lovers in Motion* does embark on a journey that results in her wholeness. Shange's integrity as a dramatist who seeks to "transcend or bypass through music and dance the limitations of social and human existence" is not compromised in this theater piece, but rather is enhanced by the depth of these characters. Not only is *A Photograph: Lovers in Motion* an exploration of lives, but it is a drama that answers some of the whys of human behavior as the heroine grows and becomes a catalyst for the growth of her lover. ⟨. . .⟩

Blacks have traditionally turned to singing and dancing as coping strategies because those areas were open to blacks in white America. Shange's dramatic structure is exciting and innovative and, in at least one play, *A Photograph: Lovers in Motion*, the poet/playwright merges traditional dramatic structure with identifiable African American self-expression.

Elizabeth Brown-Guillory, *Their Place on the Stage: Black Women Playwrights in America* (Westport, CT: Greenwood Press, 1988), pp. 97, 100

MARY K. DeSHAZER   *Spell #7* ⟨. . .⟩ focuses partly on sexist oppression but mainly on issues of color and class. The grotesque minstrel-show parody that begins the play jolts the audience with that familiar, insidious brand of racism once labeled comedy; and the magician's opening speech reveals the impact of internalized oppression on Black children who wanted desperately to be made white. "What cd any self-respectin colored american magician / do wit such an outlandish request," lou wonders as he recounts this story, besides put away his magic tools altogether, for "colored chirren believin in magic / waz becomin politically dangerous for the race." But now lou is back with his magic, he tells us, and "it's very colored / very now you see it / now you / dont mess wit me." The play quickly becomes an angry reclamation of those physical and psychic territories appropriated from Black Americans by racist terrorists: school kids, police, lynch mobs. "This is the borderline," one character, alec, claims in identifying himself and his dreams, "this is our space / we are not movin." The only safe territory, the characters reveal, is segregated space where magic rules and masks come off. But even a protected haven from which to speak cannot offset the daily horrors these unemployed performers face. Lily wishes for just one decent part, like lady macbeth or mother courage, only to be reminded by eli that she can't play lady macbeth when "macbeth's a white dude." Bettina's show remains open, "but if that director asks me to play it any blacker / i'm gonna have to do it in a mammy dress." What white audiences want is what they get, the actors bitterly remind us, and even selling out to racist taste doesn't pay the bills. Near the end of the play, alec offers one powerful suggestion that would make him less tired. A gong would sound for three minutes, all over the world, while "all the white people / immigrants & invaders / conquistadors & relatives of london debtors from georgia / kneel & apologize to us." This is not impossible, he insists; this is Black magic.

> Mary K. DeShazer, "Rejecting Necrophilia: Ntozake Shange and the Warrior Revisioned," *Making a Spectacle: Feminist Essays on Contemporary Women's Theatre*, ed. Lynda Hart (Ann Arbor: University of Michigan Press, 1989), pp. 93–94

DEBORAH R. GEIS   Ntozake Shange's works defy generic classification: just as her poems (published in *Nappy Edges* and *A Daughter's Geography*) are also performance pieces, her works for the theater defy the boundaries of drama and merge into the region of poetry. Her most famous work, *for colored girls who have considered suicide/when the rainbow is enuf*, is subtitled "a choreopoem." Similarly, she has written *Betsey Brown* as a novel and then again (with Emily Mann) in play form, and her first work of fiction, *Sassafrass, Cypress & Indigo*, is as free with its narrative modes—including recipes, spells, letters—as Joyce was in *Ulysses*. Perhaps more so than any other practicing playwright, Shange has created a poetic voice that is uniquely her own—a voice which is deeply rooted in her experience of being female and black, but also one which, again, refuses and transcends categorization. Her works articulate the connection between the doubly "marginalized" social position of the black woman and the need to invent and appropriate a language with which to articulate a self.

In their revelation of such language, Shange's theatrical narratives move subtly and forcefully between the comic and the tragic. A brief passage from *for colored girls* underscores the precarious path between laughter and pain which Shange's characters discover they are forced to tread:

> distraught laughter fallin
> over a black girl's shoulder

> it's funny/it's hysterical
> the melody-less-ness of her dance
> don't tell nobody, don't tell a soul
> she's dancing on beer cans & shingles

These images associated with the word *hysterical* in this passage show the multilayered and interdependent qualities of the "black girl's" experience: *hysterical* connotes a laughter which has gone out of control, a madness historically—if not accurately—connected with femaleness. Moreover, the admonition "don't tell nobody, don't tell a soul" suggests the call to silence, the fear that to speak of her pain will be to violate a law of submission. The onlooker will aestheticize the dance or call attention to its comic qualities rather than realize the extent to which the dance and the laughter are a reaction against—and are even motivated by—the uncovering of pain.

The key here is the complexity, for Shange, of the performative experience. In her plays, especially *for colored girls* and *spell #7*, Shange develops her narration primarily through monologues because monologic speech inevitably places the narrative weight of a play upon its spoken language and upon the performances of the individual actors. But she does not use this device to develop "character" in the same fashion as Maria Irene Fornes and other Method-inspired playwrights who turn toward monologic language in order more expresssively to define and "embody" their characters both as women and as individuals. Rather, Shange draws upon the uniquely "performative" qualities of monologue to allow her actors to take on *multiple* roles and therefore to emphasize the centrality of *storytelling* to her work. This emphasis is crucial to Shange's articulation of a black feminist aesthetic (and to the call to humanity to accept that "black women are inherently valuable") on two counts. First, the incorporation of role-playing reflects the ways that blacks (as "minstrels," "servants," "athletes," etc.) are expected to fulfill such roles on a constant basis in Western society. Second, the space between our enjoyment of the "spectacle" of Shange's theater pieces (through the recitation of the monologues and through the dancing and singing which often accompany them), and our awareness of the urgency of her call for blacks/women to be allowed "selves" free of stereotypes, serves as a "rupturing" of the performance moment; it is the uncomfortableness of that space, that rupture, which moves and disturbs us.

> Deborah R. Geis, "Distraught Laughter: Monologue in Ntozake Shange's Theater Pieces," *Feminine Focus: The New Women Playwrights*, ed. Enoch Brater (New York: Oxford University Press, 1989), pp. 210–11.

PINKIE GORDON LANE   This collection of prose and poetry ⟨*Ridin' the Moon in Texas*⟩ calls forth so many images that the reader will see him/herself in every page. It becomes an exposé of the reader's psyche. Now that's saying a lot for a slender volume that takes "old wine and puts it into new bottles." That is, Shange has employed the technique of using visual art as a takeoff for creating the substance of her verbal images. Thus, the book also contains color reproductions of exciting contemporary art in various media: painting, sculpture, and photography. ⟨. . .⟩

These short, disconnected pieces (unlike ⟨Shange's⟩ earlier, loosely joined narrative) contain lyricism, metaphor, and verbal subtleties (even elitism) that range from the vernacular to the linguistically sophisticated. The book's subjects range from a eulogy for a friend to social criticism. "Somewhere in soweto there's a small girl / she's grown thin & frightened." These lines from "Who Needs a Heart" allow us to experience what it is like living under apartheid in South Africa as seen from the perspective of a black child. ⟨. . .⟩

The book rocks, it rolls; but it also soars ethereally, shifting gears with dizzying speed. Breathless in its Joycean stream of consciousness, it just as quickly plummets to mother earth, its choice of style being adapted to the mood and subject.

Pinkie Gordon Lane, [Review of *Ridin' the Moon in Texas*], *Black American Literature Forum* 24, No. 3 (Fall 1990): 578–79

EILEEN MYLES   All of the poems in *The Love Space Demands* take up with the world. The riveting "crack annie" takes on the news. A crack mother sacrifices her seven-year-old's pussy to her dealer, and the lead poem of the book, "irrepressibly bronze, beautiful & mine," was written to work with ⟨Robert⟩ Mapplethorpe's *Black Book*. It dives in unabashedly: "all my life they've been near me / these men / some for a while like the / friend of my father's who drove / each summer from denver to / st. louis / with some different / white woman." The abandonment of the black woman by the black man is the bold angle from which Shange broaches Mapplethorpe's portraits. She looks at these men with admiration and lust. "look at me pretty niggah," she says. Is it whiteness *and* homosexuality he's leaving her for? Is that what she's saying? She moves on to "even tho' yr sampler broke down on you," a poem that mumbles in your ear as its eye grazes the rushing landscape: "(you know where my beauty marks are / all / over / HARLEM)." In "intermittent celibacy" she rears up with "all i wanted / was to be / revealed." "abstinence / is not / celibacy," she explains, "cuz / when you filled with the Holy Ghost / every man / in the world / can smell it." "if I go all the way without you where would i go?" is as formidably persuasive on sexual abstinence as it is wildly Whitmanesque about its opposite. "i open / deep brown moist & black / cobalt sparklin everywhere." In "chastening with honey," she further expounds wiseguy spirituality: "like the Passion of Christ / which brought us Lent & we give up meat." Who are we? Whose poetry is it, so supremely confident, that its "I" or "we" can finally vanish into the nightmares of the urban landscape, from there smiting the reader's sensibility with simple reportage. Ultimately, she's taken on the work the media won't do. And she's written an unconditionally sex-positive book which suggests that having control of both the yes and the no switch constitutes real power.

Eileen Myles, "The Art of the Real," *Voice Literary Supplement* No. 98 (September 1991): 13

GETA LeSEUR   Ntozake Shange strives to fill a void in the female literary canon. With novels such as *sassafrass, cypress and indigo* in 1982 and *Betsey Brown* in 1985, and her dramatic choreopoem *For Colored Girls Who Have Considered Suicide/When the Rainbow Is Enuf* in 1977, she has joined the ranks of prominent black women who are giving a voice to their sisters. Through her works, the audience is exposed to the issues facing black women as they develop into adulthood. Issues of racism and sexism must be addressed in order for her characters to grow. Although each of her characters finds a definition of herself as a black woman, the paths taken are unique to the individual. Each woman fulfills herself with a particular interest from which she derives power, be that interest music, dancing, or weaving cloth. These women must also learn to relate to and separate themselves from the men in their lives. With strength of character, Shange's women imprint themselves permanently in our memories. Shange wrote in *sassafrass, cypress and indigo* that the novel is dedicated to "all women in struggle." Within that statement lies the power of her writing. Her works are about black women, but they are indeed for ALL women.

She uses Ebonics in a manner that does not exclude any gender, class or culture. Rather it invites all readers to enjoy as well as understand and confront issues facing us.

Shange said in a 1987 interview with Barbara Lyons for the *Massachusetts Review* that "unless black women are writing the pieces we're being left out in the same way we used to be left out of literature. We don't appear in things unless we write them ourselves." This oppression of black women is addressed by the characters in her writings. Black women are often deprived of their sense of childhood because they must immediately begin striving for recognition in the home and community. In *For Colored Girls* . . . one of the dancers, a lady in brown, sings solemnly "dark phrases of womanhood / of never havin been a girl" and continues with the realization that the invisibility of black women is like death. ⟨. . .⟩ As the choreopoem continues and with the heroines of her novels, Shange sings the black girl's song. Betsey, Sassafrass, Cypress, and Indigo tackle the invisibility of black women and carve their own places in society along with the nameless women dressed in the varied rainbow colors of *For Colored Girls*. . . . This play also explores the never-ending experiences of women—rape, abortion, abuse, love/hate relationships, mothering, death, formulating philosophies of life, third world concerns, what it means to be an Egyptian goddess, and "being colored and sorry at the same time."

> Geta LeSeur, "From Nice Colored Girl to Womanist: An Exploration of Development in Ntozake Shange's Writings," *Language and Literature in the African American Imagination*, ed. Carol Aisha Blackshire-Belay (Westport, CT: Greenwood Press, 1992), pp. 167–68

◈ *Bibliography*

Melissa & Smith. 1976.

Sassafrass. 1976.

For Colored Girls Who Have Considered Suicide/When the Rainbow Is Enuf: A Choreopoem. 1977.

Nappy Edges (Love's a Lil Rough/Sometimes). 1978.

Three Pieces. 1981.

Some Men. 1981.

Spell #7. 1981.

A Photograph: Lovers in Motion. 1981.

Take the A Train. c. 1981.

Sassafrass, Cypress & Indigo. 1982.

A Daughter's Geography. 1983.

From Okra to Greens: A Different Love Story: Poems. 1984.

See No Evil: Prefaces, Essays & Accounts 1974–1983. 1984.

From Okra to Greens: A Different Kinda Love Story: A Play with Music and Dance. 1985.

Betsey Brown. 1985.

Ridin' the Moon in Texas: Word Paintings. 1987.

For Colored Girls Who Have Considered Suicide/When the Rainbow Is Enuf: A Choreopoem; and Spell #7. 1990.

The Love Space Demands: A Continuing Saga. 1991.

Plays: One. 1992.

I Live in Music. 1994.

Liliane. 1994.

Margaret Walker
b. 1915

MARGARET ABIGAIL WALKER was born on July 7, 1915, in Birmingham, Alabama. Her parents, Reverend Sigismund C. and Marion Dozier Walker, provided a culturally and academically rich environment for Margaret's upbringing. She was introduced not only to the Bible and to the standard English classics but also to black American literature and the folk mythology of the South.

Walker attended Northwestern University in Evanston, Illinois, where she became involved with the Works Progress Administration (WPA), working with troubled young women in Chicago's North Side. She began an unpublished novel, "Goose Island," about this community. After graduating from Northwestern Walker was hired as a junior writer for the WPA Writers' Project in Chicago, where she met such black literary figures as Willard Motley, Frank Yerby, Richard Wright, Arna Bontemps, and Sterling Brown. Walker and Wright became close friends and offered suggestions on the revision of each other's work. Her first poem had been published in the *Crisis* in 1934, and a few years later her poems were appearing in the prestigious *Poetry* and other magazines. Walker supplied considerable research for Wright's novel *Native Son* (1940), but in 1939 Wright abruptly broke off the friendship, wrongly believing that Walker had spread gossip about him.

Walker resumed her studies at the University of Iowa, securing an M.A. in 1940. Her thesis was a collection of poems published in 1942 under the title *For My People*, the first book by a black American woman to appear in the Yale Series of Younger Poets. The poems, written in long, cadenced stanzas reminiscent of biblical verse, utilize folk materials to illustrate the trials of blacks in America, but also stress the depth of Walker's attachment to her native South.

In 1941 Walker accepted a teaching position at Livingstone College in Salisbury, North Carolina. In June 1943 she married Firnist James Alexander, with whom she had four children. In 1949 she accepted a position at Jackson

219

State College in Jackson, Mississippi, where she would spend the next thirty years.

Walker's only novel, *Jubilee*, was submitted as her Ph.D. dissertation at the University of Iowa in 1965 and was published in 1966. This ambitious work—which Walker had conceived as early as the 1930s, and for which she received a Rosenwald Fellowship in 1944—traces the historical roots of Walker's family through the days before, during, and after the Civil War. The detailed re-creation of the daily life of a slave community reveals the exhaustive historical and linguistic research behind the work, but it met with mixed reviews.

During the writing of her novel, Walker did not abandon poetry. *Prophets for a New Day* (1970) and *October Journey* (1973) contain many poems addressing issues and personages of the civil rights movement, including elegies to Malcolm X and Martin Luther King, Jr. In 1973 Paula Giddings arranged for Walker and Nikki Giovanni to meet and discuss their views on poetry, art, and the black American community. *A Poetic Equation: Conversations Between Nikki Giovanni and Margaret Walker* was published in 1974.

Walker retired from Jackson State University in 1979. She has since devoted herself to writing and lecturing. A biography, *Richard Wright: Daemonic Genius*, appeared in 1988. *This Is My Century: New and Collected Poems* (1989) selects what the author believes to be her best poetic work, while *How I Wrote* Jubilee *and Other Essays on Life and Literature* (1990) gathers some of her essays and occasional prose writings.

◈ *Critical Extracts*

ARNA BONTEMPS   Miss Walker ⟨in *For My People*⟩ looks forward to the evolution of "The Great Society" in a "world that will hold all the people, all the races, all the Adams and Eves and their countless generations." She sees her people rebelling against hypocrisy—meaning, presumably, against the dissimulation by which the bitter, offended black man is often forced to live in some sections. She marks a struggle between pride and pain, the near-hopeless task of trying to maintain dignity under indignities. And she pins the blame for all the distress on the "money-hungry, glory-craving leeches." Simply put, her complaint is that her people are deceived and cheated.

The Negro's progress, so called, his quick achievement, his contribution to music, and all of that, leave Miss Walker quite cold. The question she asks is:

> How long have I been hated and hating?
> How long have I been living in hell for heaven?

The progress, if that is the word, has been made on the wrong fronts ("We have been believers believing in our burdens and our demigods too long"), and the result is a bitterness "flowing in our laughter," "cankerous mutiny eating through . . . our breasts." ⟨. . .⟩

One must agree with Stephen Vincent Benét, who introduced Miss Walker's work in *For My People*, that "this is part of our nation speaking."

Arna Bontemps, "Let My People Grow!," *New York Herald Tribune Books*, 3 January 1943, p. 3

ABRAHAM CHAPMAN   In its evocation of the folk experience and folk attitudes of Southern Negroes on the plantations when slavery seemed to be a permanent institution, during the Civil War and the Reconstruction years, this Houghton Mifflin Literary Fellowship Award novel ⟨*Jubilee*⟩ adds something distinctively different to the Civil War novel. Each of the fifty-eight chapters opens with lines from a spiritual or popular song of the day, and each chapter has its own title—devices which establish a broader framework and wider point of view than that of the novel's concealed, unidentified narrator. Some of the chapter headings suggest folk ways of thinking or folk wisdom: "Death is a mystery that only the squinch owl knows"; "This pot is boiling over and the fat is in the fire"; "Mister Lincoln is our Moses." Other headings suggest folk experiences: That for a chapter relating the efforts of a slave to escape to freedom is entitled "Put on men's clothes and a man's old cap"; others are headed "Seventy-five lashes on her naked back" and "They made us sing 'Dixie.' " ⟨. . .⟩

The author is so intent on presenting her historical data as accurately as possible, on correcting the distortions which have crept into so many Civil War novels, that at times she fails to transform her raw material into accomplished literary form. There are passages of very pedestrian prose. Fortunately, the colorful and musical speech of the Negro characters in the novel transcends the stilted prose of the narrator. The slave preacher, Brother Ezekiel, on his knees beside the bed of a dying slave in the slave cabin, prays: "Way down here in this here rain-washed world, kneelin here by this bed of affliction pain, your humble servant is a-knockin, and askin for your lovin mercy, and your tender love. This here sister is tired a-sufferin, Lord, and she wants to come on home."

> Abraham Chapman, "Negro Folksong," *Saturday Review*, 24 September 1966, pp. 43–44

STEPHEN E. HENDERSON   A generation ago, another beautiful black woman, Margaret Walker, focused all of that world of meaning that I have been trying to suggest in "For My People," probably the most comprehensively Soulful poem ever written. She tells it "like it is." Here is a section of that poem:

> For my playmates in the clay and dust and sand of Alabama
> backyards playing baptizing and preaching, and doctor and jail
> and soldier and school and mama and cooking and playhouse and
> concert and store and Miss Choomby and hair and company;
> For the cramped bewildered years we went to school to learn to
> know the reasons why and the answers to and the people who
> and the places where and the days when, in memory of the bitter
> hours when we discovered we were black and poor and small and
> different and nobody wondered and nobody understood;

Only a black American, I submit, can fully understand all of the tremendous emotional weight which that single word "hair" receives in this poem. It is almost as though the whole experience of blackness were there.

> Stephen E. Henderson, " 'Survival Motion': A Study of the Black Writer and the Black Revolution in America," *The Militant Black Writer in Africa and the United States* by Mercer Cook and Stephen E. Henderson (Madison: University of Wisconsin Press, 1969), pp. 101–2

PAULA GIDDINGS   Margaret Walker's philosophy of poetry fits into the structure of Christian eschatology: the preservation of the spirit beyond the flesh. But Christian explanations have never proved quite ade-

quate for Blacks whose sensibilities are deeply rooted in the folk traditions. A case in point is the "Ballad of the Hoppy Toad" in *Prophets*, which is filled with the characters and imagery reminiscent of those in works by Zora Neale Hurston and Charles Chesnutt and has the nature of African proverbs. A simple tale on the surface, it raises some of the most fudamental questions of existence.

In "Ballad," we discover that the protagonist has found some goopher dust around her door. After prayer has failed to help, she asks Sis Avery, known for her own kind of JuJu, for advice. Suddenly, the storyteller sees a horse coming toward her, threatening to trample her to death. Sis Avery grabs the creature by the mane, holding it until it starts to "sweat and shrink," becomes a little horse and finally turns into a toad. Simultaneously, the goopher man, pictured running toward the whole scene, screams for Sis Avery not to kill the animal, for he dies at the same time it does.

It is an entertaining story, but if we examine it more closely, we can see some of its deeper meaning. The toad in Nigerian myth was responsible for man's reappearance after death on earth in another and inferior form. The horse symbolizes the power to infuse man with the spirit of god, evil or good, which can completely dominate the soul. In African mythology and belief, evil not only manifests itself in an actual embodiment, but that embodiment has a protean nature. This is a key to many African, and therefore African-American, attitudes and cultural expressions. More important, the poem speaks of the relationship between an imposed belief, in this case Christianity, and the traditional formulas for living. When Christian prayer failed, goopher hexes had to be used to counter goopher hexes. It was the implementation of traditional beliefs which maintained the moral order of the community, another important theme of Black life. It is reminiscent, for example, of the Haitians who practice Catholicism as their "official" religion, but use the images and rites of Vodun to regulate their daily lives.

This folk ballad in *Prophets* is an example of the poet's coming to another kind of resolution. In *For My People*, we are told of the fascinating feats of Big John Henry, Bad-Man Stagolee, Molly Means, Poppa Chicken and Kissie Lee; that is important because it preserves our folk history. But the strict rhyme scheme for these poems in many cases seem to control their content and depth, so that they become just portraitures. In "Hoppy Toad," however, content dominates form, not only creating interesting characters, but at the same time making important comments about our culture.

To say that there is room for Margaret Walker in this age of political poetry is an understatement. Her protest against white actions or Black inaction and, even more importantly, the manifestation of her love for Black people (which should not automatically be assumed in much of the contemporary poetry) are important keys in our struggle. She not only talks about the beauty of Black people, she is a distiller of our experiences—past, present and future. And these experiences are, as she says, "the truth of our living, and the meaning and beauty of our lives."

Paula Giddings, "Some Themes in the Poetry of Margaret Walker," *Black World* 21, No. 2 (December 1971): 24–25

BLYDEN JACKSON   A poet of the forties and fifties who did capitalize admirably on the racial aesthetic in an admirably racial way was Margaret Walker. In 1942 she published *For My People*, a collection of poems which had won a competition sponsored by the Yale University Younger Poets. Her title is racial, but in a good way—a simple, forthright restatement in three very ordinary words of the whole creed and program of the New Negro. Her poem, too, is racial, and also in some good ways. She had lived through the thirties and learned to think of the Negro in the highly sociological context in which everything associated with the thirties seemed to find a frame of reference. Her "people" are the kind who often were beginning (when she wrote *For My People*) to "have" case workers in the North and about whom in the South social scientists were then writing many monographs and books. In the title poem of *For My People* she does not idealize these people. She reproduces them sympathetically, but with great fidelity to fact. Her freeverse paragraphs, in the poem, tread upon each other's heels, full of their own case histories of the actual character of life in her Negro South and Negro North. In these case histories and in her expression of a millennial hope—"for my people . . . Let a new earth arise . . . another world be born"—she speaks in a secular vein, joining the wave of social activism that would lead on to school desegregation, Montgomery, the sit-ins, and *Soul on Ice*, as well as to a changing life style for the Negro masses.

In the matter of her style, Whitmanesque as her methods appear, and to some extent are, the precedent which she follows most, nevertheless, harks back to a folkway from the Negro past that is not secular, *i.e.*, to the mourners' bench of revival time in an "oldtime" Negro church when an "oldtime" Negro preacher called not only upon the mourners to mend their ways, but also upon his whole church to "rock," to join him in the singing, shouting, praying, and movements of the body that were all done in the rolling rhythms which control the rhythmic flow of For My People. It is not only the title poem of For My People which embraces the Negro's past, as well as his present and future; all of For My People is racial. Its prevading sense impressions of the oldtime Negro church especially at the height of its evangelical fervor are no accident. They are the Negro atmosphere for a complete review of a Negro world. What the Negro was, what he is and will be, are issues of concern in all of the poetry within this book. John Henry and Stagolee are in For My People, along with Molly Means and Yalluh Hammuh, as part of the Negro legend which the past provides. The northern ghetto is in For My People as a part of the Negro's present. Apparently, the northern ghetto will be a powerful factor in his future. And, thus, it is hardly the Negro past, folk or otherwise, which finally rules in For My People. Miss Walker's poetry addresses itself to the "gone" years only in the interest of the "now" years and the "maybe" years. Her world is an intensely racial universe (in spite of the fact that she sometimes writes a sonnet). Still, she does not look back to be turned into stone, a monument of monuments. Nor does she look forward to disown a bitter and unwanted heritage. It is a function of her poetry to call for a Negro who is whole, one who accepts what he has been at the same time that he dreams of what he may become. This function of hers clearly links her with her "people" and makes of her a racial poet. And yet her racialism seems not to interfere with her Americanism. Her New Negro is neither picturesque nor exotic. Neither his citizenship nor his race is equivocal. He belongs both to America and to himself. No African paganism subverts him; but, then, neither does any monomania to be white overwhelm him. He is a mourner, but a mourner who has not lost his hope of heaven.

Blyden Jackson, "From One 'New Negro' to Another, 1923–1972," Black Poetry in America: Two Essays in Historical Interpretation by Blyden Jackson and Louis D. Rubin, Jr. (Baton Rouge: Louisiana State University Press, 1974), pp. 67–69

R. BAXTER MILLER   "At the Lincoln Monument in Washington,
August 28, 1963," presents analogues to Isaiah, Exodus, Genesis, and Deuter-
onomy. Written in two stanzas, the poem has forty-four lines. The speaker
dramatizes chronicle through biblical myth, racial phenomenology, and
Judaeo-Christian consciousness. She advances superbly with the participant
to the interpreter, but even the latter speaks from within an aesthetic mask.
The poetic vision authenticates the morality of her fable and the biblical
analogue. The first stanza has twenty-eight lines, and the second has sixteen.
As the speaker recalls the march on Washington, in which more than
250,000 people demonstrated for civil rights, she attributes to Martin Luther
King, Jr., the leader of the movement, the same rhetorical art she now
remembers him by. The analogue is Isaiah: "The grass withereth, the flower
fadeth: but the word of our God shall stand for ever" (40:8). Two brothers,
according to the fable, led the Israelites out of Egypt. Sentences of varied
length complement the juxtaposition of cadences which rise and fall. The
narrator names neither King as "Moses" nor King's youthful follower as
"Aaron," yet she clarifies a richness of oration and implies the heroic spirit.
King, before his death, said that he had been to the mountain top, and
that he had seen the Promised Land. But the speaker literarily traces the
paradigm of the life; she distills the love of the listeners who saw him and
were inspired: "There they stand . . . / The old man with a dream he has
lived to see come true."

Although the first eleven lines of the poem are descriptive, the twelfth
combines chronicle and prefiguration. The speaker projects the social present
into the mythical past. Her words come from a civil rights song, "We Woke
Up One Morning with Our Minds Set on Freedom." The social activist
wants the immediate and complete liberation which the rhetorician (speaker
and writer) translates into literary symbol: "We woke up one morning in
Egypt / And the river ran red with blood . . . / And the houses of death
were afraid."

She remembers, too, the story of Jacob, who returns home with his two
wives, Leah and Rachel (Genesis 30:25–43). Laban, the father-in-law, gave
him speckled cattle, but now the narrator understands that Jacob's "*house*
(Africa-America) has grown into a nation / The slaves break forth from
bondage" (emphasis mine). In Old Testament fashion, she cautions against
fatigue in the pursuit of liberty. Through heightened style, she becomes a
prophet whose medium is eternal language. She has mastered alliteration,
assonance, and resonance.

Write this word upon your hearts
And mark this message on the doors of your houses
See that you do not forget
How this day the Lord has set our faces toward freedom
Teach these words to your children
And see that they do not forget them.

R. Baxter Miller, "The 'Etched Flame' of Margaret Walker: Biblical and Literary Re-
creation in Southern History," *Tennessee Studies in Literature* 26 (1981): 165–66

DELORES S. WILLIAMS   In the communal life-support model,
the actions and life tasks of the major female characters sustain unity and
community within social groups in both black and white society. In Margaret
Walker's *Jubilee* the slave woman Vyry nurtures the slave master's family
and her own black family. Similarly, Vyry's mother, Sis Hetta, by sleeping
with Master Dutton (his wife refuses to do so), enables the Dutton family
to remain intact. The consciousness and actions of both women are conditioned by the demands of the slavocracy and the slave community, and
their personal needs are inextricably bound to community needs and goals.

These women undergo both positive and negative transformations. Hetta
and Vyry experience the negative personal transformation that slavery
inflicted upon black women, as Walker's description of the change in Hetta's
body—and spirit—makes painfully clear. Hetta had once "looked like some
African queen from the Congo. She had a long thin neck and she held her
head high." But as the result of bearing children for the slavocracy, she was
"no longer . . . slender and lovely."

> Her breasts were long and flabby; her belly always bloated,
> whether she was big in family way or not, and her legs and thighs
> were now covered with large broken blood vessels that made it
> painful when she stood long or walked far. . . . She was a sullen-
> looking woman . . . who rarely smiled.

Walker's whole plot is, in fact, structured around the central themes of
bondage and freedom. Vyry's character unfolds in episodes dramatizing value
conflicts between characters caught in various kinds of bondage. ⟨. . .⟩

Under the conditions of bondage, all aspects of her survival intelligence
work together to help Vyry both endure and make the transformations
needed for her family to survive the slave system. Although she emerged

from her confrontation with Master Dutton feeling hopeless, Vyry experiences many positive transformations after emancipation. Once despondent about the meaninglessness of slave existence, she becomes hopeful. Once passive, she becomes assertive in her relationship with her husband, Innis Brown. She decides when and where they will build their second home. She establishes a relationship with the town's white people, who join forces to help Vyry and Innis build their house.

Vyry is transformed spiritually. During slavery she only prayed for the safety of black children and for black freedom. After emancipation she sees herself and her family connected to all people through their common condition of sinfulness. Therefore, she prays with a concern for all humankind. She acknowledges, "Lord, we ain't nothing but sinful human flesh. . . . We is evil peoples in a wicked world, but I'm asking you to let your forgiving love cover our sin, Lord."

Out of her experience of transformation from slave to free woman, Vyry emerges a resilient person participating in making a new history for black people.

Delores S. Williams, "Black Women's Literature and the Task of Feminist Theology," *Immaculate and Powerful: The Female in Sacred Image and Social Reality*, ed. Clarissa W. Atkinson, Constance H. Buchanan, and Margaret R. Miles (Boston: Beacon Press, 1985), pp. 89, 91–92

LUCY M. FREIBERT   FREIBERT: When you write poetry, do you carry the poem around in your head first, or do you start right out putting things on paper?

WALKER: Regardless of the medium, whether you are a musician, a painter, a graphic artist, a plastic artist, or a sculptor, whether you are a writer or an architect, you begin the same way. Creative writing grows out of creative thinking, and nothing begins a work before the idea as a conceptualization; that is the beginning. All writers, all artists, all musicians, all people with creative talent begin with that creative thinking. They begin with conceptualization. You get an idea, and sometimes the whole process moves on mentally and unconsciously before it is given conscious artistic form, but the process begins with the idea.

Everything begins in the mind. You have an idea, and you may not know for a long time what form this idea is going to take or what you are going to say or how you are going to say it, but you have that first. For me it is intuitive. Some people are not intuitive. I'm intuitive. I in-tu-it. For me it begins with a concept, maybe before it is even an idea—a concept before it becomes thought or idea. It may begin with a picture. For the musician, I am sure it begins with a musical motif or a sound that the musician hears or senses. It is a process using the sensory perceptions, I guess you would say. You perceive or conceive. You perceive what is outside. You conceive what is inside. And you move from the perception of a concept or thought or idea to a figuration and a configuration.

The poet has nothing but words and language to be used as tools. And the poet—I think my father taught me this—the poet in my instance uses rhetorical devices. I have been told by some poets and even by some teachers that I am too rhetorical. I cannot conceive of writing poetry without metaphor and simile, synechdoche, metonymy, hyberbole. I grew up with that, and my work is rhetorical, but I think it is rhetorical in the best sense of the word. I had teachers who tried to break me of the habit. My father taught me my first lessons in rhetoric from an old English book that he had brought to this country. It gave all the rhetorical forms. I don't think a poet writes simply in grammatically correct language. I think all the greatest poets in the world were rhetoricians, and I believe in the rhetoric. Paul Engle has criticized me for it. He said, "Margaret was just too rhetorical." I laughed, because I am still rhetorical, and I always will be.

FREIBERT: That's what makes your voice so distinctive. What or who helped you find your voice?

WALKER: My father, really. I think Stephen Benét tells it in the introduction for For My People. It was not just that I heard the sermons my grandfather and my father preached, but it was that training my father gave me in the use of rhetoric. And I really didn't believe when I was a teenaged youngster growing up that you could write poetry without the use of simile and metaphor. I thought you had to use them. After I was older and had gained my own voice, I realized that I had read the Bible all my life and that the use of parallelism was what I had learned from the Bible: cataloguing and repetition and internal rhyme—not so much end rhyme, because that was what I had learned from ordinary poetry. I didn't think of the poetry in the Bible as ordinary, I thought it was extraordinary.

Lucy M. Freibert, "Southern Song: An Interview with Margaret Walker," *Frontiers* 9, No. 3 (1987), p. 32

ELEANOR W. TAYLOR   As the journey of memory, *This Is My Century: Black Synthesis of Time* reclaims the four matters of Afro-American poetry as *écriture*. Before the publication of "For My People" in 1937, these four matters had become traditional: the matter of Africa, the matter of America, the matter of the South, and the matter of the North. By 1773, the matter of Africa had been inscribed in the poetry of Phillis Wheatley, especially in the dedicatory "To Mycenaes." The African matter expands to embrace the Caribbean (Claude McKay), South America (Robert Hayden), and Europe (Langston Hughes). The matter of America begins with Lucy Terry's "Bars Fight" (*circa* 1746), not only the first extant poem by a person of African descent in the English colonies but one which establishes a distinctive sign of the Afro-American speaking mask in poetry: that of witness. Moreover, the matter of America expands to include the matter of the New World, adapting and metaphorically re-envisioning Caliban and Prospero in Shakespeare's *The Tempest*. And the matters of South and North configure regions in tropes and in linguistic particularities revealing, for one thing, how formal English is expanded and transmuted by black speech and music idioms. Along the axis of these matters, Margaret Walker's poetry references, mainly, the matter of America. It stands as a port of trade transacting the linguistic yield of what Richard Barksdale has called Southern Black Orature as that transforms the cadences of Southern and Midwestern American *parole* and formal English. Yet much of her prosody gains resonance from biblical cadence; her allusions range the mythical matter of the African discursive world.

   This Is My Century also reclaims the major themes of the pre- and post-industrial world which play about the matters of Negro poetry before 1937: colonialism, mercantilism, slavery, imperialism, racism, and gender chauvinism. And texturing the matters of Africa, America, North, and South before 1937, black poets weave the major ideas affecting the twentieth century which, in Margaret Walker's *Century* poem, become revolution, psychoanalysis, relativity, existentialism, and Pan-Africanism.

   Eleanor W. Taylor, " 'Bolder Measures Crashing Through': Margaret Walker's Poem of the Century," *Callaloo* 10, No. 4 (Fall 1987): 582

JOYCE PETTIS   The vital elements of Walker's work—its identity with the South, its historical perspective, folk tradition, and racial themes—

remain consistent in *Prophets for a New Day* as well as in the poems of *October Journey* (1973), a brief book (thirty-five pages) of mostly previously published poems. The title poem of the volume is notable for its thematic consistency with earlier ambivalent poems about the South. "October Jour-ney," however, excels those earlier poems in its extravagant imagery of the physical appearance of the Southland in the fall, when the land is awash with warm autumnal colors. As in the earlier poems, landscape and memory change when reality intervenes and displaces the visual scene in the mind of the traveler.

The rigorous depiction of realism in the South and the demand for social, political, and economic changes for black Americans have been consistent characteristics of Walker's work. Her knowledge of tradition and history has constituted fecund sources from which she has extracted material for its transformation into art. Additionally, she has located her themes and insistence for change within a humanistic framework and within a tradition accessible to nonacademic as well as academic readers. But more than anything else, Walker has anchored her work in the love and experiences of her people.

Margaret Walker, Southern black woman poet and novelist, occupies a unique position in American literary history through her inclusion with two generations of writers. It is a well-earned position, however. Walker's work since the 1930s illustrates and confirms an unquestionable dedication to art, determination to survive as a writer, and refusal to be defeated by the "silences" that have often shut off women writers' voices. The second phase of her career, beginning with the appearance of *Jubilee*, affirms her commitment and perseverance. Since many of the pressures that have the potential for silencing have lessened during Walker's lifetime, readers can anticipate that her voice will continue to be raised strong and vibrantly among the current generation of Southern women writers.

Joyce Pettis, "Margaret Walker: Black Woman Writer of the South," *Southern Women Writers: The New Generation*, ed. Tonette Bond Inge (Tuscaloosa: University of Alabama Press, 1990), pp. 18–19

FLORENCE HOWE   *For My People:* More than any other poet I can think of, Margaret Walker's first poem in her first volume strikes the note that persists through her half-century of writing poems. Walker herself says she has selected ⟨for *This Is My Century: New and Collected Poems*⟩ 100 poems from 1000 she has written through this lifetime, but there are very few poems in this volume that one might call "personal." ⟨. . .⟩

When she says she "belong[s] to all the people I have met, / Am part of them, am molded by the throng," she is describing herself as a poet of history. For those who remember the sixties' civil rights movement, Walker's poems stir memories of the fearless children who ignored threats and attended Freedom Schools, of the sit-ins, of the demonstrations and of the deaths— Medgar Evers, the children of Birmingham, Andy Goodman, Michael Schwerner and James Chaney, Malcolm X, Martin Luther King. Much of this poetry is inspirational, often in elegies, the heroism of people who stood for human—not national or racial—dignity. It is not that Walker ignores race; the poems more often than not speak to "the color line." Rather, she speaks to it and beyond, perhaps because of that visionary quality her poetry has had from the first. Walker is the least sectarian Christian I can name. Steeped, she tells us, not only in the Bible, but in the "wisdom literature of the East," she values the lessons of the past, especially when they offer evidence of the human energy for spiritual as well as material survival.

Ultimately, then, as a poet of history, she is a poet of vision, of the flow of past not only into present, but of a reach into the future. The seven new poems called "Farish Street" that close the volume focus with camera-like intensity on the Southern street, its shops and people, and, at the same time, recall an ancestral African village, the "Root doctor, Hoodoo man" then and now. And in the series' final poem, "The Labyrinth of Life," Walker presents herself as "traveler," looking down the road "to the glory of the morning of all life." But the poems that precede this final group remind us of the terrible world still needing mending: "On Police Brutality," "Money, Honey, Money," "Power to the People," "They Have Put Us on Hold," "Inflation Blues"—the titles themselves a litany of troubles for all the have-nots, all the powerless who would have space to live.

Florence Howe, "Poet of History, Poet of Vision," *Women's Review of Books* 7, Nos. 10 & 11 (July 1990): 41–42

▩ *Bibliography*

For My People. 1942.
Jubilee. 1966.

The Ballad of the Free. 1966.
Prophets for a New Day. 1970.
How I Wrote Jubilee. 1972.
October Journey. 1973.
A Poetic Equation: Conversations between Nikki Giovanni and Margaret Walker (with Nikki Giovanni). 1974.
Richard Wright, Daemonic Genius: A Portrait of the Man, a Critical Look at His Work. 1988.
This Is My Century: New and Collected Poems. 1989.
How I Wrote Jubilee and Other Essays on Life and Literature. Ed. Maryemma Graham. 1990.

❖ ❖ ❖
Phillis Wheatley
c. 1753–1784

PHILLIS WHEATLEY'S exact birthdate is unknown, but it is estimated at 1753 or 1754. She was possibly born in Senegal. It is certain that Wheatley arrived, in bondage, in New England in 1761. She was purchased by John Wheatley—from whom she took her surname—as a present for his wife Susanna. She was a precocious child who, according to her biographer, William H. Robinson, mastered the English language in sixteen months. Phillis soon acquired the fundamentals of a classical education, becoming acquainted with the Bible as well as a good deal of English literature and Greek and Latin literature in translation. She also learned Latin. The Wheatleys, who were proud of Phillis, introduced her to the affluent and educated circles of Boston society, where she was received warmly for her erudition and charm, and also for the fact that she was an educated slave— a rarity, and some thought an impossibility, in the Boston of that day.

Wheatley's *An Elegiac Poem, on the Death of That Celebrated Divine, and Eminent Servant of Jesus Christ, the Reverend and Learned George Whitefield* (1770) was her first separate publication, though it is thought that she wrote many poems earlier than 1770, such as "On Being Brought from Africa to America" and "To the University of Cambridge, in New England," some of which appeared in various periodicals. "On Messrs. Hussey and Coffin," published in the *Newport Mercury* for 1767, is her first known appearance in print.

Wheatley's elegy on George Whitefield garnered much attention because of the popularity of the evangelist and because of the delicately crafted lines in which he was celebrated. Yet it was the publication of *Poems on Various Subjects, Religious and Moral* (1773) that solidified her reputation as a poet. Just before its publication in England, Wheatley was received with fascina-tion and hospitality in London society under the sponsorship of the Countess of Huntingdon, to whom Wheatley dedicated the collection. The voyage to England provided a strong draft of freedom for Wheatley, and some speculate that she was freed as early as a month after her return, but certainly by 1778.

Poems on Various Subjects is marked by a strong neoclassical influence. Alexander Pope, perhaps Wheatley's favorite poet, is especially reflected in the carefully wrought lines, use of the heroic couplet, highly restrained, impersonal tone, and classical allusions. Wheatley's familiarity with the Bible is also evident in her verse, especially in her numerous elegies. She is often criticized for not addressing the position of her race in colonial society, but this was not Wheatley's focus. She did, however, follow political events: many of her occasional poems were inspired by the early flickers and later flames of revolution. This is reflected by her poetic appeals to such men as King George III (1768), the Earl of Dartmouth (1772), and George Washington (1775), and titles such as *Liberty and Peace* (1784). Yet political events so overshadowed interest in her poetry that her publications became less frequent after 1773.

Phillis Wheatley moved with her master John Wheatley to Providence in 1775 but returned to Boston after the British evacuation in 1776. After the death of John Wheatley on March 12, 1778, Phillis married John Peters, a free black Bostonian with whom she had three children. The marriage proved to be an unhappy one marked by financial difficulties. Phillis Wheatley died, apparently abandoned by her husband, in a boarding house on December 5, 1784.

▦ *Critical Extracts*

THOMAS JEFFERSON   Misery is often the parent of the most affecting touches in poetry. Among the blacks is misery enough, God knows, but no poetry. ⟨. . .⟩ Religion, indeed, has produced a Phyllis Whately; but it could not produce a poet. The compositions published under her name are below the dignity of criticism.

> Thomas Jefferson, *Notes on the State of Virginia* (1784), *Basic Writings*, ed. Philip S. Foner (Garden City, NY: Halcyon House, 1950), p. 146

G. HERBERT RENFRO   Having learned to read, Phillis readily learned to write, her own curiosity prompting to it, as her master testified.

Possessing at first no writing materials, her genius improvised some for the occasion. Not being supplied with pen and paper, she found ever-ready substitutes in a piece of chalk or charcoal and brick wall. In this and other ways indicating unusual ability, much attention was directed to her from the Wheatley household. That excellent family soon learned that, instead of obtaining a spirit born to serve, there had come among them a spirit born to create. In her twelfth year Phillis was able to carry on an extensive correspondence on the most important and interesting topics of the day with many of the wisest and most learned in Boston and London. Having mastered the English language within the short period of four years she began the study of the Latin tongue, and her progress in this was only paralleled by her remarkable record in the study of English. She soon made a translation of one of Ovid's tales. It was considered so admirable for one so young, and so extraordinary for one of the African race, that friends insisted on its publication. The translation was received with great favor, and on her visit to England, a few years later, it was republished, calling forth many encomiums from the public press.

The news of such progress, made even in the large city of Boston by an unknown African slave, could not be concealed. Public attention was directed toward her. Friends of the Wheatleys, refined and intelligent, came to visit the African prodigy, to witness her proficiency, and to cultivate her friendship. Thus becoming acquainted with many of the best people of Boston, she was often invited to their homes, and, during these visits, mindful of the prejudice against her race, she always conducted herself in so becoming a manner, while a recipient of honors, as to give no offense to the most prejudiced mind whom accident or design might cause her to meet on these occasions.

The city of Boston was even then the intellectual metropolis of the New World, having within her confines a numerous class of men distinguished for their literary attainments. Yet, education was not so widely disseminated as to be regarded as universal. The illiteracy of the master was often covered by the pride of his station, but that of the slave was exposed to the sunlight. Hence, we can account in a measure for the indulgence shown to Phillis, and the curiosity excited by her efforts. Here was a slave girl, just entering upon her teens, whose entire education was gathered from private instruction of a few years at her master's house, who was able to converse and discuss with the most learned and cultivated people of Boston; many of whom sought her society, loaned her books, gave her encouragement, acknowledged her merit and respected her abilities. Nor is this the first occasion in history that the wise and intelligent have found worth and merit in the conversation and virtues of a child.

> G. Herbert Renfro, "A Sketch of the Life of Phillis Wheatley," *Life and Works of Phillis Wheatley* (Washington, DC: Robert L. Pendleton, 1916), pp. 11–12

JAMES WELDON JOHNSON   Phillis Wheatley's poetry is the poetry of the Eighteenth Century. She wrote when Pope and Gray were supreme; it is easy to see that Pope was her model. Had she come under the influence of Wordsworth, Byron or Keats or Shelley, she would have done greater work. As it is, her work must not be judged by the work and standards of a later day, but by the work and standards of her own day and her own contemporaries. By this method of criticism she stands out as one of the important characters in the making of American literature, without any allowances for her sex or antecedents. ⟨. . .⟩

⟨. . .⟩ Only very seldom does Phillis Wheatley sound a native note. Four times in single lines she refers to herself as "Afric's muse." In a poem of admonition addressed to the students at the "University of Cambridge in New England" she refers to herself as follows:

> Ye blooming plants of human race divine,
> An Ethiop tells you 'tis your greatest foe.

But one looks in vain for some outburst or even complaint against the bondage of her people, for some agonizing cry about her native land. In two poems she refers definitely to Africa as her home, but in each instance there seems to be under the sentiment of the lines a feeling of almost smug contentment at her own escape therefrom. ⟨. . .⟩

What Phillis Wheatley failed to achieve is due in no small degree to her education and environment. Her mind was steeped in the classics; her verses are filled with classical and mythological allusions. She knew Ovid thoroughly and was familiar with other Latin authors. She must have known Alexander Pope by heart. And, too, she was reared and sheltered in a wealthy and cultured family,—a wealthy and cultured Boston family; she never had the opportunity to learn life; she never found out her own true relation to life and to her surroundings. And it should not be forgotten that she was only about thirty years old when she died. The impulsion or the compulsion that might have driven her genius off the worn paths, out on a journey of exploration, Phillis Wheatley never received. But, whatever her limitations, she merits more than America has accorded her.

James Weldon Johnson, "Preface," *The Book of American Negro Poetry* (New York: Harcourt, Brace & World, 1922), pp. 25, 28–29, 31

BENJAMIN BRAWLEY   *Poems on Various Subjects* lists thirty-eight titles, aside from "A Rebus by I. B.," to which one of the pieces is a reply. Fourteen of the poems are elegiac, and at least six others were called forth by special occasions. Two are paraphrases from the Bible. We are thus left with sixteen poems to represent the best that Phillis Wheatley had produced by the time she was twenty years old. One of the longest of these is "Niobe in Distress for Her Children Slain by Apollo, from Ovid's Metamorphoses, Book VI, and from a View of the Painting of Mr. Richard Wilson." This contains two interesting examples of personification neither of which seems to be drawn from Ovid, "fate portentous whistling in the air" and "the feather'd vengeance quiv'ring in his hands," though the point might be easily made that these are but the stock-in-trade of pseudo-classicism. "To S. M., a Young African Painter, on Seeing His Works" was addressed to Scipio Moorhead, servant of the Reverend John Moorhead, who exhibited some talent with the brush and one of whose subjects was the friendship of Damon and Pythias. The early poem, "On Being Brought from Africa to America," consisting of only eight lines, is one of the few pieces with autobiographical interest, and there is also a reference to race in the lines addressed to William, Earl of Dartmouth; but in general Phillis Wheatley is abstract, polite, restrained. "An Hymn to Humanity" is one of the most conventional pieces in the volume. One can but speculate upon what the author might have done if she had lived to see the French Revolution and to feel the glow of romanticism of Wordsworth and Coleridge and Scott.

Yet, when all discount is made, when we have spoken of the influence of Pope and of the few examples of lyrical expression, we are still forced to wonder at the ease with which the young author, technically a slave, could chisel the heroic couplet. Her achievement in this line is as amazing as it is unique.

Benjamin Brawley, *The Negro Genius* (New York: Dodd, Mead, 1937), pp. 25–27

JULIAN D. MASON, JR.   It is quite clear that Phillis Wheatley
was not a great poet. She was not a poet in the classical Greek sense of
maker, seer, creator, nor were her concerns really with Emerson's meter
making argument or Poe's rhythmical creation of beauty. Phillis Wheatley
had aspirations, but she also knew her shortcomings; and her concerns were
less august, less pretentious. Her primary endeavor was to put into rhythmical,
poetic forms those thoughts which came to her or which were brought to
her attention by the small crises and significant experiences of the people
of Boston as they met life and death from day to day. Most of what she
wrote of was not noted by the world outside of that city, though she
occasionally did treat more general topics and there is some evidence that
before and after the Revolution her poetic horizons may have been broad-
ening.
     On the basis of the poems which have survived her short career, she
must be labelled as primarily an occasional poet, one interested in the clever
crafting of verse. Such a craftsman is not as concerned with selecting topics
and creating patterns as with taking a given or obvious topic and fitting it
skillfully to an already existing pattern. However, if he is a good craftsman,
he is distinctive in his own right and possesses a great gift which is worthy
of the world's attention, if not its lasting praise. Such was Phillis Wheatley's
gift and her concern, as she was a better craftsman of verse than most of
the others attempting the same type of thing in America in the 1770's, a
time and place which certainly produced more craftsmen than true poets.
Her reward was in immediate praise—not the type which echoes through
the ages, but which appropriately sounds again from time to time for only
brief periods.
     Julian D. Mason, Jr., "Introduction," *The Poems of Phillis Wheatley* (Chapel Hill:
     University of North Carolina Press, 1966), pp. xx–xxi

M. A. RICHMOND   The crowning legacy of the poet's time in
London was a volume of her verse, the first book by a black woman to be
published. It was entitled *Poems on Various Subjects, Religious and Moral* and
dedicated to her patron, Selina Shirley (Lady Huntingdon). Her ladyship
graciously permitted the dedication, and for this dispensation the poet and
her mistress were effusive in their gratitude.

The poet's thanks included a shrewd calculation and a jolting lapse from her literary style. "Under the patronage of your Ladyship," she wrote, ". . . my feeble efforts will be shielded from the severe trials of uppity Criticism. . . ." Uppity?

If one realizes that the Wheatley volume, appearing more than a century and a half after the first pilgrim landing at Plymouth, was still among the first volumes of verse by a colonist to be published, one may appreciate how rare a phenomenon it was. For a woman slave, barely turned twenty, it was a dazzling triumph. The gift of the black slave could not be placed on the market without a white testimonial that it was genuine.

Appended to the volume was a statement by eighteen prestigious residents of Boston, attesting to its authenticity. Among the eighteen were Thomas Hutchinson, royal governor of Massachusetts Colony; James Bowdoin, who was to be governor of the state of Massachusetts; John Hancock, possessor of the most celebrated signature in American history; and seven ministers. Men of substance all, conscious of it, affixing their valuable signatures to the ponderously drawn affadavit designed to impress even the most skeptical with its judicious restraint. It was a strange introduction to poetry:

> We, whose names are under-written, do assure the World, that
> the Poems specified in the following Page were, (as we verily
> believe) written by Phillis, a young Negro Girl, who was but a few
> years since, brought an uncultivated barbarian, from Africa, and
> has ever since been, and now is, under the disadvantage of serving
> as a slave in a Family in this Town. She has been examined by
> some of the best Judges, and is thought qualified to write them.

M. A. Richmond, *Bid the Vassal Soar: Interpretative Essays on the Life and Poetry of Phillis Wheatley and George Moses Horton* (Washington, DC: Howard University Press, 1974), pp. 33–34

MUKHTAR ALI ISANI   Phillis Wheatley not only gained her initial fame with an elegy, the celebrated poem on George Whitefield's death in 1770, but over the remaining years of her life retained her place in the public eye in no small part because of her facility with the elegy. A third of her compositions in *Poems on Various Subjects, Religious and Moral* (1773) are elegies. Elegies appear in like proportion among the poems she tried in vain to publish as her second collection, in 1779. She received little recognition as an elegist, but these poems have merit. They make effective use of the mix of elegiac traditions prevailing in the poet's time. While they are comparatively numerous, they are genuine effusions of a feeling heart. While they appear to be composed with rapidity and sometimes even in haste, they are generally the result of careful planning and thoughtful revision. Their faults are obvious but their strengths must also be noted. Certainly, these poems lent her much of her contemporaneous fame. ⟨. . .⟩

More than personal piety is responsible for the religious flavor of Wheatley's poems. The influence of the tradition of the New England funeral elegy is especially evident. By Wheatley's time, the funeral elegy, once the prerogative of the clerics, was almost entirely the work of laymen, including those with no special call to letters. Broadsides remained in vogue, but increasingly such verse was appearing through the cheaper media of newspapers and magazines. The didactic emphasis and the use of mortuary detail continued, but the latter was declining. Wheatley's use of pentameter couplets and emphatic mortuary reminders is in the tradition of the New England funerary verse. Current practice was responsible for encouraging the use of the stock image and phrase. The recurring personification of Death, the frequent return to "the mansions of the dead," the visions of spirits, and the sounds of angelic choirs had the sanction of the time. Occasionally, the poet can be accused of sentimentalism, but the neoclassic restraint which was changing the tone of the Puritan elegy was also an influence on Wheatley's poetry.

In its choice of elements and in its emphasis, Wheatley's elegiac verse bears a stamp of its own. The poet set up a pattern and, unfortunately, often repeated herself. Her typical elegy is not principally a song of sorrow. It is a poem of solace through praise. It often relies on dialog to achieve *anagnorisis*. Its setting is not in this world but in the next, and its comfort is based on the pious philosophy that the world to come is a happier place than man's terrestrial home.

> Mukhtar Ali Isani, "Phillis Wheatley and the Elegiac Mode," *Critical Essays on Phillis Wheatley*, ed. William H. Robinson (Boston: G. K. Hall, 1982), pp. 208–10

WILLIAM H. ROBINSON   It is true that practically all of her writings are informed by a lifelong preoccupation with orthodox Christian piety. But that fundamental fact will not form the basis for deducing that her range was limited to Christian or Biblical or even pious concerns. Phillis composed over one hundred poems and published more than fifty pieces in her lifetime, certainly enough to display a wider range of topics than that for which she has been credited. In the thirty-eight pieces in her 1773 volume alone can be seen pieces on such matters as reconciliation, "the works of Providence," delightful companion lyrics of the Morning and the Evening, two Biblical renderings, a Latin translation, a tribute to a fellow black Bostonian who was also a poet and an artist, the human imagination. Most of these pieces are, however, variously structured elegies, versified comfortings for recent widows, widowers, parents grieving the death of their children or relatives.

In poems published before and after the 1773 volume, her range of poetic concerns includes topics of American patriotism, simple friendship, pioneering tributes to black Africa. Indications of still other topics may be reckoned from some of the titles of the thirty-three poems listed in her proposals for a 1779 volume, a volume that was never published: "Thoughts on the Times," "Farewell to England," "Epithalamium to Mrs. H——," "A Complaint." Likewise, her letters reveal a lively interest in several issues: antislavery, her chronic sickness, her ordeals as a bookseller and distributor of her own book, her manumission, the onset of Christian redemption of "heathen" Africans. The charge that she versified nothing but piety cannot be documented.

She may have written heartfelt condolences for personal Tory friends, but Phillis was plainly a Whig or American Patriot in her deepest political sympathies. This much is clear in a half-dozen poems she wrote. One of her very first efforts, "America," is a versified, allegorical chiding of Mother England for the imposition of unduly inhibiting taxation on her vigorous, growing son, New England, or America. Hailing King George III for his repeal of the Stamp Act, so despised in the colonies and especially in Boston where it had triggered mob riots, Phillis wrote two versions of a poem of American thanks to his majesty. The Earl of Dartmouth was appreciated in some of the colonies as a sometimes sympathetic recourse for American grievances. Congratulating him on his royal appointment as Secretary of State for North America, she greets his "blissful sway," because

> No more, *America*, in mournful strain
> Of wrongs, and grievance unredress'd complain;
> Which wanton *Tyranny* with lawless hand
> Had made, and with it meant t'enslave the land.

She also took occasion in this piece to testify of her own experiences as a kidnapped African slave to underscore the great hope with which, she was sure, her fellow colonists must greet Dartmouth's tenure. As she was herself a slave or unpaid servant, however indulged, when she wrote this poem, the piece can easily be read as her disdain for all kinds of slavery.

William H. Robinson, "On Phillis Wheatley's Poetry," *Phillis Wheatley and Her Writings* (New York: Garland, 1984), pp. 91–92

HENRY LOUIS GATES, JR.   Imitating Pope in rhythm and meter, Wheatley wrote in decasyllabic lines of closed heroic couplets. There is much use of invocation, hyperbole, and inflated ornamentation, and an overemphasis of personification, all of which characterize neoclassical poetry.

Seventeen, or one-third, of her extant poems are elegies, fourteen of which appeared in the first edition of *Poems on Various Subjects, Religious and Moral* and five of which have been revised from earlier published elegies. In one of the few close readings of Wheatley's verse, Gregory Rigsby demonstrates conclusively that her elegies are a creative variation of the "English Elegy" and the "Puritan Elegy." Wheatley's elegies are threnodic after the fashion of the "Renaissance Elegy," in that they are meant "to praise the subject, to lament the death, and to comfort the bereaved." Yet they are "Medieval" rather than "Elizabethan" insofar as they prefer a sublime resignation to an unrestrained death force, and seem to avoid the protest against it. The medieval resignation toward death, the function of the "Renaissance Elegy," and the form of the threnody as it developed in Elizabethan poetry were fused together in the "Puritan Funeral Elegy," a form peculiar to colonial America.

The Puritan funeral elegy, in turn, derived its specific shape and tone from the early American funeral sermon, based as it was on energetic exhortation. But, as Rigsby argues, Wheatley utilized the triple function of the Renaissance elegy within "her own elegiac structure and established more elaborate conventions." Rigsby then identifies these elements to be the underlying "structure of a Wheatley elegy": (1) the deceased in Heaven, (2) the deceased "winging" his way to Heaven, (3) an appreciation of the deceased's work on earth, (4) seraphic strains of heavenly bliss, (5) consolation of the living, (6) exhortation. The identification of the conventions of her elegies indicates that Wheatley was an imaginative artist to a degree largely unrecognized in critical literature. Although her remaining occasional verse lacks the irony, the contrast, and the balance of Pope's poetry, which she cited as her conscious model, her critical reception since the eighteenth century has failed in a remarkably consistent way to read her verse in comparison with the various literary traditions that she so obviously attempted to imitate and by which she just as obviously sought to measure herself. Curiously, all of her extant poems, except five, utilize the heroic couplet. Vernon Loggins traces, albeit vaguely, the influence of Milton in her hymns to morning and evening, as well as in her poem to General Lee, as he does Gray's influence on her elegy to Whitefield and Addison and Watt's presence in "Ode to Neptune" and "Hymn to Humanity." But these, again, are suggestions of influence rather than practical criticism.

> Henry Louis Gates, Jr., "Phillis Wheatley and the 'Nature of the Negro,'" *Figures in Black: Words, Signs, and the "Racial" Self* (New York: Oxford University Press, 1987), pp. 78–79

HENRY LOUIS GATES, JR.   That the progenitor of the black literary tradition was a woman means, in the most strictly literal sense, that all subsequent black writers have evolved in a matrilinear line of descent, and that each, consciously or unconsciously, has extended and revised a canon whose foundation was the poetry of a black woman. Early black writers seem to have been keenly aware of Wheatley's founding role, even if most of her white reviewers were more concerned with the implications of her race than her gender. Jupiter Hammon, for example, whose 1760 broadside "An Evening Thought. Salvation by Christ, With Penitential Cries" was the first individual poem published by a black American, acknowledged Wheatley's influence by selecting her as the subject of his second broadside, "An Address to Miss Phillis Wheatly [*sic*], Ethiopian Poetess, in Boston," which was published at Hartford in 1778. And George Moses Horton, the second Afro-American to publish a book of poetry in English (1829), brought out in 1838 an edition of his *Poems by a Slave* bound together with Wheatley's work. Indeed, for fifty-six years, between 1773 and 1829, when Horton published *The Hope of Liberty*, Wheatley was the *only* black person to have published a book of imaginative literature in English. So central was this black woman's role in the shaping of the Afro-American literary tradition that, as one historian has maintained, the history of the reception of Phillis Wheatley's poetry *is* the history of Afro-American literary criticism. Well into the nineteenth-century, Wheatley and the black literary tradition were the same entity.

Henry Louis Gates, Jr., "Foreword: In Her Own Write," *The Collected Works of Phillis Wheatley*, ed. John C. Shields (New York: Oxford University Press, 1988), pp. x–xi

JOHN C. SHIELDS   Wheatley, who wrote most of her extant verse by the age of twenty, has been censured for her alleged dependence on and imitation of neoclassical conventions and poetics, and she has been denigrated for lack of sympathy with her people's struggle for freedom. An investigation of her poems and letters proves these charges false. In a letter treating the slavery issue written in February 1774 and addressed to Samson Occom, the American Indian Missionary, Wheatley forcefully and eloquently states, "In every human Brest, God has implanted a Principle, which we call Love of Freedom; it is impatient of Oppression, and pants for Deliverance." She made this statement some four months after her own manumission. Not only was Wheatley vitally concerned for the plight of her enslaved brothers and sisters, but she fervently sought her own freedom, both in this world and in the next. So complete was her absorption in the struggle for freedom that this endeavor governed her conception of poetry, causing her to be no more imitative than any other good student and writer of literature.

Wheatley articulates the theme of freedom in four ways. The first may be surprising, especially from the pen of a black slave: she sometimes uttered passionate political statements supporting the American colonial quest for freedom from Great Britain. Although not as readily observable, the second way is much more prevalent. Wheatley displays numerous examples of what Jung called the mandala archetype, a circular image pattern closely associated with a psychological attempt to discover freedom from chaos. The persistence of this pattern suggests Wheatley's discontent with her enslavement and indicates a means by which she adapted to it.

One conscious poetic escape from slavery was the writing of contemplative elegies; this was the third means by which Wheatley achieved freedom, not in this world but in the next. So enthusiastically does she celebrate death and its rewards in her numerous elegies that she becomes more clearly aligned with the thanatos-eros motif of nineteenth-century romantics than with her eighteenth-century contemporaries. Her poetics of the imagination and the sublime, comprising the fourth representation of freedom, even more strongly attests her romantic alignment. This young poet's intense longing for the spiritual world motivated her to use her poetry as a means of escaping an unsatisfactory, temporal world. The imagination and the sublime become tools by which she accomplishes her short-lived escape. She presents so sophisticated a grasp of these two eighteenth-century aesthetic ideas, which emphatically heralded the romantic movement, that their consideration deserves extended attention.

> John C. Shields, "Phillis Wheatley's Struggle for Freedom in Her Poetry and Prose," *The Collected Works of Phillis Wheatley* (New York: Oxford University Press, 1988), pp. 230–31

BLYDEN JACKSON   No black poet until Paul Laurence Dunbar in the 1890s was so widely known as Phillis Wheatley, and probably none should have been. She was not only much more a beneficiary of training in literacy than either Lucy Terry or Jupiter Hammon. She was also born, apparently, with more of a native endowment for poetry than either of them. Neoclassicism was the prevailing mode for writers of her time. It was a mode to which she gave a close and conscious allegiance. She was sympathetically acquainted with such Latin poets as Virgil and Ovid, exemplars of the poetic art from classical antiquity whom neoclassicists revered. Milton, incidentally, clearly appealed to her, and Miltonic influences may be detected widely in her work. Even so, Pope, the arch practitioner of English neoclassicism, was her model of models. Of the thirty-nine poems in her *Poems on Various Subjects*, all but five are not only in the neoclassical heroic couplet but also in that particular form of couplet—to the full extent, apparently, of which she was capable—precisely in both the manner and spirit of Pope. Pope preeminently affected satire, often of the most virulent tone and the bitterest, most savage content. Phillis Wheatley—perhaps, it can be conjectured, because of her vulnerable position in society—was one neoclassicist who did not turn to satire. But in every other significant respect, she followed Pope and the neoclassicists religiously. She invoked the muses. She wrote elegies, fourteen in her *Poems on Various Subjects*. She adopted subjects which permitted her to expatiate on abstractions, as in her "On Recollection" and "On Imagination." She indulged rather freely in personification, as became an orthodox neoclassicist, and always in that special neoclassical way which is divided by all too thin a line from abstraction, not because, in it, the process of abstraction has been too personified, but because, in it, the purported process of personification has been too abstract. She was urbane, logical, impersonal in tone (even when writing, as she did in her elegies, of people she knew), and prone to the use of poetic diction— all of these as a good neoclassicist should have been. Her poetry functioned to remind its audience of mankind's universal traits and sentiments and of the occasions in human experience which all men tend to share. Thus, it is axiomatic with her critics that she was an occasional poet, very much in keeping with her neoclassical bent.

Blyden Jackson, *A History of Afro-American Literature* (Baton Rouge: Louisiana State University Press, 1989), Vol. 1, pp. 42–43

Bibliography

An Elegiac Poem, on the Death of That Celebrated Divine, and Eminent Servant of Jesus Christ, the Reverend and Learned George Whitefield. 1770.

To Mrs. Leonard on the Death of Her Husband. 1771.

To the Honorable Thomas Hubbard, Esq. on the Death of Mrs. Thankfull Leonard. 1773.

An Elegy, to Miss Mary Moorhead, on the Death of Her Father, the Rev. Mr. John Moorhead. 1773.

Poems on Various Subjects, Religious and Moral. 1773.

An Elegy, Sacred to the Memory of That Great Divine, the Reverend and Learned Dr. Samuel Cooper. 1784.

Liberty and Peace: A Poem. 1784.

Memoir and Poems of Phillis Wheatley. Ed. Margaretta Matilda Odell. 1834.

Letters. [Ed. Charles Deane.] 1864.

Poems. 1909.

Poems and Letters. Ed. Charles Frederick Heartman. 1915.

Life and Works of Phillis Wheatley. Ed. G. Herbert Renfro. 1916.

Poems. Ed. Charlotte Ruth Wright. 1930.

Poems. Ed. Julian D. Mason, Jr. 1966, 1989.

Collected Works. Ed. John C. Shields. 1988.

Title Withdrawn